HO MONK U LES

10 Rules for
Not Screwing Up
Your Happily Ever After

TOUCHSTONE

New York London Toronto Sydney New Delhi

I Suck at Relationships So You Don't Have To

Bethenny Frankel

with Eve Adamson

Touchstone
An Imprint of Simon & Schuster, Inc.
1230 Avenue of the Americas
New York, NY 10020

First Touchstone paperback edition April 2016

TOUCHSTONE and colophon are registered trademarks of Simon & Schuster, Inc.

For information about special discounts for bulk purchases, please contact Simon & Schuster Special Sales at 1-866-506-1949 or business@simonandschuster.com.

The Simon & Schuster Speakers Bureau can bring authors to your live event. For more information or to book an event contact the Simon & Schuster Speakers Bureau at 1-866-248-3049 or visit our website at www.simonspeakers.com.

Manufactured in the United States of America

10 9 8 7 6 5 4 3 2 1

Library of Congress Cataloging-in-Publication Data

Frankel, Bethenny.
  I suck at relationships so you don't have to : 10 rules for not screwing up your happily ever after / by Bethenny Frankel ; with Eve Adamson.
     pages   cm
1. Man-woman relationships.   2. Interpersonal relations.   3. Interpersonal attraction.   4. Couples—Psychology.   5. Dating (Social customs).   I. Title.
  HQ801.F747 2015
  306.7—dc23   2014043140

ISBN 978-1-4516-6741-7
ISBN 978-1-4516-6742-4 (pbk)
ISBN 978-1-4516-6745-5 (ebook)

*This book is dedicated to women
who have the best intentions in love and matters of the heart,
but at times fall short. To those who believe in relationships and
partnership but have somehow lost their way. You can see the island,
but you simply don't know how to make it there.
Let's make it there together.*

A Special Thank-You

I'm no professional, and I make that very clear throughout this book. However, there is somebody who *is* a professional—my therapist and renowned psychologist Dr. Xavier Amador, who is a leader in his field. My association with Dr. Amador has always been fruitful for me, and so I was honored when he said he would be willing to contribute his thoughts throughout the book. When I am in the heat of a relationship issue, sometimes I don't see things with perfect clarity until after I've had some time for reflection, but Dr. Amador does. This is the gift he has bestowed upon this book—shining his light on the parts where his commentary might add extra insight or even tell me when I'm being over-the-top.

I want you to know that Dr. Amador's opinion is worthy of serious consideration. Thank you, Dr. Amador, for your contribution to what I hope will be a game-changer for modern relationships!

Contents

Introduction 1

Something to Think About 7

Chapter 1: Understand the Man 9

Chapter 2: Woman, Know Thyself 30

Chapter 3: Master the Catch and Release 65

Chapter 4: Don't Hate the Player, Hate the Game 89

Chapter 5: Control Yourself 117

Chapter 6: Get a Life 146

Chapter 7: Trust Your Gut 165

Chapter 8: Manage Your Money (Noise) 211

Chapter 9: Getting It On 232

Chapter 10: Don't Let Cracks Become Craters 264

Epilogue: Remember Who You Are 295

Acknowledgments 299

Index 301

Introduction

Here's my confession: I suck at relationships.

Now that I'm in my forties, I have a lot of life experience. I've weathered the ups and downs of press and fame, of being broke and having money, as well as having my relationships largely documented on television. I would say that I've been pretty successful in most areas of my life. I'm a mom to an amazing little girl. I've always been good at generating ideas and marketing. I've built a brand and I have good business sense. I know when something can be fixed and when it's time to move on. I'm decisive, I have good gut instincts, and I know how to get what I want.

In my own love life, however, I'm a disaster. As good as I am in business, that's how bad I am at love. I find relationships to be just about the most impossible thing in the world, and I've done so many things the wrong way that I've become, strangely, a sort of expert at what not to do. Here are just a few things I've done wrong: I play games. I get afraid. I run. I shut down. I fall in love with the wrong men. I can't deal when things get uncomfortable. I ignore, I retreat, and I get very confused. Over the years, I've settled for less than I deserve. I've looked for an out. I've set people up to fail. I've sabotaged my relationships. I've wasted time. I've convinced myself to be with someone who I knew wasn't right for me. I've been afraid to be alone. I've asked anyone who will listen what I should do (something I rarely do in business). I suck at staying put and being content. I've misjudged people and situations, and I've ignored my gut instincts. I've trusted the wrong men and forced a relationship with men who weren't right for me. I've tried to force a square peg into a round hole. I've called when I shouldn't have called. I've texted when I shouldn't have texted. I've *not* called when it would have been the kind thing to do, and I've worried about getting someone to love me before I worried about whether I loved them. I wanted the ring and got the ring, many times, but then I didn't want it anymore. I've wasted time and energy and money in relationships. I've fallen for being in a relationship with someone who loves me more than I love him. I've been with men who made a lot of money and supported me and I've been unable to handle that. I've been with men who had no money, who turned out to be gold diggers. I've been with men because they were the father I never had. I've been with someone who could handle my career but wasn't strong enough to handle me, and I've tried to be with someone who needed me to take care of him. I've done all the things that women do badly in relationships, and then some.

Sometimes I wonder if I have unrealistic expectations. Will good enough ever be good enough for me? Do I just choose poorly, or have I really not met the right person yet? We often make decisions out of fear, which can cause us to settle for Mr. (or Miss) Right Now. In the moment, it seems so much safer and easier than striking out fearlessly to find the truly perfect match. Is that what I've done? I'm not sure. I'm still working it out, but in doing that, I've already learned many, many things that I don't want, that I won't accept, that I shouldn't settle for. And I still believe in love.

You might wonder why I would write a book about something I admittedly suck at. I must have some set of balls. I was recently chatting with somebody who doesn't have a lot of relationship experience, and she asked me, "So, given your relationship history, what makes *you* an expert?" I have grappled with this question for a while, and here is what I've come up with: When I write a book, I write about what inspires me, what pours out of me, what I need to talk about. The things I've learned about what *not* to do could fill volumes, and this is a book about what not to do, as well as a book full of strategies you can use to tackle your relationship issues without blowing the whole thing up, based on what I know because of the many, many mistakes I've made. Trial and error is a great teacher, and this is a subject I've been schooled in over and over. It is also a subject that is important to me. It's close to my heart. It's *about* my heart, and I have a lot to say about it, so hear me out.

I don't know all the answers. In fact, I probably know hardly any of the answers. The irony of me giving relationship advice is not lost on me. This book is not about me putting myself out there as someone who knows more than you do, or someone who has any kind of professional qualifications for counseling (other than having been on the couch end of plenty of years of it). Fortunately for all of us, I've got a psychologist and a psychiatrist weighing in throughout this book. It's no secret that I'm going through a very negative and public and nasty divorce. Right now, I'm in relationship recovery. In my last significant relationship, I hit rock bottom. I think people thought that I sold my company, I landed on the cover of *Forbes* magazine, and my life was now perfect. Actually, as I'm writing this book, I don't even have a home. I'm the richest homeless person you know. I'm like a vagabond with no personal belongings, running from hotel to corporate apartment to the homes of friends, because at this time, getting an apartment isn't possible for me. Trust me when I tell you that no amount of money will ever make you happy.

I've been going through an ordeal, as many of you have. Whatever you are going through, I want you to know that you will figure out why it happened. You might not figure it out today or tomorrow, but the answer is coming. I know I'll eventually learn why I've gone through this personal hell. There is always a lesson. You keep making the same mistake until you learn the lesson. Time does heal all wounds, and eventually, the things that tore you apart start to become less painful. The things you were obsessing about become less important. It gets better. The answer is coming.

Whatever has happened to you—infidelity, money issues, abandonment, the inability to sustain a long-term relationship, constantly replaying your past mistakes, even abuse—a lot of us out there have been through it, too, and have come out on the other side. Maybe you trusted someone and you were duped. Maybe you feel confused, or lost, or angry, or just hopeless. Maybe you feel bad about yourself, or you just can't seem to find that special relationship you believe in. Pick up this book if you haven't been able to figure it out yet. Pick up this book if you don't understand why your relationships aren't working, or because you feel bad about yourself, or because you can't find the relationship you dream about. Pick up this book if you, like me, were duped into trusting someone, or if your relationship is in a lull and needs a jump-start, or if you are constantly rehashing the details of a difficult decision, or obsessing, or beating yourself up, or if you just aren't happy. Your life can be so much better than it is right now, and I want to help you get there because I have learned hard lessons and experienced enough heartbreak for all of us. You probably feel like you have, too.

When a recent relationship fell apart, I beat myself up. I obsessed. How could I have been so stupid? How could my judgment have been so poor? How could I have been so blind? I kept going back over it, re-hashing all the details, all the decisions that seemed right at the time but that I now see were so wrong. I kept asking why it was happening to me. I kept wondering when I was going to realize why it happened, what the purpose was, what it was all for. Where was the silver lining? Of course, Bryn is the silver lining, but still sometimes I feel like I can't get through it. Then I see the light at the end and I know there is something better for me up ahead. I'm not angry. I'm not bitter. I still believe in good people and happiness. I still believe in love, and I still come from a place of yes. That doesn't mean I don't sometimes get grouchy, bitchy, unhappy, or mean. But I always know I go through what I go through for a reason. Maybe the reason is you.

If you still haven't found the reason behind your personal heartbreak, that's okay. You don't always need to know everything right now. Your life doesn't have to be all wrapped up in a perfect little blue Tiffany box with a bow. This book will help you wait until you are really sure about the relationship before you start clamoring for the ring. This book will help you figure out if the relationship is right for you or if you are wasting your time, or worse, getting into something you won't be able to get out of easily. I hope this book will save you weeks, months, even years of misery and heartache.

Now, I'm really not so sure I ever want to get married again. I want a life partner, but ten years ago, I thought marriage was the ultimate goal. I'm no longer certain that it is. I'm genuinely not sure about this question, and maybe we'll figure that out together, because I really don't want to screw it up again. I know a lot of you have found the right man for you, and that's inspiring to me.

The upside is that I've learned a lot about what makes a poor choice.

I've learned that the ones you think are trustworthy are very often the ones who aren't, and the ones who seem like they wouldn't be trustworthy sometimes, surprisingly, are. Still waters run deep, and I'm here to help open your eyes and help you see what's really going on in *your* relationship, or in your strategy to find the right relationship. Many women think there are no good men out there, but even with everything I've been through, I'm here to tell you that there are a lot of great men out there. You just need to know how to find them, and once you find them, you need to understand how they think.

Finally, despite all my relationship disasters, I remain an optimist. I know that one of these days, I'm going to get it right. I'm in my forties and while writing this book, I have been dating, and I keep learning more because every relationship is different. Then again, some things remain the same. I remain the same, and so do you, so that's where I want to focus. What can we do to make it better? What can we do to make our relationships more successful? I keep going, I keep trying, and I keep opening my heart to love. This book is my offering of hope.

So take this journey with me. Relationships aren't easy, but neither is life, and a good, strong, nurturing, and supportive relationship certainly makes life better. You have your own stories that could help me and other women as well. I want this book to be a launching pad for a network where we all share stories to help each other. You can come from a place of yes. You don't have to suck at relationships. You can have any life you want. You can break the chain and not repeat the mistakes you've made in the past. That's what I intend to do. We'll do it together.

Something to Think About

In this book, I talk a lot about women and men, but I do not in any way want or intend to exclude same-sex couples from the discussion. Partnering with another human being is a challenge no matter your gender, and I hope that all women can get some help from my observations about women, and all men can get help from my observations about men. However, it would have become unwieldy to keep saying "he or she" when referring to the reader's boyfriend/girlfriend. For that reason, and because in my personal experience my partners have been male, I generally use "he." Please forgive the exclusion of the female pronoun if that is what applies to you, and please also, if you don't mind, just put an "s" in front of "he" in your mind, so you don't feel like I'm not talking to you. Because I am. I am talking, with all humility, to every one of you who has struggled with relationships. We are all human, and we are all the same in how we feel love and suffer and care. I hear you. I feel you. Let's have the discussion, because we all need to know that we are not alone in our failures and that we all have the potential to find love.

CHAPTER 1

. . . .

Understand the Man

*Men always want to be a woman's first love. That is their
clumsy vanity. We women have a more subtle instinct about
things. What we like is to be a man's last romance.*
—Mrs. Allonby in Oscar Wilde's
A Woman of No Importance

Women. Men. Were there ever two more completely different animals working at cross purposes? It has taken me many years, many failed relationships, and a lot of time with my guy friends, but I think I am finally beginning to understand the man. This wasn't always the case. For much of my life, I didn't understand what men need. I thought they pretty much wanted the same things women want. *Wrong.* Men not only want different things than we do, but they think differently, they process differently, they love differently. They are a completely different animal.

The first time I really began to understand what men want was when I dated a very confident and very good-looking bachelor whom I really fell for. We really connected and had a very passionate relationship, but I didn't understand why he did a lot of the things he did. Why wasn't he interested in talking about our relationship for hours? Why wasn't he upset about things when I was upset about things? Why didn't he feel guilty when I nagged him? Why did he feel like doing things without me sometimes? If I hadn't loved him so much, I wouldn't have done the work to figure out the puzzle that is Man. So I watched him. I observed. I listened to the things he said to me and others. And I got some ideas.

One day I decided to try something. He had a friend visiting for the weekend, and I decided not to nag him even one time about anything. I decided to be an easygoing person. I was light and bright and pleasant and sweet, and he didn't know what hit him. I went out with his friends and partied and laughed, and that was the day he opened up to me and decided he loved me. He bought me a beautiful gift, totally committed to me, and gave me everything I wanted. I was as surprised as he was—could it really be this easy? He just needed to know I could hang out and not bust his balls and control every minute of our interaction. Mind-blowing.

Of course, I can't change completely. Even though I know what men want, I still forget. I still slip up. I'm a ball buster by nature and you can't change your nature. But it was enlightening to recognize how easy it is to give men what they want, and to know that all it takes is to be easygoing, fun, and interesting is a huge relief, at least to me.

Maybe it can be a relief to you, too, to know that men really aren't that complicated. Women spend so much time obsessing about men and what they want, but it's not calculus. It's more like basic arithmetic. The number one most effective thing you can do to improve your relationship with a man is to practice rule #1: Understand the Man. When you get how men think, what they want, and how totally different they are from women, you will break the code. Otherwise, being in a relationship with a man can feel like going to a foreign country without learning any of the language. If the local people don't speak your language (and most guys do *not* speak Woman), then you're going to have an awful time communicating. But if you at least get some basic vocabulary down, you can begin to find your way around. Your native language will always be Woman, but it's time to get bilingual.

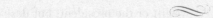

DR. AMADOR SAYS . . .

In my experience—and the research agrees—there really is a code. Men are socialized to see a complaint, concern, or hurt feelings as a problem to be solved. We fix. We are men of action who focus on the thing before us—the computer giving us trouble, or the woman. This often results in our looking for the source of the problem in the woman we love (the machine we are repairing) rather than in ourselves, or our relationships. Like Bethenny says, it's truly not personal—even though it feels that way.

Women, on the other hand, are socialized to value relationships first. Listening and being heard are what are important. Not understanding these differences and taking them personally ("He never listens," "He doesn't care," or "She's acting crazy and all emotional and not letting me fix the problem") is a recipe for conflict and misery.

—XAVIER AMADOR, PH.D., PRESIDENT,
LEAP INSTITUTE, WWW.LEAPINSTITUTE.ORG

• •

What's with Men?

If we really, truly comprehended what men are thinking most of the time, many of us would seriously consider giving up men completely. Men are little boys. They are babies. They are cavemen. They are animals. They are morons. They are all these things, and sometimes they seem totally clueless about relationships—at least in the way we see them. They don't know how to behave, they don't know how to give us what we want, and they have no idea what we are thinking. Are we really that complicated?

Yes.

Here's the truth: Men are simple. Really simple. It's not that they aren't smart. Some men are extremely smart and have big intellects and high IQs and run major corporations and countries and all of that, but even super-smart men are simple. Your husband or boyfriend could be a rocket scientist or nuclear physicist or the president, but despite what they do in life, how intelligent they are, and how supposedly interested they are in the women in their lives, I have learned over the years, through much study, that men mainly care about a few basic things:

- Food
- Drinks—usually the ones containing alcohol
- Guys' night out
- Sex
- Masturbation
- Sleep
- Taking a shit
- Power over the remote control
- Gadgets and technology
- Watching sports
- Playing sports (often golf)
- Vegas
- Scratching or rearranging their balls
- The fantasy of a ménage à trois
- Appearing cool to other men

That's about it. There is a kind of elegance to the list—if a list that contains "Taking a shit" can be elegant. Why clutter your mind with a bunch of useless chatter if you don't have to? And most men don't have to.

Some men (but not all) are also very invested in their careers and they work a lot. To them, this is also very important because they are earning a living and they want to feel successful in the world. But when they come home to the women in their lives, and they are done working, the above list pretty much sums it up. They might feel temporarily prone to over-analysis if their actions have consequences—like the woman they love leaving them—but otherwise, it's pretty much business as usual. You get up. You do your work. You finish your work. You go home. You relax and focus on pleasure—food, drink, sports, sex—and then you go to sleep. It actually sounds like a blissful existence to me. I *wish* I could keep it that simple.

I don't think I'm being chauvinistic to see it this way. In fact, a lot of my guy friends see this list and totally agree. Some are offended, though. They think that they are complex. They worry. They have emotions. They consider problems. They want to hear about how their partner feels. They know how to "do relationships." Okay, I can accept that, but here's what

I think: The degree to which men do all these things is 1 percent of the degree to which women do these things, in general. Women are complicated, to the extent that we totally overcomplicate everything. Most women could probably benefit from a good lobotomy. Men are simple. They come pre-lobotomized. Lucky men. There are always exceptions, but hey, I'm just calling it like I see it.

· ·

DR. AMADOR SAYS . . .

I wish men were as simple as Bethenny suggests. However, men are every bit as emotionally complex as women. It just doesn't seem that way to women, because from early childhood, men are taught to hide our feelings, wear our armor, "man up," and worse. The truth is that men want to be loved and to give love as much as women do, but to admit that in daily life is . . . well, it's "acting like a girl." We only have brief windows when we feel safe enough to reveal our hearts (proposing marriage, saying the vows, the death of a parent, the birth of a child, to name a few examples). I understand why Bethenny says things like this, as it's a way to understand the surface level of interactions, but remember not to let labels keep you from looking, listening, and digging for deeper truths.

—Xavier Amador, Ph.D., president,
LEAP Institute, www.leapinstitute.org

· ·

Realizing that this is how men see the world is enlightening and actually takes a lot of pressure off. They don't necessarily understand all your complex thoughts and feelings and anxieties, and they don't necessarily want to. They definitely don't want to hear about them—at least not for more than about thirty seconds. If a man thinks you have a problem, he wants to fix it. The most frustrating thing in the world for a man is to sit and listen to you go into detail about a problem for an hour and then tell him, "I don't want you to fix it. I just want you to listen." (I think this was a concept first publicized in the book *Men Are from Mars, Women Are from Venus.*) Listening with no active purpose makes men crazy. They think, *What the hell was the point of listening to all that if I wasn't supposed to do anything about it?* Men are doers. They aren't thinkers. Even the philosophers, even the psychologists. They want to fix the problem, not just go over it and over it until we feel better. That's not a fix-it method they recognize or acknowledge.

To know this is to change your expectations, and that will change your relationship for the better. Expect your man to give you what he's good at giving (love, sex, protection, fondness, nonverbal support), and don't expect him to give you what he isn't good at giving (emotion, long conversations about feelings, knowing what you want before you say it, understanding your every nuance). If you can recognize this and adjust your expectations, you will be much more content with your relationship. If you want men to care about and talk endlessly about your specific problems, forget about it. If you talk for too long, trust me when I tell you that your man feels like saying, "Shh! Stop talking!" The only reason he doesn't say it is because he knows that for some odd reason, you might be offended. But if you want a man to care about *you* and help you *fix your problems*, then that is totally doable. Isn't that more important anyway? You can always save the obsess-about-it-from-every-possible-angle conversations for your girlfriends.

Things to Remember About Men

When your husband or boyfriend is frustrating the hell out of you or pissing you off, give yourself a reality check. These are some basic things to remember about men:

Men Like Easy

Not easy like slutty (although some of them like that, too—but only for test drives, not for the long haul). Men like easy as in *not so fucking difficult all the time.* Guys like you to be easy and life to be easy. They might be fascinated by your complexity in the beginning. It might attract them like a moth to a flame, but once they have you, they want you to be simple. Not a doormat, not subservient, not simpleminded, but just easy to be with. They don't want you starting shit with them every day, telling them how they're doing everything wrong or how they don't understand you. *Of course* they don't understand you. You are a complete mystery to them, and it benefits you to keep it that way.

This is hard for women to understand. We meet an interesting man who seems complex and mysterious, but when we get to know him, he's about as complex as a caveman, with needs about as demanding as the needs of your dog. Don't expect men's baffling behavior to reflect their true feelings. Those feelings are pretty basic. We just can't quite believe it. Could men really be that simple?

Yes! The sooner you get this into your complicated, overanalyzing brain, the easier life will be. Being easy isn't actually that easy for a lot of women, myself included. You have to lay off. Just relax. Just let each other be who you are. This isn't easy, either. When I dated someone ten years younger than me, it was like going through immaturity boot camp. How many hours in a row can you bowl, drink, play poker, and hang out at a sports bar? Apparently, more than I ever imagined. It was very hard to just let him be who he was at that moment in life. However, when you can achieve this, a lot of the stress you thought was part of your relationship will melt away. Accepting leads to understanding.

Again, I'm not saying men are stupid. Far from it. Men can be confident, controlling, rule-the-world types who master the boardroom or run the company or have mad skills at whatever, but when they get home at the end of the day, they are babies who want to feel good. Period. They want love and they don't want to have to ask for it.

Most men are all soft inside, even the hardest ones. And here's a surprise: They are more romantic than us! Men want to conquer the world, but with you, they need to be built up, supported, adored, and made to feel manly. If you do that, then they will worship you like the goddess you are. If you beat them down and refuse to build them up, if you nag at them constantly for everything they do to disappoint you and never show them how much you appreciate what they do that you love, they will eventually drift away from you—if not physically, then emotionally.

You want to be worshipped, right? You don't mind the view from that pedestal, do you? Of course it's uncomfortable if your guy has totally unrealistic ideas about you. He has to know who you really are, including all the crazy (which we'll talk about later), but overall, if you just relax and go with the flow a little bit and stop trying to change him into something else, then he'll do the same and you can both just have a nice time together, support each other, and feel good about your partnership. It's win-win.

At the same time, you need to keep a guy on his toes, and that's part of your natural allure. Guys also want to know that they got a good one, that you are sharp and independent and you have your own life. They want to be amazed that you are with them because you're so interesting and mysterious and sexy. So relax into your relationship, but at the same time, keep your own life fully intact (see chapter 6).

This is the magical formula for mastering the male of the species and being happy in your relationship with one of them:

Easygoing + loving + mysterious + independent + fun
+ sexy = the woman of his dreams

Men Don't Like to Fight

This is related to the previous item about men liking things to be easy. Men do not want to fight with us. They will go to great lengths to avoid an argument, and they opt out of all but the most important of the battles (and even some of those). You might think you don't like to fight, but a lot of women seek out drama even without realizing it. I certainly do, although I don't like to admit that. Arguments help women resolve issues and help relieve intense emotions. Men would much rather skip right to the makeup sex. You could be in the heat of the most important argument of your life, sobbing and pouring out your heart, and a guy could actually fall asleep, as if he doesn't have a care in the world. You can have the most intimate, tear-jerking sex and when it's over, he can turn on the TV like it never happened. He doesn't question these things because he assumes everything is fine. How can they possibly fall asleep when you are crying? Turn the TV on after mind-blowing sex? Because they are men.

If you want to resolve an issue without getting into a fight, take a cue from men, who have the ability to wait to talk about something. Can you think about what you want to say before you say it? Let it marinate overnight so you can get some clarity. Boil it down to a single issue. It might not seem like such a big deal tomorrow, or maybe you'll realize it wasn't about what you thought it was about. Save drafts of e-mails so you can remember what you've already said and what he said back. Even if you feel like the world will come to an end if you don't talk about something, see if you can wait until you're not feeling so emotional. See if you can get comfortable with not knowing exactly what's going to happen.

Also remember that men are much less likely to understand or want to participate in an argument about feelings. If it's about something solid and tangible, they will be more willing and able to communicate. Money, infidelity, trust, living situations, specific behavior of friends or family, how much time you spend together—those are all concrete things. See if you can focus the discussion there. It might still turn into an argument, but at least you will both know what you are arguing about. Or just be vulnerable. Admit you are feeling insecure, or you just need a little bit of self-esteem boosting. Men understand that and will probably find your admission disarming.

. . . .

DR. AMADOR SAYS . . .

No one wants to fight when one or both sides fight dirty: name-calling, insults. This always ends with silence, sulking, or screaming. Fights hurt relationships when we make the other person defensive. This is *toxic* fighting. Instead, practice the 7 habits to healthy fighting from my book *I'm Right, You're Wrong, Now What?* and focus on your contribution, not his. You can't control what he does but you can learn to stop throwing gasoline on the fire.

The 7 Habits to Healthy Fighting

1. **Stop insisting you're right.** If you've said your piece twice and he still doesn't get it, it's time to stop.

2. **Don't engage in insults or name-calling.** "That's stupid," "You're an idiot," "You don't care," "Bastard," and worse just lead to defenses going up.

3. **Pick the right time.** Don't argue drunk, when he's exhausted and trying to sleep, when he's trying to rush out the door to work, etc. Use common sense. It can wait.

4. **Never use absolutes.** "You always . . ." or "You never . . ." tell him he's been tried, found guilty as charged, and convicted. Expect an angry defense.

5. **Don't "kitchen-sink it."** If you're upset about last night, don't bring up last Tuesday, last week, or last month. And don't add other complaints. Fight one battle at a time. Throwing everything in but the kitchen sink escalates a single argument into a war.

6. **Listen without defending.** If you're defensive, he will be defensive. He won't feel heard and he won't be interested in hearing you because he will be busy defending himself.

7. **Reflect back what you have heard.** Instead of a boxing match where you block and counterpunch, practice verbal Jujitsu. If he insults you, reflect it back. "So you're saying I'm being unreasonable? Is that right?" He will feel heard, calmer, and off balance.

—Xavier Amador, Ph.D., president,
LEAP Institute, www.leapinstitute.org

. . . .

Men Can Wait

Another thing that baffles women about men is how good they are at not bringing up things that bother them. We don't understand this at all. If a woman is upset with her husband or boyfriend, he could be giving the inaugural address and she would want to interrupt him to talk about their relationship issue. When we are upset about something, we want to talk about it right here, right now. A man doesn't feel compelled to do this at all. Maybe he's upset that you were flirting with an old boyfriend at a party and he was jealous. Yet he could wait three weeks to even bring it up. Or maybe he knows there is an issue you have to talk about, like whether to be exclusive or move in together, or whether it's time to have kids, or maybe he knows you both need to discuss something that happened with your child at school that day. He can be fully aware that this is an issue that needs a serious discussion, and he can go out and spend the day playing golf or go to work or go to a meeting and *not even think about it once*. It baffles me that men are so good at not bringing up things that bother them.

One of the main reasons, I think, is that men can compartmentalize everything, and they want everything to happen in its own time. I used to date a guy who worked in the stock market, and when the market was about to open, he got irritated if I tried to talk about anything. Personally, I could be just about to walk onstage or in front of a TV camera and I would probably talk to you if we were having an issue. Men are more likely to say those dreaded words women hate to hear: "I can't talk to you right now."

Women are not like this at all. Our default mode is, "What is wrong with the relationship?" and/or "How can we make the relationship better?" A man's default mode is, "Everything's fine." We are obsessed with relationships and constantly trying to tweak them. Men want to leave things alone. We want to deal with a problem in the moment, as soon as we realize there is a problem. Men wait for the right moment. They do not have that feeling of urgency because, as I said before, they take the relationship for granted. Whatever it is can wait because it's probably not really that big of a deal. If he's used to you making a big deal out of every little thing, he will assume nothing is a big deal. It's the boy-who-cried-wolf syndrome. The discussion about it is really just something that happens because you say it must, so there's no particular urgency. After work or after the weekend or three months from now should be just fine for the "big discussion" or "fight," and if he can enjoy a martini and have the game on while it's happening, so much the better. Weird, I know. But that's how they are.

But when it's really not fine for a man, it's not fine. It's important to remember this. Men are not mercurial the way women are. I can break up with somebody every month, or every minute, and then be ready to get back together. When a man is done, he's done. It's hard to pull him back in. Much harder than it is to pull a woman back in. For this reason, it's useful to kick back and chill out and reduce the drama. Take it down a notch, so you don't get yourself into a position that is irreversible.

• •

DR. AMADOR SAYS . . .

You can't have intimacy without disagreements, arguments, and fights. When you do it well, when you practice healthy habits for fighting, you'll find the conflict almost always leaves you both feeling closer, safer, and more in love.

—Xavier Amador, Ph.D., president,
LEAP Institute, www.leapinstitute.org

• •

Men Don't Need to Talk

They can talk, of course. They are even willing to do it, on occasion. Sometimes they might actually enjoy it. But the way a man likes to talk and the way a woman likes to talk are totally different. He has no interest in calling Freud or going for therapy or asking what you learned in Psych 101 that totally applies to him. He doesn't want to go back to the womb to figure out why he feels something. He feels what he feels, things are what they are, and that's that. They are very black and white in their thinking.

It's not that he doesn't love you, or care about your feelings, or have any feelings of his own, although that's what it can feel like to a woman when a man doesn't want to talk. It's not that he isn't interested in the details of your life. (Maybe not *all* the details . . .) The truth is, your boyfriend or your husband is probably smitten with you and wants to rip your clothes off every second of the day, and if he knows you are feeling sad or upset about something, that's going to bother him and he's going to want to fix it.

But what he *doesn't* want to do is sit there and listen to you talk about feelings. Men tend to think in a more straightforward, linear, and logical way about situations, and they can sum up the gist of things in a few words, not involving feelings. We need more than a few words, and most of them have to be about feelings. The one thing guys tell me they dread hearing about the most is your feelings. Or his. Or your opinion of what his feelings are (or should be). None of that makes sense to him. His feelings are what they are, period. He certainly doesn't want to talk back to you in the same way you talk to him, because he doesn't feel the need to do anything about his own feelings. Either he's fine with them, or he knows he'll get over it. And please don't start analyzing his feelings. That's prickly and uncomfortable territory for a man. As for your feelings, unless you are one of those few women who never talks about her feelings at all, he already has all the information he needs and more on that subject. You don't need to give him hourly updates.

This isn't a weakness in men. It's just a difference. Sometimes I wish I was more like this. Sometimes I feel like I need to spit it all out before I even know what it's about. The next day, I often realize that what I said wasn't how I really felt, and then I have to go back and apologize or redo the whole conversation.

Men don't need to talk to figure out their own minds or process their feelings. They already know what they think and feel, and they don't understand why we don't know what we think and feel, or why what we think and feel is always changing or even up for debate. That's a mystery to them, and it's a big part of the reason why they think we are so complicated. But this is a mystery they'd rather not solve. They like you *without* knowing how you feel or why you feel it.

• •

MAN-FORMATION

Here's something men want: They want to be taken care of by someone. They just don't want you to make a big deal about it. They want you to take care of them and do little things for them and build them up and make them feel manly without calling attention to it or even consciously letting them know you are doing it.

• •

Men Respect the Bro Code

You might want to tell your partner everything, but guys not only don't feel the need to do this, they have a personal code that tells them not to do this, especially when it comes to gossip. Gossip is a primarily female (and gay male) phenomenon. We are fascinated with other people and we want to know everything about them. Guys have an unspoken agreement that what happens in Man Land stays in Man Land. (The one exception I see over and over is when men are with their mothers or their families. They suddenly turn into gossips. "Grandma said she didn't invite your sister to the wedding!" Men get involved in that, for whatever reason.)

For example, a guy I was dating had a bachelor party in Vegas. When he returned, I asked him how it went. He said it was fun, good guy bonding, great, etc. No details. Later, I found out that one of the guys on the trip almost died from alcohol poisoning and had to go to the hospital. Any girl would *lead with this story*, but my guy didn't even mention it. It's the Bro Code.

The Bro Code even extends to you, to some extent. If it's personal information and it doesn't directly concern you, your guy—indoctrinated as he is in the Bro Code—probably won't mention it. *Especially* if he thinks it may upset you, make you jealous, or make him look bad in your eyes. Have you ever noticed how guys rarely talk about their past relationships, never point out old girlfriends, and give no details about their exes, not to mention their more interesting indiscretions, like their three-ways, prostitutes, and other sexual exploits? (I know not all men have done those things, but they've all done *something* they're not telling you.)

In other words, men keep their secrets. It's the Bro Code, but it's also just a natural tendency for self-preservation and keeping the peace. To guys, talking too often ends up causing trouble. He'll still *do* whatever he wants—a guy might have been with five hundred women, or gambled away a fortune, or done drugs, or had some other sexual or illegal exploits—but he won't tell you anything about it. It seems like the more skeletons a guy has, the less he talks about them. We have the exact opposite impulse, but it's nothing to take personally. Your guy doesn't withhold information because he doesn't trust you. It's the Bro Code, and it has nothing to do with you.

• •

MAN-FORMATION

Things men don't care about:

- When your anniversary or any other "meaningful" date is
- Having time to "just talk"
- Your opinions about other people
- The emotional thing that happened to you today (unless it directly impacts him and/or your relationship)
- What any of your friends said about anything
- What restaurant you are going to, or what you are going to make for dinner (unless it's something they don't like, e.g., too healthy or weird)
- Getting gifts from you

Things men do care about:

- That the relationship is going well and that you have fun together (preferably including lots of sex)
- Your general happiness
- Being able to be proud of you and show you off
- Being comfortable in the home environment
- Getting to do what they want to do (eat something, take a nap, go back to work when necessary) without being nagged or barked at

• •

Men Bond Over Stuff and Action

Women connect with other women over feelings, emotions, and shared experiences, like being moms or sharing similar interests that they feel passionate about. Men can feel bonded to someone even if they never once mention their feelings. They connect about superficial things—sports, gadgets, work issues, mutual glee over girls in bikinis. It's not emotional, and that's how they like it. When women bond over sports, it's usually about the emotions they share, connecting with the athletes or the crowd, or loving watching the emotional reactions when a team wins or loses. While men are discussing or at least thinking about the technical aspects of a play or the mechanics of a race car, women are trying to see the faces (or cute butts) of the athletes. Who *is* the quarterback and what is he like? Who is the guy driving that race car, and how does he feel about his life? Male bonding is a way to relax and escape all the emotion men have to deal with from women.

Men Move On

If you do have an emotional discussion with a man, and then the discussion ends, it's actually over. This is also hard for us to comprehend because to a woman, the end of an emotional relationship discussion is just the beginning of a long and convoluted mental process of analyzing and reanalyzing the contents of the discussion to figure out what it was really about. Men don't do that. They don't want to linger over an argument, and they especially don't want to linger over an emotion. If you've wrapped up the argument and come to some solution, even a temporary or unsatisfactory one, your man will consider this discussion and issue checked off his list. He probably won't give it much more thought, so even if you obsess for weeks, don't assume he's doing the same. Trust me, he's not.

. . . .

JUST THE TIP

Men aren't very comfortable with their emotions. It's not their fault. Our culture has drummed it into their heads that they aren't supposed to be emotional or show any weakness. It's cruel, in a way. Women get to process their emotions, but men are made to feel ashamed of doing that. This is why we have phrases like "man up" and "cry like a woman." Crying is especially touchy for men. Women need it because it's like an emotional release valve. Men don't love a good cry the way we do. In fact, they hate it because it makes them feel weak. They will do almost anything to avoid crying in front of you. If they do it in spite of themselves, they will pretend it never happened, and so should you. If your guy cries in front of you, be cool. Don't make it worse by making a big deal about it or calling attention to it or even mentioning it. Whatever you do, don't tell him that he shouldn't be ashamed of it. It's too late for that. Just be there, be supportive, and then be a sealed vault. Whatever you do, never ridicule or belittle a man for showing emotion or tell anybody else that he cried. Your man would see that as a betrayal.

· ·

Men Don't See Marriage the Way Women Do

Most men definitely get to a point in life when they want to get married, but the notion doesn't consume them from childhood like it does us. We've been conditioned to want and desire the security of marriage, to have someone and to be had by someone officially. We are implanted with the notion of marriage in childhood by watching movies featuring Disney princesses who live happily ever after. The societal pressure is so strong on women that it's hard to avoid it. Nobody wants to be a spinster.

Bachelors, however, are seen as romantic, charmingly incorrigible guys' guys who just can't settle for one woman. Why would they want to give that up? Societal pressure practically tells them *not* to get married (even if their mothers press for it). The whole idea of the ball and chain, never sleeping with another woman for the rest of your life, being trapped by a nagging wife who never wants to have sex anymore, and having a bunch of shrieking kids terrifies some men, and yet the ones who shy away from it seem somehow heroic. It's totally unfair but that's how it is, so men don't typically feel the urge to get married unless they have a good logical reason.

This is something new about society. A century ago, a respectable man would "take a wife" because it would increase his standing in society or in his career. That may be true in some cases now, but more likely, it's not an issue for men anymore. Instead, the reasons most men finally decide to get married are:

- They're tired of sleeping around. The single life is getting boring and the security of a really good woman who can keep them in line and make a permanent home becomes more attractive as they get older.

- They meet someone who seems perfect for them and they are so happy that they realize they aren't interested in other women anymore. This is usually unplanned and "just happens."
- They've been with someone for a long time (sometimes many years) and are happy, but the woman they are with wants to make it official, so they finally decide it can't hurt.
- There are financial reasons. Maybe a two-income household sounds appealing.
- They are getting older. They have considered growing old alone and don't like the idea. They want someone to take care of them.
- They decide they really do want to be a dad. This is a big one!

All of these reasons develop with age and maturity. You can't rush them. They happen when they happen.

· ·

CELEBS SPEAK OUT

If you do get married, get a prenup. It's not about money at all. It's about having a document that states how you'll dissolve your marriage while you still have a shred of respect for each other.

　　—ALEC BALDWIN, INTERVIEW WITH THE *DAILY NEWS*

· ·

Rubber Bands and Ceramic Bowls: How We Fall in Love

Over the years, I've noticed something interesting about the way women fall in love versus the way men fall in love. It is my opinion that, in general, women fall in love more easily, and fall out of love more easily, too. A woman's mind is better at multitasking and transitioning than a man's, so even though we may be the ones who act all romantic and smitten and then heartbroken and destroyed, the truth is that a pint of ice cream and a good cry and one (or a few) therapeutic girls' nights out are all we need to move on. We move on because we've learned that we have to. Our hearts are good at rebounding. We are rubber bands, opening our hearts over and over, so we get used to rejection and become truly resilient. Women are strong, and we have a long evolutionary history of disappointment and bearing up under impossible odds and terrible conditions and still doing what we need to do for ourselves and our children. If you've gone through a horrible and heart-wrenching breakup, maybe you disagree because you are still healing, but you are strong and you know how to heal your heart. Women as a gender and as historical figures are as experienced at heartbreak as anything.

Men, on the other hand, are less experienced in love. They may be more experienced in lust, playing the field, sleeping around, and being cavalier about relationships, but when it comes to deep authentic love, they are much more cautious, much more hesitant, and much more easily destroyed when it doesn't work out with the woman they really believed was the one for them. Because men so rarely let themselves be vulnerable, men fall in love less often than women, and less easily, but when they do fall, they fall hard. For a man, no amount of ice cream or even single-malt scotch will heal the ravages of a broken heart. Most men will always remember that girl in high school or college whom they first loved and who wrecked them. Many of them will admit if pressed that they vowed never to let that happen again, and some of them even admit that they went on with their lives determined to get back at as many women as possible for the pain they suffered. It's not rational, obviously, but it's a guy thing, apparently.

A man's heart isn't like a rubber band that bounces back. It's more like a ceramic bowl. If you shatter it, it's going to be a long hard job to mend it and it will never be quite the same as it was before it was ever broken. This is why emotional connection terrifies many men. A broken heart stings like a beast to them. We look back on a past relationship with an eye roll and a "Thank God I got away from that one," or maybe a wistful "Oh, that was a good guy who got away." Men can't do that.

There is a popular song out right now by the group 5 Seconds of Summer called "Amnesia" that says, "If what we had was real, how could you be fine? 'Cause I'm not fine at all." This exactly describes what I'm talking about. The girl in the song has recovered and is happy now, long after the breakup, but the guy singing the song can't get over it. This is classic.

It's my opinion that part of this difference has to do with how men and women think. In the movie *Sex, Lies, and Videotape*, James Spader's character, Graham, says: "Men learn to love the person that they're attracted to, and women become more and more attracted to the person that they love." This is so true. Men think with their penises, and they are sexually attracted first. When the sex is good and other things fall into place, then they start to fall in love. Women, on the other hand, think with their hearts. They engage their hearts first and fall in love. Then, when they really feel connected, they want to have sex. We are polar opposites in this way. This is one of the reasons why women start worrying about a commitment, or where the relationship is going, long before men do. They take longer to get into that head space, but when they get there, then it's a freight train.

Heartbreak isn't easy for women, either, and we can also have serious consequences from a broken heart. I've been in a relationship where I was positive I knew the person, and when it turned out that I never really knew him at all, I felt like I couldn't trust my own judgment anymore. Now I second-guess myself in every relationship. That one relationship ruined it for all the future ones because I have massive trust issues now. But I still don't think my pain is the same as a man's heartbreak. I've bounced back a hundred times and gone on with my life and never lost faith that I would find love again. Even when I'm commitment-phobic, I'm still an optimist. It's like dieting. We have such high hopes and we jump in with such optimism with every new diet that makes big promises, and then we get crushed by failure and finally we just can't do it anymore. But deep down, we still believe we will find the diet or food attitude that will work for us. Men lose all faith, all hope, and are truly slayed.

The reason I think it's important for women to understand this about men is that you really do need to be careful. If you can tell he's falling in love with you and you aren't really in it, you need to end it before it gets too serious. You need to be kind and take care of a man's fragile heart. It's the right thing to do. And if you are all in? Then if he's falling hard, you've probably got him for as long as you want him.

So that's men. You can't live with 'em and you can't kill 'em. But somehow, you gotta love 'em. And we do. When you understand them, you can love them even better.

CHAPTER 2

. . . .

Woman, Know Thyself

A woman who has never changed her mind doesn't have one.
—UNKNOWN

Now that we've talked about men, you might be feeling pretty superior, what with your complex intellect in the face of your drooling, burping caveman boyfriend or husband. But hold on. We have our issues, too. We do some pretty stupid things, and also some things that seem totally logical to us but that completely and utterly baffle men. In the service of greater communication, I want you to think about these things, too, and cop to them and see where you can let it all out and when it makes more sense to hold back a little bit. Because here's a fact: Women are a little crazy. We can't help it. It's hormonal.

In fact, the influence of hormones is hugely important in making a woman the way she is. We can be the smartest, sharpest, most savvy people on the planet, and then hormones suddenly turn us into raving lunatics. PMS has almost taken me to the edge and over. Once, I was in a sensitive place. I was indulging in a lot of inner dialogue about my relationship and convincing myself that the guy I was dating had been recently very selfish on multiple occasions. I was talking myself into a really emotional place, and I was obsessing and feeling needy. Then I had to attend a wedding.

My boyfriend at the time was the usher at a wedding for one of his friends, and I was his date. Women are good at multitasking and especially good at doing weddings, but being involved was a lot for him to handle and he was really stressed out and overwhelmed. Because a wedding wouldn't stress me at all, I didn't understand that he had a lot going on and had bitten off too much. I was impatient. I thought he was whining. I didn't see his stress.

Then, on the morning of the wedding, I found out that my mother provided gossip stories to the rags. Then I bombed during an appearance, and everything else started going wrong. I cracked a black eye shadow all over my bathroom, the toilet flooded, and I was an hour late to the wedding.

When I got there, my boyfriend pretty much left me to hang out with his friends from the cocktail hour all the way through to the appetizers. His friends were engaging me, but I was spinning out internally, obsessing about where he was and how he had abandoned me. Just another selfish gesture on his part! When he came to sit with me for a while, he looked miserable. Then I saw him laughing with his friends. My interpretation was not that he was revealing his stress to me but playing it cool with the dudes. I just thought he didn't want to be with me and was having more fun with his friends. I was in my head and brought all my baggage to the current situation. After the appetizer, I walked outside to find him and told him the relationship was over, and I was done. He'd never heard me say anything like that to him before. Then I turned around and walked out.

Even my girlfriends told me walking out of a wedding meant I had screwed it up big-time.

But I was absolutely sure I was in the right. In the moment, and all that night. He deserved it. He'd abandoned me. He wasn't giving me what I needed. I had had a really bad day, and he left me alone.

The next morning, things started to look a little different. I woke up and tried to call him and text him for hours. He ignored me. Finally, he texted back that we were over—as I had made clear to him the night before.

I panicked. I realized I had made a mistake. I always say you have to know when to hold 'em and know when to fold 'em, and I failed. This was a time to hold 'em—I folded because I was feeling insecure and thinking he wasn't paying enough attention to me. I should have held it in. It wasn't the time or place to react to my extreme emotions and I realized it too late. For the entire day, I cried and begged. Finally he said he was willing to see me. I apologized and then I gave him space. Eventually he came back to me, but with reluctance. I had done a lot of damage to us.

One week later, I got my period.

We finally repaired our relationship, but it was at a great cost. Sometimes you need to wait before you say something or do something based on emotion because it will make a much bigger emotional mess that you have to clean up.

The booze at the wedding didn't help, either—booze and emotions don't mix, and booze and PMS are the worst combination ever. But the bottom line is that PMS is the devil. If you have it, know that it has the power to destroy everything you love the most.

Welcome to being a woman.

Hormones aren't our only failing. Women also tend to overcomplicate things. As simple as men are, that's how complicated we are. I have battled my tendency to overcomplicate things for years and made plenty of mistakes in my attempts to both overanalyze and overcommunicate with men. I've also wasted a lot of energy trying to justify my own crazy. I've been all over the place, and it's made many of my relationships more difficult over the years. Maybe you can relate. Maybe you can't quite admit that you're overcomplicating practically everything to do with your relationship. Maybe you can't admit that PMS turns you into a crazy person. And maybe your guy is at fault, too. Maybe he doesn't understand you at all and doesn't even try. Maybe he thinks that when he's blanking out in front of the TV, he's actually thinking deep thoughts. But here's the bottom line: If you like penis but you suck at relationships like I do, you need to deal with the facts of what a woman is. Understanding yourself a little better will help.

. . . .

DR. AMADOR SAYS . . .

Hormones and emotions are not failings! Neither is thinking deeply. They don't make you crazy. Bethenny can be hard on herself. She is very intelligent and looks at problems from multiple angles. She can't help but analyze. That's who she is and that means this quality is not a bad thing. Like most women, she's especially adept at seeing the emotional side of a situation. However, talking about every angle you see every time the thought occurs to you can certainly overcomplicate your relationships. Control what you can and don't label your style of thinking as a failing or "crazy." It will only come back to bite your self-esteem, give ammunition to a man who is a toxic fighter, and excuse you from doing anything about the part you really can control: learning when and how to talk about what you see and are feeling.

—XAVIER AMADOR, PH.D., PRESIDENT,

LEAP INSTITUTE, WWW.LEAPINSTITUTE.ORG

. . . .

What's with Women?

Despite the many ways in which women are more complex and arguably more interesting than men, sometimes the nature of being a woman ain't so pretty. Let's break it down. First, women need more than men. Good or bad, it's the truth. The list of things we need is big and unwieldy and complicated, and what makes us even more challenging is that our list of needs is constantly changing. What we desperately need in one moment is irrelevant in the next.

There are some basics, of course. We want love and support, we want security and attention, and we like our lives to be enjoyable, but that's just the beginning. We also want to feel feminine, beautiful, and strong, and we want to be worshipped. At other times, we feel vulnerable, like the girl who needs to be rescued, and we want to be swept off our feet and be protected. We want somebody to make it all okay. But then, we also want power, success, and recognition, and we don't want anybody telling us what to do. Next, we want freedom, independence, self-reliance. And then we are dying for a relationship again, for physical affection and emotional support and somebody to listen and understand and truly know us. And then we want attention. And then we want someone to take the reins so we can stop trying so hard to control everything. And then we grab the reins away again. From the outside, this is all very confusing. You can't stereotype a woman because we constantly defy stereotypes. A guy who understands women based on movies or television will never have a chance at understanding a real woman, because we aren't like that. We aren't the "career-focused ice queen" or the "sweet helpless damsel in distress" or the "manic pixie dream girl" or the "poor little rich girl with abandonment issues" or the "MILF" or the "man-hating dyke" or the "relationship-obsessed single girl" or the "sex-crazed divorcée" or the "girl next door" or the "tomboy" or the "Madonna" or the "whore" or any of those things. But at times, we might be some of them. Or all of them. And then we'll change again, into something much more complex. You can't pin us down.

We also want to talk through everything in great detail so we understand it. This is how women's minds work. If we don't talk it out with somebody, we don't fully understand what we think about something, so when our partner's eyes glaze over and we realize they have no interest in hearing us talk, it's a blow not just to our egos but to our sense of the relationship and its depth. If we can't verbally work through things to understand how we feel, we get as frustrated as a guy who can't get laid.

And then, on top of all that, we want to get laid—but we have many more requirements for a successful sexual experience than most men do. We also want to feel protected, nurtured, carried away, and emotionally bonded. And after it's over we want to be totally secure we were right to let somebody inside of us. We want to know not only that it was pleasurable but that it was worth it and added to our relationship, personal security, and emotional growth. Sex is never just sex to a woman. There are a few exceptions, but they are as rare as a unicorn.

Add to that the not-insignificant hormonal aspect of the female personality. Whether it's adolescence or PMS or pregnancy or postpartum or perimenopause, hormones literally make us a little bit crazy. I'll talk more about this later, but we can be the most loving, nurturing partner in the world, and then the next day (or the next minute), we can hate somebody with every cell in our being for absolutely no reason. I have a friend who is totally in love with her boyfriend, but she says that one week per month, she eyes the cast-iron skillet hanging in her kitchen and seriously considers whether it would be an effective murder weapon. The very next week, she's head-over-heels about him again. What we want, what we like, what we hate, what we need is constantly changing. You can't predict it with much accuracy. All you can do is go with it.

· ·

JUST THE TIP

Women need and want so much in life that they can't possibly get it all from one person. Don't make the mistake of expecting your partner to fulfill all your needs. Spread it around to your girlfriends, family members, career, even your yoga or exercise time. All these things will help to fulfill you. No one person will ever "complete you" (sorry, Renée).

· ·

You need to admit all of this about yourself. If you are in denial, if you think you are perfect or the one who is right all the time and you aren't recognizing how complicated and baffling you are to your partner, you will just come off as inaccessible and difficult. I have another friend who says that whenever she gets on her high horse about something in an argument, her husband says, "You think you're such a badass." At first, she didn't realize what he meant. She would get angry and deny being a badass or thinking she was a badass, and berate him for even calling her a badass. But then she noticed that he always said this when she was refusing to admit any fault in a situation and blaming it all on him. What she thought of as righteous indignation, he thought of as her being a badass (and not in a good way, like Chuck Norris). Now, "badass" has become her cue that she's being stubborn and superior, and that she needs to back down and look at her own position more realistically.

Men don't just want but need to feel respected, and if you spend all your relationship time punishing your partner for not living up to your standards or expecting him to just go along with your moods, you aren't being a fair partner. Maybe he isn't either, but you can be the one to re-calibrate the relationship. If not you, then who? Men don't usually know how to do this, but we do. We obsess about it. And the first step is to know yourself.

Know your strengths and also your weaknesses. Know how you tend to treat people, and compare that with how you know you should treat your partner. And know your own personal crazy. We all have a little crazy in us, and if you want to come together with another human being, you have to know what your crazy is, so you can find somebody willing to deal with it. Maybe it's PMS-related irritability, or depression, or hyper-emotion. Maybe it's a hot-button issue you have, like always seeking men who won't abandon you like your father did but then being afraid to commit because if you leave them, they can't leave you (ahem). Maybe it's insistently putting your career first and resenting anyone who wants more attention than you can give. Maybe it's refusing to tolerate anybody's help or participation in raising your children. Maybe you're chronically jealous or suspicious or you tend to get prematurely clingy or you think you are too independent to ever really give yourself fully to someone. Or commitment just terrifies you, for whatever reason.

There are a million forms of crazy. Know yours, and work on it at your own pace, but don't fool yourself into thinking you don't have any issues. Easy relationships are casual relationships with low stakes. Real relationships that matter are tough, especially for complicated people, and if that's you, then you are in for a challenge. Know yourself and work on being better every day, and you can get there.

. . . .

DR. AMADOR SAYS . . .

"Know your own personal crazy" really means "Know your emotional triggers." Emotional triggers are those events and relationships from your past, especially your early childhood, that lay in wait like land mines. Bethenny's father left her at a very young age and had almost nothing to do with her growing up, so she has a heightened sensitivity to abandonment. This is a common issue with many people, and the result can complicate relationships. An unreturned call, text, prolonged silence, or a partner spending the night out with the boys triggers this deep well of feeling. Feelings that are actually voracious memories can momentarily devour reality, so that all you see is that you are being left again. Knowing the source of such overwhelming sensitivities is the first step to understanding that they are not necessarily about what actually happened today.

—XAVIER AMADOR, Ph.D., PRESIDENT,
LEAP INSTITUTE, WWW.LEAPINSTITUTE.ORG

. . . .

Things for Women to Remember

You've got plenty to remember about how to deal with men, but let's add some important things for you to remember for yourself. You can only control your own behavior, so here are some things you can do to make your relationship easier.

Shut the Hell Up

No offense, but you talk too much. You also text too much. Not in my opinion, but in the opinion of most men. It's not just you. It's me, and most women. We can't help it. Who hasn't been a little buzzed or a lot excited and gone off on a tangent about her latest girl drama, job drama, friend drama, fashion obsession, or new hair color, or that article she read that totally explained her relationship issues? I'll tell you who hasn't: most men. They don't care about these things, and if you really need to let it out, they will probably tolerate it, but they are more than likely thinking of something else while you talk and would fail any quiz you gave them afterward about what you just said.

Women don't just like to talk. We need to talk, especially about our feelings. Men don't. This is one of the most basic, square-one differences between men and women, so to even the playing field a little, sometimes you need to shut the hell up. Just give it a break once in a while. I'm not saying you should never talk, but see if you can cut the chatter by, say, 25 percent. Try some silence and see how it goes. What happens? A girlfriend might be startled and offended if you stopped talking to her, but a guy will likely find it a welcome relief. Guys love silence. I've heard they can make their minds go totally blank and think of absolutely nothing. This is why men sleep like rocks (and the ones who don't are too complicated to deal with). I can't even begin to imagine how not to think about anything, but men seem to have that special skill.

We get into trouble when we start reading into those silences, assuming a man is thinking the way a woman is thinking. When we experience a silence, we go into a complicated internal drama about all the problems the silence must surely indicate, when the guy is probably not thinking anything at all, or something totally mundane, like why the car engine is making a strange noise or how awesome sex was last night.

· ·

GIRL TALK

Girlfriends exist for the sake of talking. Girls *want* you to talk, and they want to talk back to you. They especially want to talk about feelings—your feelings, her feelings, his feelings. A group of girls can sit down together and the talking won't stop for seven hours. It's therapeutic and we love to do it. So have your girls' nights out. Make them a priority. Have coffee with your best friend. Go on walks with your sister or your mom. Meet your coworkers for happy hour and talk your ass off. Your gay best friend is great for this, too—gay men love talking much the way women do. So go to town—fill the air with chitchat and gossip and noise. Then go home and reel it in. Say one thing at a time. Be friendly, light, easy, and if you need to discuss an issue, keep it to one subject only. Trust me—your relationship will improve, and there are plenty of other modes of communication he probably prefers.

· ·

See what happens if you let the silence be.

I've often seen a statistic quoted, that women say three times as many words every day as men do. Then I read something else that contradicted this and said that actually, men and women say about the same number of words every day but talk about different things. I'm not sure what I think of this because I know some pretty talkative men, but on the other hand, only a few compare to most of the women I know when it comes to sheer number of words. In my world, men talk when they have to, when they want something, or when they have something funny to say (or something they *think* is funny, like a dumb movie quote). Sometimes they like to ramble on about some silly story nobody wants to hear, and they never seem to realize you aren't captivated by their words.

Sometimes men ask questions about what they are interested in, but what they want back from someone in a conversation is not what we want. They want straightforward, simple answers to their questions. They do not want a novelized version of a reply to "What are we doing for dinner?"

Men are not big on small talk.

I have a girlfriend whose husband complains that she talks in paragraphs. He says that by the time she is done, he can't even remember what they were talking about because she has switched subjects so many times. On a normal day, she probably does talk more than he does, but I've gone out with them at night and when he starts drinking, he won't shut up and she clams up because she's annoyed. Maybe it evens out at the end of the day. Another friend says that when her boyfriend can tell she wants to talk about something, he heaves a big sigh and says, "Okay, *go*." She says that drives her crazy, like he's gearing himself up to tolerate whatever she's going to say because he knows it's going to take too long and he's obviously not really going to be listening.

So if you want to make things easier, shut the hell up. Not with your girlfriends. Not with your family. Not at work or in class, when it's appropriate to be heard and make your voice and opinion and intelligence evident. Not anywhere where your interesting ideas and verbal prowess can improve your life.

But whether you're in a new relationship or you've been married for fifty years, try the power of silence. Just try it. Try talking in sentences instead of paragraphs. Text less. Don't think out loud. Bring up one subject at a time, or offer your opinion on something and then don't say anything else. Let what you said hang there for his contemplation. Because in your relationship, excessive talking is *not* improving your life. It's making your life worse. He isn't listening, and you already know that every time you realize he isn't listening, you feel like a loser.

And if you still think he cares about how well Estée Lauder's new cream works, then you are the one who is a moron.

A benefit to this strategy is if you talk less, he will talk more. If you've been wanting to draw him out more, this is the way. If there's one thing I learned being a talk show host, it's that the less you talk, the more the other person talks. Then you'll learn more about him, not just tell him all about you. That's valuable information you're getting.

• •

GIRL TALK

I enjoy the occasional juice cleanse, or cleanse from alcohol, meat, or sugar. When you've been eating badly, drinking too much lately, or you just don't feel great, nobody else might notice, but you know you could use a reboot. Cleanses allow the body to rest and focus on healing rather than processing food. Recently I thought, *Why not try this with relationships?* That's when my assistant Leslie and I both decided to try a communication cleanse.

The essence of the communication cleanse is to consciously decide to take some space from each other when the relationship is a little rocky. You know you want to be together but you haven't been appreciating each other. It is a kind of maintenance effort before things go downhill and someone "needs space" in that bad way that means "I really want to break up but I don't know how to say it."

Whether you have a specific goal in mind, like deciding whether to move in together, deciding whether to have kids, deciding what you need from someone, are in a lull, bored, or bickering a lot, or you just need some time to think and be by yourself, a communication cleanse can be just the relationship reboot you need. Just be sure it's mutual and you both feel good about it. Set a specific date and time to get back together to discuss how it went, then go and enjoy the physical and mental peace and quiet.

My communication cleanse was refreshing. It didn't come out of a fight. It was more like a mutual "I love you, we're on the same team, I think about you all the time, but let's take a breather" kind of situation. It quieted everything down. Sometimes two passionate people need to be quiet for a while. It's the only way you can hear yourself think and get clear about what you need and want.

Leslie's communication cleanse had a more specific purpose. Here is how she describes it:

This week, my boyfriend and I tried a communication cleanse from Monday through Thursday. We had both been having hard times at our jobs and with our living situations. He is changing careers and I am in desperate need of a new apartment. He's not ready for us to live together, even though I am. This month is also the anniversary of a terrible car accident I was in, during which I could have lost my life, so this time of year is always difficult for both of us. We recognized that outside forces were straining us, so we decided we would each take some space to reevaluate our lives and our relationship and figure out what each of us needed for support. We didn't speak to or see each other for four days. The only communication was when I needed help with my fantasy football team, so that was five minutes over text on Tuesday morning. My only cheat!

On Thursday night we got back together and exchanged handwritten letters about what each of us felt we needed. He wrote that he wanted unconditional support with his career change, even if that means no vacations or fancy date nights since he will be taking a huge pay cut and working long hours. I wrote that I wanted more affectionate interaction between us, and I want us to have a long-term plan (such as, "By September 2015, we will be living together," etc.), so I feel like we have a future we are both working toward.

The result was fantastic. We have a healthy, strong relationship already and don't argue much. We're best friends and we've been together for six years, but life is hard sometimes and we all get battered by circumstances. The positive time we took apart allowed us both to focus on the big picture, rather than on specific petty disagreements that can fool us into thinking we want to part ways. We were both able to clarify what we needed to get us through the next few tough months, and today we couldn't be happier.

Keep It in the Safe

I'm the queen of TMI and I've had to learn the hard way that you shouldn't divulge everything about yourself—not to anyone, but especially not to the person you're interested in. You can steal from the guy playbook for this one. The more you tell about yourself, the less control you have over that information. Even your husband doesn't need to know everything about you. Remember that once it's out, you can never take it back, and maintaining an air of mystery, no matter how long you know someone, will always make you more intriguing.

Yet, unlike guys, who hardly ever reveal anything, we tend to be open books. We want to tell our partners everything about us *on the first date*, even the embarrassing and not-so-flattering things. We can usually restrain ourselves somewhat, but eventually it all comes out, for better or for worse. I know I can tell myself a thousand times not to say something, but then all of a sudden one day when I'm not even thinking it, out it comes, like a bad batch of oysters. Verbal diarrhea. It's a problem. (It tends to be worse when you are younger, before you hit your 40s and realize nobody gives a shit about your big opinions.)

There are many downsides to being too open about yourself. Talking about mistakes from the past can give people the wrong impression about who you are now. Maybe you had a promiscuous period of your life, or you used to shoplift or get a little loose with the nose candy, or someone knows what you did last summer. If that's not you anymore, why subject yourself to irrelevant value judgments? Do you think he will like you more because you had a fucked-up childhood? Don't wear your story. Everybody deserves a second chance, but if you really are over what you did in the past, there isn't really any need to bring it up. At least not right away. Let your partner get to know who you are right now first.

. . . .

BATTLE OF THE SEXES

In my opinion and based on what I've seen, men and women cheat on their partners about equally. I think the notion that men cheat more is a myth in the twenty-first century. However, how they cheat is different. Women cheat to feel loved and get attention, and they are more stealthy and better at doing it without getting caught. Men cheat to feel cool and to validate their masculinity. They are also more obvious.

. . . .

You might also be tempted to detail your past accomplishments (business, career, or financial success; mastery of some complicated subject; fame; your high IQ; that cool thing you invented and patented), but that's just obnoxious. Let your stellar qualities unfold naturally, so he can continue to be ever more impressed with who you are. And you won't sound braggy. Besides, men don't care how much money you make, unless you make more than they do, in which case you could intimidate them. They don't care about all your other so-called fantastic accomplishments, either.

It's also a bad idea to talk about your past relationships, whether it's the rich boyfriend who gave you all that cool stuff or took you on those jet-setter weekends or the psycho ex-husband who hired a PI to follow you around after the divorce. Either way, it will only reflect badly on you and your choices. Some guys might like a damsel in distress. They might want to sweep in and save you. But is that what you want in a relationship? To be chosen for your weaknesses and problems? Other guys will be scared away by this kind of information.

It's better to let information trickle out in bits and pieces here and there, good and bad and neutral, so you are a puzzle, a mystery to decipher, a challenge. Don't show your whole hand right away. What's sexy about a girl who blabs about everything? Even if it's clear that whatever you are revealing is in your past, it doesn't help you to lay all your cards on the table. A girlfriend might think such disclosures mean you are intimate friends. To a guy, it's TMI.

Sometimes they will ask, though, just to see what you say. They may be trying to figure out if they like you, or they are testing you, or they genuinely want to know more about you because you haven't revealed very much. A guy I was dating recently asked me whether I was ever pregnant aside from Bryn. I felt safe with him and I was just about to launch into a story about a past pregnancy . . . but then some instinct kicked in and told me to just sit there and let it breathe. There was no reason to reveal that intimate detail of my life right there and then. What good would it do? Would it move our relationship forward? Would I be proud of myself for admitting it? No and no. He didn't press the topic. When I didn't answer, we just changed the subject. Men are so ADD, he totally forgot he ever asked and it hasn't come up since, and I feel better about having kept something to myself for once. If he ever reads this, he probably won't even know what I'm talking about. And considering how guys are usually pretty selfish, I doubt he'll ever read this anyway.

Another time, a guy who is a good friend asked me if I had slept with the guy I was currently seeing yet. In a moment of weakness, I blabbed. Why did I do that? How did it benefit me? How was it his business, or anyone's? Just because someone asks you a question doesn't mean you have to answer it. I regretted it. It felt like a betrayal of relationship trust. Men don't tell. Why did I?

It's also important to keep your relationship private from all but your closest girlfriends. Obviously you have to process it with somebody, but a new relationship might not be able to withstand a series of Twitter updates to your thousands of followers or constant Facebook posts about how you think you "found the One." Just cool it. If you end up having issues or the relationship doesn't work, you'll feel like an idiot, and being too public about your personal life can actually cause the destruction of your personal life. Trust me. I know this firsthand.

· ·

GIRL TALK

If you are obsessing about your relationship, get moving or get busy. Do yoga, take a walk, go running, or immerse yourself in a project. If you don't exercise or think about something else, you can get mired in your thoughts, and an idle mind is the devil's playground. Writing this book has kept me sane during my divorce because it's given me something to focus on.

· ·

Eventually, you can disclose personal things, but not all at once and definitely not too soon. Be like an onion, with layers to peel. Don't act mysterious. Be mysterious. Let who you are unfold rather than explode. Be that girl who people wonder about. *Who is she?* The less you say, the more they will want to know, like an outfit that reveals enough to entice but still leaves something for the imagination.

It's not about lying, or withholding important information when you are getting serious about someone, but the first few dates are not the time to show your whole hand. If you're not oversharing, you're a lot less likely to:

- make yourself look bad
- be boring
- get misquoted (or just quoted)
- compromise yourself
- kill the intrigue
- seem crazy or desperate
- be too obvious

Meanwhile, you can do your own private investigation. You can find out a lot about your new interest without necessarily asking questions outright. You can talk all day at someone and learn nothing about them, but you want to know as much as possible. Listening is your opportunity to find out what your guy might otherwise not tell you. Chat with his friends. Pay attention to what other people say about him. Find out how he feels about his mother, his work, his health. Be interested in him. When you find out things (which you will), keep them to yourself. If they are bad and worth ending the relationship over, at least you found out before you got in too deep. If they are good, then you can feel more confident about pursuing the relationship. In the movie *Wall Street*, Gordon Gekko famously said, "If you're not inside, you're outside." Be inside.

Even if you are married, let your life, especially your past, be yours. You can reveal little bits here and there, but why not always remain a little bit inscrutable? Don't play hard to get—be hard to get. It's an ancient instinct for men to chase, and an ancient instinct for us to be hard to catch. Even when you are technically "caught," you can still be hard to catch. You can still inspire the chase. Men need to be the pursuers, even in marriage. If you keep them engaged, they will never get bored. My assistant

Julia once told me that when you chase a dog, he runs away. When you run away from the dog, he chases you. Run away from the dog.

. . . .

JUST THE TIP

"Keeping it in the safe" applies not just to relationships but to everyday life. Do you want to be known as the girl who can't keep a secret, who gossips and spreads rumors, or do you want to be the cool one who stores and processes the information but doesn't use it? So you know a guy friend of yours has a secret girlfriend? Keep it to yourself. You know your husband's friend is cheating on his wife? Keep it to yourself. Your boyfriend's best friend's wife tells you something shocking? Don't go telling your guy. Nobody likes a gossip. Period. The end. Personally, I'm a steel trap. A safe. Everyone tells me everything. Celebrities, regular people, perfect strangers—they tell me because they know I won't tell. And I don't. You can do this, too. Store it all away. You may never need to know it, but even if you never tell, it could turn out to be useful information for your life.

. . . .

Just Say It

On the flip side of zipping it, I also want to talk about how to talk to a man. Sometimes, you have to say something important. Talking is required. When you have to talk to your guy about something that really matters, you need a plan. This isn't necessary with your girlfriends. If you have an issue with your girlfriend, you can both talk all around the issue, considering every possible angle, and finally come to the real problem at the end of the second bottle of wine. However, this approach is a disaster if you try it with your boyfriend or husband (or brother or father, for that matter).

When you have something important to say to your guy, you need to remember just two things:

1. Keep it very simple. Core issue only, no other issues thrown in. Don't globalize. This is not the time to kill two birds with one stone. *One subject at a time*, and stick to the issue.

2. Take the emotion out of it. Don't be snippy or mean or weepy or needy or melancholy or a drama queen. Be even and calm and get right to the point.

If you want to have a real conversation that actually has good results, you have to do these two things. You have to be straightforward and direct. No sniping, no insults, no taking shots at the other person, no hinting, no being so polite that you never actually say anything, no criticism, no getting back at him for something he did yesterday, no tit for tat (but tit on its own might work). It's not about scoring points or winning or being right. It's about fixing a problem.

This can be difficult if you are in the habit of being emotional when you talk about emotional subjects. Most women are. It comes naturally to us and there is nothing wrong with it, *when talking to other women*. But sometimes we have to suck it up if we want to get something done right, and that means flatlining the weepy and the needy to get our message across. Your guy would rather hear it straight out. As long as you are calm and sweet about it, then direct is always best—and a huge relief to your guy if he is used to your being passive-aggressive or thinking he will read your mind or intuit your meaning. Trust me: He doesn't know what you are thinking, and somehow believing he does is just a waste of everybody's time and annoying as hell. What you want him to guess will remain a complete mystery, plus you've ruined his day by getting mad at him for not being psychic.

Let's say, for example, that you really want him to make plans for your nights out once in a while. Or maybe you want him to be more physically affectionate or say he loves you more often. Maybe you would like a little romantic gift once in a while.

This is what *not* to say:

You: We need to talk. I feel like something is really really wrong with our relationship.

Him: Huh?

You: Well . . . [long dramatic pause] I don't want to be annoying or demanding, but I feel like there are so many little things you would do if you really cared about me, and you don't do them. Or you used to do them and you stopped. You know what I mean?

Him: Um . . . no?

You: Are you being purposefully dense? You don't know me at all! That must be why you never ever make the plans for our nights out and I have to do it all. In fact, I do everything. You bring nothing to the table. Why don't you ever send me flowers or listen to what I want so you know that I like romantic presents? And last week you didn't answer my text. And then you went out with your friends when you could have had dinner with me. And you left your towel on the floor.

Him: Blbbblblllbblb . . . [and then his brain explodes]

This conversation could quickly descend into hell. Your words are full of negativity. Instead, what if you just tried this approach?

You: Can you make the dinner plans tomorrow?

Him: Okay.

You: I love it when you take the initiative. It's sexy to me. Thank you so much. I love you!

The end.

Obviously there is no perfect conversation, but you have to pick your battles. What are the things you are and are not willing to live with? What is the biggest problem or the thing you want to solve first? Whatever the issue, present it in a straightforward and loving way with a direct request. Follow up with positive reinforcement, and deal with the other little issues later (they might even take care of themselves).

Relationship harmony restored.

Women like to see progress and evolution, while men like to stay in a flow that works for them. With the above method, you make it seem like you are in the flow, but you are also prompting subtle progress. It's win-win. It's not less romantic if you have to tell him what to do. Trust me, if you tell him you want flowers more often, and a month later, you get a big bouquet of flowers for no reason at all, it's going to be romantic and you're going to love it. He'll be happy because he did something right, and you'll be proud that he heard you and actually responded to your needs.

A lot of guys complain about how girls don't just say what they want. A lot of women expect men to know, through some magical psychic man power, what they want. *If he really knew me, if he really understood me, if he really loved me, he would just know.* Forget that. Men are simple, and you want them to read your mind? Nobody knows what you want until you tell them. Not even your "soul mate." Even if you drop what you think are really obvious hints, he's not going to get it. Or he'll get it but he might choose to ignore it because you are being annoying. Just say it.

Here's an example from my life. I had been dating a guy for six weeks, and I felt like we were getting pretty emotionally and physically intimate, but I never saw him during the day, and sometimes I only saw him once a week. Some people might be okay with an arrangement like that, but personally, this bothered me because if I'm sleeping with someone and being intimate, I want to hear from that person the next day. I want to know there is some kind of connection and structure to our relationship.

I didn't want to be a crazy person and I didn't want to confront him with every issue all at the same time. I thought about what to say before I said it. I planned it out and stuck to the issue. I was calm and confident, and I laid it out:

Me: Look, if we sleep together, I need to know that you'll call me the next day.

Him: Okay.

And he did. Our relationship progressed. I was pretty proud of myself for keeping it simple.

There is one caveat to being straightforward, however. Once you are honest with yourself and know what you really need or want, you have to be willing to give up something in return (fair is fair) or be willing to walk if you don't see the possibility of getting what you need. You might not always get everything you want immediately and there has to be give-and-take, but think about whether it might be something you will get eventually. Sometimes what you need is in the cards, down the road, but your relationship has to mature into it.

Not all men and women have difficulty communicating; however, there are noticeable gender-related styles to speaking and being understood. Men tend to accept words on face value and are not always aware of the underlying emotion in a statement. Women tend to be better at emotional awareness. A conflict can occur when women feel like their emotions are being ignored and men simply are like "Huh?? I didn't know you felt like that!" The lesson is to be specific about the issue and how it makes you feel. Many men also will shy away from confrontation, which can feel like you're being ignored. Instead of turning up the volume to make sure that you're being heard, it's good to tune in by staying focused on the issue at hand.

—Janet Taylor, psychiatrist from
New York City, www.drjanet.tv

Also consider how reasonable your demands are. If you like someone who is complicated and interesting, then you can't complain when he gets moody. If you like someone who is stable and steady, then you can't complain that he isn't spontaneous and passionate. You can't order your partner's personality traits à la carte.

Think about what you are willing to live with and what you are willing to live without. Think about the consequences of asking for that thing you think you need or want. Do you really want him to change his personality? Or grow up immediately? Or sacrifice something he loves for you? Those things aren't reasonable and probably can't happen. Do you really need to know right now where the relationship is going, or are you just anxious to get proof that he really likes you? Do you really want a ring right now, if it means risking losing him before you really know each other when you scare him away with a demand like that? What's it really about?

Sometimes, if you really think about it before you say anything, you'll realize that you are actually getting what you want already. Look at what's bothering you and look at the balance of give-and-take. You might give some things, and he gives different things. Also look at what you love and what you are getting, and find the balance there, too. And be careful what you wish for—if you want him to do more and more and more, and then he starts doing everything and you're not in control anymore, you might not like it or you might push him away.

But if you know you need something and you don't see it happening, or if you are intimate and what you are asking for is important to you and reasonable, then you have to mean what you say. If he calls your bluff and says he's not willing to do what you want, and you cave in and stick around anyway, you are a doormat. You're basically telling him that you don't mean what you say and he can treat you however he wants, not calling you after you sleep together, or not letting you meet his parents, or whatever it is.

Instead, you need to do what's right for you. Mean what you say. If you need time to get it straight in your head before you actually say it, then take some space to process the situation. Be sure what you need is worth the risk, and if it is (and if it's important to you, it should be), then rip the Band-Aid off and move on with your life. Either you'll be free, or it will be a wake-up call for your partner, who might just come crawling back. If not, the relationship wasn't right and probably never will be. The truth is more important than what you want. Some people aren't right for each other, period.

Being married complicates this strategy, of course. You can't just walk out because your husband doesn't put his arm around you anymore or because you feel disconnected, and pulling the divorce card every time you fight is hitting below the belt. If you have issues that aren't huge and fundamental, you can probably work through them with some mutual compromise. Isn't that what you agreed to do when you decided to get married? What you can't work through is finding someone you are attracted to and love. If you have that, it's a valuable thing. You can't just go out and grab someone off the street to be in love with. If you have a foundation of love and connection, don't let something silly break you up. The wrong kind of fighting causes damage that can be difficult to repair. If you miss him when he's gone, if the sex is (or was) really great, if you feel like you are really a part of each other's lives and that means something to you, then you can work out the irritating details. I have a girlfriend who told me that she and her husband have agreed they will always stay together. No matter what they argue about, no matter how upset anyone gets, they have that baseline, so nobody fears the other person will leave. There is a comfort, safety, and security in that knowledge. They know they are in it forever, so they have motivation to work problems out in a way that will be successful in the long term. I like that; however, it's not an excuse for complacency.

. . . .

JUST THE TIP

When to bring up an issue:

- When you are both calm and in a logical mood.
- When he isn't obviously busy doing something else, especially working or watching TV.
- When you are in public, to keep it light and avoid a scene (unless that doesn't work for you). Stay out of earshot of other people. A secluded booth at a restaurant or a park bench is a good option.

When to shut the hell up:

- The minute your partner walks in the door. Give him some transition time.
- When you have PMS. Just stop. Whatever it is, don't bring it up. You are currently possessed by the devil.
- After sex. This is the time for sweet pillow talk, not problems, especially sexual problems. Never talk about sex while in bed.
- When either of you is angry or emotional. This is really hard to do because this is exactly when you want to start something, but breathe through the strong feelings and try to bring the issue up later when you are calm.

. . . .

Timing Is Everything

When they think of something that bothers them, many women tend to get all wound up and they just have to get it all out and talk about it in the moment. It's very hard for us to mull it over or wait to say it. We can't help it. We are dying to say it. We have to say it out loud, right then and there. As much as I tell you not to do this, I know that it is practically impossible and I break my own rule all the time. It's hard not to deal with something right when you are feeling the strongest emotions about it, even though that's the worst time to deal with something in an effective way.

The problem is that if you bring up an issue before you are really ready to deal with the consequences of saying something about it, then suddenly you're in a fight and being judged by what you say, which might be more rude or harsh than you intended or not precisely what you mean because you haven't actually thought it through first. Then you're into something you really don't want to be into.

If I feel something, I say it, and if I don't get the reaction I want, I harbor resentment, which often puts me and my partner in a worse situation than we were with whatever the original problem was. This is an example of where we can steal a strategy from men. A man can wait three weeks to mention something that's bothering him, and then he can do it calmly. He can think it through like a chess game before he makes his move. He won't do it until he's ready, and if you bring it up, then he's likely to say, "I can't talk about this right now." That's smart. Nearly impossible for a woman, but smart.

So let's say you're going to wait it out. When should you bring it up? The first thing to consider is timing. I know a guy who says that he always gauges his wife's mood and what she is doing before he brings up anything at all because if he doesn't time it right, he won't get a good reaction. He can wait two months for the right moment. Women often think that whenever they are ready to talk, other people will automatically be ready to listen. Not true! The next time you get the urge to bring up a sensitive subject, step back and look at what your man is doing and what kind of mood he's in. Is he distracted by a big business deal? Did he just visit his mom in the hospital? Is he exhausted from a long day at work? Is he watching a game? Is it really urgent or time-sensitive? Remember, men process issues one at a time. If something else is already taking up his attention, he's not going to give his full attention to the issue you want to discuss. Has he had a chance to relax for a few minutes and get into a more receptive frame of mind? Is he already in a bad mood, or is he looking around to see what you are doing and wants to engage?

Bringing up problems at the wrong time could just result in a big fight and won't solve the problem. If talking about something *right this minute* is going to start an avalanche of accusations and you're going to start picking on every little thing that irritates you all at once, then it won't take very many words before he can't even hear you anymore. You can do real damage saying things when you're emotional that you don't really mean or aren't ready to say. You could blow up a whole relationship by triggering the wrong subjects or emotions or by hitting below the belt. Don't open Pandora's box when the relationship is worth having. Remember, bring up one issue at a time. Don't set your partner up to fail. Don't push buttons when you aren't prepared to deal with the aftermath. If you are arguing about the division of housework or who does what with the money, don't suddenly throw in something sensitive, like, "Oh, and by the way, your mother came over today and told me XYZ about you," or "Oh, and by the way, when are you going to get a real job?" The fact is that you aren't perfect either, and you can't start keeping score, because you don't want him keeping score. Seek professional help if you can't get there on your own, but don't just throw it away lightly. If your connection existed once, you can find it again.

• •

DR. AMADOR SAYS . . .

If you don't want to push buttons then *practice restraint of tongue and thumbs*. Never send a text or an e-mail without waiting at least two hours after you've finished furiously typing out your complaint. It can wait. What's the hurry? No matter how calm and reasonable you think you're being, what you've written will likely just push his buttons if you rush to push that send button! Put it aside and give yourself a little time to reconsider. Let me explain *how* to do this and *why* it works.

When the wait time is up, read what you wrote and you will almost always see why it was wise to wait. Delete any criticisms, name-calling, tit-for-tat attacks, defensive comments, or higher ground proclamations such as "I would never treat you the way you treated me." In other words, delete the toxic argument you've made. Then, if what's left is a pure expression of how you feel about something he said or did, press send. If this advice feels too difficult, then don't text or e-mail anything! Let it go and revisit when you're calmer.

Why It Works: Bringing up problems in an e-mail or text almost guarantees your "innocent and reasonable" note will trigger a negative reaction and a fight. Why? Your old habits of kitchen-sinking, name-calling, defending, etc., will color your carefully chosen words an angry, attacking red. And there is too much room for interpretation. There's no tone of voice, eye contact, or body language in a text message or e-mail to help him understand you feel hurt and vulnerable and that this is ultimately the reason you said those things.

—Xavier Amador, Ph.D., president,
LEAP Institute, www.leapinstitute.org

. . . .

Here are some things to ask yourself the next time something is really bothering you and you have the urge to start throwing grenades:

- What is he doing right now? Is he in a mental space to hear you, or is he tired or in the middle of something else he's concentrating on (even if it's something you think is idiotic, like a hockey game on TV)?
- Can you give it a day, or even an hour, before you open Pandora's box and the whole thing takes on a life of its own and ruins everybody's day and you end up arguing about nothing because you just feel like arguing right now? I know at least for me, I'm like lasagna—I'm better the next day, after I've had a chance to cool off.
- How are you going to present this issue? If he keeps forgetting to take the garbage out after he says he will, or if he leaves food crumbs on the counter, are you going to be rude about it? Are

you going to say it's his fault the whole apartment smells like a sewer? Or are you in the mental space to be calm and rational and keep your request simple? "Hey, babe, do you mind taking the garbage out?"

When the time is right, say what you need to say. You always have the right to ask for what you need, but you will be more likely to get it if you consider your communication strategy and choose something most likely to work with your partner.

It's Never About What It's About

Sometimes women fight with men unnecessarily because it is a way to process the feelings they have about themselves. Have you already been having an internal dialogue with your partner that you totally made up, and are you already annoyed at him because of what he said or did during the internal dialogue that didn't actually happen? Maybe you imagine asking him to take out the trash, and him ignoring you, and you feeling neglected and telling him he never helps out around the house, and him saying he makes more money than you do so he shouldn't have to take out the garbage, and now you feel hurt and dejected and inferior, when he is totally innocent.

More often than not, internal dialogues like this actually reveal your own insecurities about yourself, rather than anything your partner thinks. Maybe you feel inferior because you never really found a career or a passion. Maybe you aren't even upset about the garbage. Look at those feelings instead of pointing the finger at someone else. Most of the time, I find that when I just present the issue calmly, nothing even resembling my internal dialogue ever happens.

Even without the internal dialogue, it might not be about what it's about. Are you sure you know what you are actually upset about? Is it that thing he said or did, or is that really a symptom of something bigger? Is it the towel on the floor, or do you feel like it's just a sign that he doesn't care about what's important to you (such as a bathroom that doesn't look like a men's locker room)? Or are you just insecure, so you are bringing up things that aren't that big of a deal, just to engage him?

Maybe whatever it is really is something you can just let go. Sometimes you just want to fight, or you just want to initiate a conversation. If that's the case, it's very helpful to recognize this. Can you just let this go and connect in a more positive way? Here's a shocker: *Not every issue you think up in your head is actually a problem you need to discuss with your partner.*

Sometimes, you just want to fight. I think that women like to fight more than men do, even if they say they don't. They like the drama. Or you just want to talk. Or the thing that annoys you in the moment won't be a problem later and you can choose to just let it go. Don't do this if it's something really important, obviously. But if it's not, is it really worth a scene? Maybe not.

• •

DR. AMADOR SAYS . . .

When Bethenny says, *"Not every issue you think up in your head is actually a problem you need to discuss with your partner,"* I say, "Amen!" I am not sure I agree that women always like drama, but I am impressed by the simplicity and the power of her insight. Couples in strong, loving relationships that last know and practice this simple truth.

—Xavier Amador, Ph.D., president,
LEAP Institute, www.leapinstitute.org

• •

Here's an example. Recently, a guy I was dating told me he wanted to see me that night. When he texted me to say let's get together, I dropped what I was doing because I wanted to see him. Then some friends of his showed up, and he really wanted to hang out with them. I could tell he was worried that I would be mad at him if he didn't ditch his friends to come see me. *Even though it was his idea for us to get together.* But I was okay with it, if slightly annoyed. I told him to go ahead, and I went back home. I was proud of myself for not saying anything or turning it into a big bitch session. That is rare.

The next night, however, he wanted us to have plans. I was home, and he got there at 8:20 p.m. He'd already had several drinks and was kind of buzzed. He wanted to hang out and have sex. This was all normal to him, but I was still annoyed from the night before, so this very small transgression (making me wait until 8:20 and then coming home buzzed because he'd already been having a good time while I was waiting around) really pissed me off. I was upset with him not because of this one night alone, but because it was on the heels of the night before. I felt like he was jerking me around, making me play second fiddle to his social life. Because the night before was long gone from his mind, he thought I was completely crazy. "What's the big deal?"

I could have launched in and turned the evening really nasty, but I stopped, stepped back, and thought about what the *real* issue was. It wasn't that it was already after eight. I actually had a lot to do and I'd been getting it done. It wasn't that he was buzzed. God knows I'm often buzzed by 8:20. It wasn't that he wanted to have sex. I was fine with that. But I was pissed, and I needed to figure out why before I said anything. I was calm and rational and I figured it out. Then I said: "Can you do me a favor and let me know what's actually happening ahead of time? I need to know if we have plans or don't, and when, so I don't drop everything for no reason, or so I'm not left hanging because I don't know what we're doing."

That, he understood. He wouldn't have liked that, either. That was the core issue, and so that was the only thing I said. It had the right impact, he apologized, and we didn't get into a nasty fight. I considered it a major victory for all womankind.

Ultimately, we should want our partners to be happy, but sometimes we don't act that way. If you really love someone, you really do want them to be happy, but it's easy to let pettiness and hurt feelings get in the way. This is why it's so important to stay calm when you bring up sensitive issues. If you can keep your eye on the goal—a stronger bond and a happier relationship—then you might do less damage.

I'm not always as successful as I was that night. Sometimes I can feel the harmful words coming out and I know there's not much I can do to stop it, especially when I'm PMS-ing. Nobody should have to feel like they aren't allowed to express themselves. You *should* be allowed to express yourself. But what I'm talking about is about timing and tone. And if you really can't help it, if it's coming out despite your best efforts, then let it out, but have a plan. Decide on the one thing to say. Vow not to bring in every other little thing you are feeling in that moment. Then let it rest. Let the one thing reverberate. It's the best way to be heard.

. . . .

THE SILENT CONTRACT

No one can do everything. There should be a silent contract that each person should do what he is good at doing and let the other person handle the other stuff. Nobody signed a contract that said they promised to be romantic every day because you are, or like all the same things you like, or be the one to write all the thank-you cards. If you're the one who is great at planning, if you're the one who enjoys buying gifts, making cards, writing poems, then you can't beat the other person up for not doing it as much as you do. Your boyfriend or husband can't help it if he's not a good planner or not crafty. If you're the one good at making money, or managing the money, or cooking, or cleaning up after your partner cooks, or keeping the house neat, then go with your strengths and let your partner go with his. Be good at the job that is yours.

It has to even out, of course. He might be the one who is better at fixing things, or doing the yard work, or maybe he makes most of the money, or is better at cooking, or does most of the cleaning. If it's pretty much equal in the big picture, then maybe you can live with that. However, you do have the right to say, "Look, I do thoughtful things for you and I would love it if you would do them for me sometimes. Once out of ten times, can you do something romantic? Because it would mean a lot to me." Or, "Hey, I know I'm usually the cook, but can you cover dinner once a week? It would really help me out." Anyone can do something once in a while, even if they don't like it or aren't good at it, to please the person they love. Then, if he does it, fair is fair—it's only right that you also offer to mow the lawn once in a while or do something else you wouldn't normally do for him. Like give him a blow job on his lunch hour. I'm pretty sure he would appreciate that.

. . . .

Check Yourself Before You Wreck Yourself

Sometimes, despite all your good intentions, you're going to launch into an argument prematurely and get in deeper than you intended. If you go ahead and say what you're thinking without considering the repercussions and the whole thing starts to go south, you can still rescue yourself. This is the time to *change your trajectory*. Step back, and say, "You know what, I don't want to say something I'll regret. Let me sit back and think about this so I know what I really think, and I'll get back to you." Then go give yourself a time-out.

· ·

DR. AMADOR SAYS . . .

How do you give yourself a time-out? What I taught Bethenny and countless others is to exit toxic arguments using *BET*. "Bet" on the power of time to make you better at getting what you need. BET stands for:

- **Breathe:** When he's yelling or striking back with hurtful words or the silent treatment, take three deep breaths from your abdomen. This actually changes your neurochemistry from the fight-or-flight response to a much calmer state.
- **Exit:** Now, from a slightly calmer place with your eye on the prize—ending the fight feeling closer—exit the argument. Say, "I'm sorry. I'm too upset to talk now and don't want to say anything I'll regret. Let's talk about this later. I promise we will." Then leave the room, hang up the phone, stop texting. Do whatever you need to exit the argument.
- **Think:** Consider what it is you *want* versus *need*. You likely *want* to "win," to have him admit he's wrong and you're right. What you *need* is to have a conversation in which you both feel listened to, respected, and closer when it's over. With your focus on that goal, and the 7 habits of healthy fighting I wrote

about earlier, it's time to keep your promise and have that conversation.

—Xavier Amador, Ph.D., president,
LEAP Institute, www.leapinstitute.org

. . . .

A common guy response is, "How do you not know what you think?"
because guys almost always know what they think at any given moment.
We are not wired that way. We can be totally sure we think something one
moment (like, "OMG, I can't stand him!") and then absolutely positive
we think something completely different an hour later (like, "I don't know
why I was complaining, he is such a good man"). It isn't easy living with
a brain that does this, so that's why you need to give yourself a time-out
and take a break. If your brain is feeling scrambled, just stop. Nobody
says you have to keep arguing, especially when the argument becomes
about something other than what you wanted to say. Seal the dam. Shut
your mouth. Walk away. When an argument takes on a life of its own and
becomes destructive, cut it off at the pass.

Here are other mistakes women make when fighting:

- **We want instant results.** We spew out fifty problems and want
  him to fix them all immediately. It's not going to happen. He
  probably only really heard the first problem.
- **We are dogs with bones.** If something is still bothering you,
  don't send him fifty texts while he's at work. I could be on the
  phone with President Obama discussing the economic crisis,
  and if somebody I'm dating sends me a text that upsets me, I'll
  drop everything to obsessively text him back about nothing to
  do with anything important. I always regret it when I overreact
  like that. I feel like a loser.
- **We kitchen-sink it.** That means we throw every single thing that
  bothers us into one argument even if most of those things have
  nothing to do with what we are really talking about. When you
  feel compelled to bring up everything that person has ever done
  to annoy you, there is no logical response. Guys have told me

that this can feel like bullets or missiles coming at you in the dark. You don't know where they came from or which ones to respond to.

- **We exaggerate (and totally believe it at the time).** We tend to say things in a moment of anger that are not really representative of our true feelings. Your partner can think, *Wait a minute, she's been thinking* that *all along and I never knew it?* This can create resentment and distrust, even though you haven't actually been thinking that all along—you only think it sometimes. Later, when you calm down, you're going to wish you'd toned yourself down a bit.

- **We blame our partners for our own insecurities.** As I said before, it's never about what it's about. When we are upset about something, it often really means that 1) we don't feel loved enough, 2) we feel insecure about ourselves in some way, or 3) we feel like we aren't getting enough attention from our partners. It's hard to admit these things, but think about it. If you just say, "I'm feeling a little insecure right now," that might be all you need to say. It took me six months to be able to say that to a guy I was dating, but sometimes it opens you both up for a much deeper and more meaningful conversation. He might even admit he'd been feeling insecure, too.

So avoid the fight if you can. Be truthful with yourself and your partner about who you are, and if what you really seek is connection, reach out gently and honestly and ask for it.

About PMS

Every month it's the same—we turn irrational, become psychotic, pick fights, are impossible to please, and it happens like clockwork but somehow it always takes us completely by surprise, like it's the first time we've ever had a period. This is the time of month when you might need chocolate injected into your veins, or you could randomly start screaming at and wishing death upon the girl behind the counter because your frozen yogurt portion isn't big enough. If you've ever thought you seriously needed a divorce or you never want to see your boyfriend's face again, only to realize a week later that your relationship is actually just fine, you know what I mean. When you have PMS, your brain can be thinking, *Don't say it, don't say it*, while you hear yourself saying it anyway.

• •

DR. AMADOR SAYS . . .

Although men don't get PMS, we can be moody, and definitely have emotions—whether we sit on them or abrasively read you the riot act. Welcome to being a human being. Both sexes are in the wild ride of handling our neurochemistry and emotions together. I am not saying all things are equal. I am saying let's not forget to see our commonality, our sameness. If we must use the word "crazy," then let's be honest with ourselves: Neither sex has the market on crazy.

Yes, PMS is real and some women have an easier time with it than others. Some learn that when hormones and emotions run high, it's better not to run headlong into a confrontation. Bethenny offers some timeless advice in this section.

—Xavier Amador, Ph.D., president,
LEAP Institute, www.leapinstitute.org

• •

A friend once told me that her husband said, "If you know you've got PMS, then you've got to be extra careful not to start all that shit." He was obviously missing the point—having PMS means you *completely lose control* over your ability not to "start all that shit." However, the guy has a point, even if it wasn't well expressed and made his wife want to roundhouse-kick him in the face (she had PMS at the time). If you have PMS that makes you irrational, then you do need to have a plan. The minute you start getting that feeling (like the car in front of you is going too slow and must be forcefully rear-ended, or the sound of a busy signal on your phone makes you want to hurl it through the window), go into your predetermined default mode—you have to remember that you *cannot trust yourself at that moment*.

In fact, no matter what happens, when you have your period or PMS, no matter what you think or feel in the moment, even if your husband sleeps with your sister (Joking!), apologize because you are wrong. Just lead with that.

Unfair as it may seem, you have to cop to PMS. Just say it. "Look, I have PMS, I'm sad, and I'm sorry. Can we start over?" You also need to remember to hold off on major relationship decisions and discussions until you feel back to normal again. *Do not make important decisions* while under the influence of PMS, menstruation, or menopause. *Do not have important, life-changing conversations.* It's too easy to forget that your emotions are exaggerated, and you could say or even do something you'll regret forever.

Of course this is difficult. All you want is sugar, alcohol, fried food, and for everybody to just shut up and understand that you are right about everything. You can't give in to any of these impulses (at least not too much) or you will just make the whole situation worse. We already know that sugar, alcohol, lack of sleep, and lack of exercise will definitely affect and worsen PMS symptoms. You need to take care of yourself, even when all you want is a chocolate martini. So take a seat. Treat yourself to a massage. Have a therapeutic night out, do some yoga, go for a walk, eat your vegetables and maybe have just a few French fries. Get as much sleep as you can. Then do your best to ride the mood swings without doing too much damage to your relationships. And know thyself. You are no good to anyone when you are acting crazy.

It sucks that women have to deal with this, and not every woman has this problem, but if you have it, you have it, so the reality is that you have to deal with it as well as you can. Just remember that next week, you'll be back to normal again.

That's my take on the gender wars. Men are simple and easy to understand if you know what they're about. Women are crazy and impossible to understand, but if you know that, then you can accept it in the woman you love. Neither one of us is better or worse, but we are all out there trying to come together, so we might as well make the best of it.

Now that we've got some basic understanding, let's start looking at the actual coming together. Let's talk about how to bait a hook.

CHAPTER 3

• • • • • • • • • • • • • •

Master the Catch and Release

To catch a husband is an art; to hold him is a job.
—Simone de Beauvoir

What attracts you to a man? A friend once told me that this question came up when she and a big group of girlfriends were having breakfast at a diner. At first, everyone had the typical responses: cute butt, nice eyes, sense of humor. Then one of them made a confession. She was one of those intellectual hipsters who was also smokin' hot, who seemed like exactly the kind of girl who would be in total control of all her relationships, who could choose anyone she wanted. She said: "Honestly, the one thing that attracts me to a man more than anything else, and the one factor that has determined which relationships I get into, is that the guy is persistently attracted to *me*."

After they all thought about it for two seconds, everyone at the table admitted that, for the most part, the partners they had pretty much chose them, instead of the other way around. These women weren't out there hunting down the cute butts and nice eyes and the guys with a sense of humor. Guys were hunting *them* down, and they had let themselves be caught. A further analysis determined that many of their boyfriends or husbands did *not* have many of the items on their lists of what attracted them to men. Some said their husbands had no butts at all, or had somewhat asymmetrical eyes, or told terrible jokes. But all the men attached to the women in that group had one magical quality in common: *They wanted us.* Whether or not a man is right for us, we fall for this relatively random method of pairing.

Guys are pretty smart like this. They are the fishermen, and we are the fish. We swim along happily in our little schools and then we get hooked by the guy who decides, "I want *that* one." This can be fun, and flattering, and a sweep-you-off-your-feet kind of situation, and I'm the first to agree that men need to be the pursuers in the relationship. They need to be the pursuers and the providers. It is in their nature, and trust me—if it isn't, then something is off. But here's the problem with this scenario: You might not decide whether the guy with the fishing pole is the guy you actually want. You might just go along with the romance of the situation, and before you know it, you are in a relationship with somebody who isn't right for you. The men have traditionally been in charge of who gets paired up with whom.

This is something I have always known to some extent, but I've never put that knowledge into practice very well. I've been successful at figuring out how to get a guy to want to hook me, and I enjoy that game. I know how to intrigue, engage, entertain, and excite. Unfortunately, I tend to do this indiscriminately and irresponsibly, without spending enough time assessing the fishermen. I get into relationships with men who aren't right for me, who can't handle me, or who don't want the same things I want, and I ignore all that because I'm too caught up in getting caught and being desired. I don't determine which man I really, ultimately want before getting too hooked. Knowing what you want is essential for choosing the right person. If you get hooked first and then realize you didn't make a good choice, you can break a lot of hearts, your own included.

There was once a cute guy I was intrigued by, and I wanted to like him. I also wanted him to like me. On our first date, he happened to mention, "I eat to live, I don't live to eat." What? I looked at him like he was an alien. Who eats to live? What kind of person doesn't live to eat? Food is everything to me. It is my greatest passion and a huge part of my life. I couldn't imagine being with someone who didn't share my fascination and pursuit and enjoyment of food. It might seem like a trivial issue, but to me, it was a fundamental difference that resulted in being a deal breaker. I unhooked myself.

Women can be so concerned with getting into a relationship that they forget about who they are getting into a relationship *with*. While men say that when they meet the right person, they are suddenly ready to commit, women often decide they are ready to commit before they find the right person. They are looking at their clocks and saying, "I've got to do this now." It's their instinct. The next guy who comes along simply has good timing, and the women allow themselves to be hooked.

Why aren't we the ones reeling in the fish? Because men need to be the ones casting out, looking for us, finding us, pursuing us. But that doesn't mean we can't be choosy about whether or not we get hooked. So often, I think women don't even realize they have this power. We let ourselves be hooked, maybe not by just anyone, but by anyone who appears decent on the surface and who expresses desire toward us and shows up at the right time, when we think we need to be getting married or at least paired up with someone. We think we need to get into a relationship, so along comes the fisherman, and we take the bait. Then, once hooked, we will often go to great lengths to justify and defend and stick with a relationship, when we might never have given that person a second glance had he not cast his pole (ahem) in our direction.

In my experience, the men who were the most in love with me were the ones who pursued me the most ardently, but the ones I've been the most in love with were the ones I played a conscious role in choosing. I allowed them to hook me when I was more sure of the match. They were the ones I was able to step back and evaluate to determine whether I felt a strong passionate connection to them, too.

Often, the man who chooses you does so because he is genuinely fascinated by you. He genuinely wants *you*. A man should treat you like you are the greatest prize he has ever won, or he should be working in the direction of realizing that is what you are for him. But you also have to play a role. You can choose him right back. To do this, you need to understand, consider, and make decisions about your own relationship based on what men are like, what women are like, and what *you* are like. Only you can decide if a relationship is worth investing your time, energy, and love into. Only you can determine your relationship's potential, and only you can recognize whether you will ever get what you really need, and whether or not it's time to move on. This is even more crucial to do if you have children.

Look back over your past relationships and think about this. How often were you the unwitting fish, and how often were your strategies instrumental in who you ended up with? A clever guy will make you think you chose him, when really, if you examine how it all transpired, it was actually the other way around. A clever girl will make a guy think he did all the choosing, when in reality, she decided *he* was the one. Be the clever girl.

You can be the chooser without taking over as the fisherman. You can be the one who looks up at the line of fishermen on the shore and decides which one you will allow to catch you. Survey them with discretion and intelligence, and then you can choose which one you want. Mastering the catch and release means mastering who catches you and releasing the ones who don't make the grade. It's about having standards and requiring that they are met before you give your heart away to the next meandering fishhook. Decide what you want up front before you get stuck in something. This is how you build a good foundation, rather than one patched together with tape and staple guns.

But finding exactly the guy you want—not just the one with the cute butt or attitude but also the one who understands you and shares your values and frame of reference and wants to go in the same direction as you in life—that's the tricky part. Let's start there.

What Kind of Fish Are You?

Before you even look at all those hooks in the sea, the first thing I want you to do is sit down with yourself and figure out what you want out of a relationship. Your list might change tomorrow, but be honest with yourself right now. If your list is true to who you are today, then you will be an intelligent and discerning fish. To do this, put yourself into a calm state and go to a quiet place, because a lot of things can distract you from what you really want. Loneliness, the fear of being alone forever, anxiety about your biological clock, and even the pressure to have a date by New Year's Eve can all interfere with your ability to honestly assess your needs right now. To help you think about this, answer these questions about yourself as honestly as you can:

- *Am I looking for a long-term relationship with possible marriage potential, or do I really just want to have fun right now?* If you want to have fun, you can be less choosy and play the field, using that as a learning opportunity. If you are seriously in the market for someone with long-term potential, don't waste your time on the guys who don't even have that on their radar. It's always possible that the person you are interested in could change priorities based on knowing you, but you can usually tell pretty quickly whether somebody is in the market for a serious relationship or not—or whether they might be open to it, even if they aren't quite ready right now.

- *Do I need to be taken care of financially, or am I okay with being financially independent?* If you really want to stay home and raise kids, or just pursue your own interests without having to make money, you have to consider this before you invest too much in that drummer who still lives with his parents. Maybe you are looking for someone to share financial responsibilities with. If this is the case, also avoid that drummer! If you really do want to be supported, keep in mind that this will mean giving up a certain level of control. If you think men don't use money for control, you are fooling yourself. No matter how rich, poor, generous, or stingy a man is, no matter what his mother was like, the bottom line is that money equals control, and if a man is paying your credit card bill and knows everything you are spending, he controls you. It doesn't mean he will abuse that control, but the control is there. (For more on this, see chapter 8.)

- *How important is passionate sex in a relationship?* If you don't have a sexual spark with someone, you can't manufacture it. This is important to most people (although wild, passionate sex isn't everybody's cup of tea), so pay attention to the chemistry when you meet someone. If it's not there, you can try to convince yourself it doesn't matter but eventually you may find that all those other qualities you loved (great job, good looks, financial security) don't add up to much. I've had a sexual spark right from the beginning with some guys I've dated. With others, it wasn't there in the beginning and that was telling, because it never developed.

- *How do I need to be treated?* Know what you need and never settle for less than you deserve. Every woman deserves respect, consideration, and to be treated like something precious. Know your worth and don't forget it or let your biological clock or fear of being alone eclipse these basic rights. But think beyond this. Do you need someone who can handle your strong personality, your neuroses, your high-powered career, your weird hobby? Do you need someone who is particularly gentle with you? Who will love your kids and be a good parental figure? Do you like to be treated like a goddess? An intellectual equal? A buddy? Do you like intelligent and witty repartee? Do you need a best friend? Someone to laugh with? Do you like chivalry? Do you like your independence? Do you like your privacy and someone who won't intrude on it too often? Know these things about yourself.

. . . .

DR. AMADOR SAYS . . .

How do you know you are being treated well? Looking and listening to what he does and says will tell you a lot about how he's treating you, but it's not enough. This is one of those times you need your emotions and feelings to help you know how you are being treated. Your emotional compass is a more sensitive and powerful source of information. Emotions can be tools, not weapons. What is your heart telling you? Ask yourself: *Do I feel safe in the relationship? Do I feel safe talking about what's bothering me? Do I feel attractive when I'm with him?*

*Does he make me feel sad? Happy? Anxious? Lonely? Connected? Do
I feel cherished and loved?*
                    —XAVIER AMADOR, PH.D., PRESIDENT,
            LEAP INSTITUTE, WWW.LEAPINSTITUTE.ORG

• •

- *Is my deal-breaker list realistic?* You might be quite sure that you
  want the big house, the hot car, the huge diamond, the husband
  with the prestigious job, but you can't love a piece of paper. If
  your deal-breaker list is full of material things and not substance,
  you might want to rethink it, because a Ferrari and a five-carat
  diamond are not going to make you happy all by themselves.
  They will not keep you warm at night and you can't have wild,
  passionate sex with them. Once, I was in a very serious relationship with someone who was good-looking, had an amazing job,
  made a good living, was a very nice person, and loved me very
  much. He was everything I thought I wanted, and yet, inexplica-
  bly, I didn't want him. I remember sitting in the bathtub at night,
  saying, *"Please, please, why can't I be happy with the perfect guy?"*
  I tortured myself because my deal-breaker list was all wrong.
  I forgot about love, chemistry, and making a good match for
  me. I needed someone who stimulated me, challenged me, and
  could handle me, but it turns out what I didn't need was someone who everybody else thought was perfect. We tend to make
  men into Mr. Perfect, and when things go wrong, we blame
  ourselves. Never marry a piece of paper, but do look for someone
  who is on the same page.
- *What are my standards?* Know what matters to you. Are you
  religious? Do you always put family first? Do you know you definitely want children? Do you live a creative life? Are you political? Are material comforts and financial security important
  to you? Are you cerebral? Do you like to read? If you want to
  discuss that article in the Sunday *New York Times* and he just
  wants to watch *Two and A Half Men,* that will probably start to
  grate on your nerves. Do you have a passion and your happiness

depends on it? Do you have strong moral beliefs about something? Never compromise your standards for anyone else. You
have to hold true to those, no matter what. If you compromise
what really matters to you, you will never really be content or
feel like yourself in a relationship.

- *Is this relationship too far outside my comfort zone?* It can be exciting to challenge yourself with someone outside your frame of
reference, but if someone is too far outside—for example, from
a completely different culture, religion, or even social status,
or much older or younger—it can cause a lot of problems for
the relationship. What if he's young and you're going through
menopause, or if he comes from a blue-collar background and
you come from a blue-blood background, or if he is Jewish and
you are a Baptist? What if he's a partier and you're a homebody?
What if he's really into fitness and you hate to work out? What if
you're a liberal tree hugging yogi and he is a right-wing conservative? What if you like to read and go to museums and he likes to
hang out in sports bars and binge-drink? What if you like to be
with people all the time and he would rather live on the couch
in front of the TV? If it feels like a problem at the beginning, it
will only get worse, so trust your gut on this.

There is something very comforting about being with someone of a similar age, who has similar beliefs, and/or who grew up
in the same time you did and shares your cultural references.
For example, growing up in this country Caucasian is a much
different cultural experience than growing up Latin or Asian. It's
also easier if that person is from the same area of the country
(East Coast, Midwest, South) or even the same town. This isn't
a requirement, of course. Even if you come from drastically different backgrounds, you can make it work. Many people have.
Just know it will be more difficult if you are far apart in culture,
age, experience, or important issues.

I had a girlfriend who was twenty-three and she married a
man who was fifty. They had a lot of chemistry, but she was just
getting started with her life and he was already established in

his, so she didn't get to share the excitement of building a life together, buying their first house, succeeding at their careers. She missed having that bond with someone her own age, and it was difficult for her to just step into his life. He had lived in his home for twenty years and had a well-established career, so she didn't have to work but she wanted to make it on her own. He didn't necessarily remember what it was like to be twenty-three and just starting out. The marriage ultimately did work out, but they both had to give up some things. She was outside his comfort zone as well because she didn't share his history or know about any of the things he grew up with. Life is about sharing experiences, so if you can find a way to do that, then you might be okay.

- *What does this person's family reveal about him?* We aren't always like our families, but families can be revealing. One crazy uncle isn't necessarily a cause for concern, but I was once in a relationship with someone who had one cousin who was caught stealing someone's identity, another who was on drugs, and another who was in jail for something nobody in the family wanted to talk about. It's tempting to overlook these things at first, in the initial passion of a relationship, but later on when you have to actually deal with your partner's family, you might find yourself judging a little bit. Is your partner's family racist? Do they gay-bash? Are they substance abusers or prone to violence? Also look at the family dynamics. How do his parents treat each other? How do they treat their kids and grandkids? Your partner might not be like any of his family members, as far as you know, but serious family issues can be a sign of trouble. The apple doesn't fall far from the tree, as they say. This is not a guarantee of trouble, but a sign. What does the tree look like? You might end up having to spend a lot of time with those people. Also, it's difficult to completely reject what you were raised with and taught as a child. Many people successfully rise above their circumstances, but it's always a struggle.

Even if his family is just fine, you might not get along with them. Is your partner a mama's boy? Does he still take money from his parents or live with them? If so, run! If he puts family before you at first, that's not huge, but once you are in a serious relationship, will you become the priority? It can't be your partner and his family against you, or you will be living in hell. It's important to make an effort to get along with each other's families, but the relationship has to come first. You need to be a team, a unit, and if your partner isn't capable of that, this is something to look seriously at before committing.

- *Can I live with imperfection?* This is a trick question because the truth is, there are no guarantees in life and nobody is perfect. You might make a bad choice. You might get fooled. You might get your heart broken. And even if you really do find mutual love, respect, affection, and marriage, anyone you decide to love is going to have faults and plenty of shit that drives you crazy, and you're going to drive him crazy sometimes, too. That's life, and that's love. If you can't live with that, then you probably aren't ready for a relationship right now. Go back to the first question in this list.

- *Does this person get me?* Maybe the most important thing of all is to find someone who understands you and everything you come with. Women are complicated, and in order to accept you, the person you are with needs to understand your particular brand of crazy and not give you a hard time about it every second. We don't always have total control over our dysfunctional parts, and when you both understand that about each other, the relationship becomes a huge relief. This takes compassion, but it is essential.

. . . .

MAN-FORMATION

Just as the guys who look great on paper aren't necessarily the best partners, in my experience, the most unlikely suspects can turn out to be great partners. When they meet the right girl, men who never wanted to commit can suddenly realize what they've been missing and decide to change completely. These guys might turn around and be fully in it with you. Men who don't necessarily make a great living might be warm, supportive, loving, and everything you really need—and maybe you already make a great living on your own. Guys who seem irresponsible might fall so hard for you that they grow up and change their lives. You can't change anyone else, but anyone can choose to change in order to be with you. Keep an open mind. There are many different types of guys who could potentially make great partners.

. . . .

Choosing someone to commit to is always a risk. Why else would it be so scary to so many people? But going into it with both eyes open, with your illusions dispelled and a realistic picture of who you are, who he is, and whether you really want to be with that person for the rest of your life, will create a solid foundation. You can build on that. Of course, you could be totally certain and still get blindsided, but at least you will increase your chances of success. These are just criteria that might help.

Now let's get to the fun stuff. You know what you want, so let's talk about how to go out and get it.

. . . .

JUST THE TIP

A lot of people ask me what they should wear on a first date. My advice is to think sexy but not slutty. First, you need to be comfortable. If you are pulling at your clothes or sitting weird all night because your skirt is riding up or you're self-conscious that your dress is hugging you in all the wrong places, you won't have fun and you will seem uptight. Second, pick your spot. Choose one thing to reveal, then pull back on the rest. Choose something low-cut (but not too low-cut) so you reveal a little cleavage or side boob. There should be no danger of a nip slip. Or choose a lot of leg via a short skirt or cute shorts with heels, but if you do that, keep your cleavage to yourself. The other option is to show bare shoulders, but if you do that, be more conservative with the leg and neckline. The trick is to offer a hint, not a big reveal. Leave the rest up to the imagination.

. . . .

How to Bait a Hook

You spot him across the room and you wonder, *Who is* that? Your eyes meet and you feel a tingle of chemistry. Maybe someone introduces you at a party, or you've noticed him at a club, or maybe it's even a very promising blind date. Now what?

Now you have fun. You engage him. You are light and bright—the most interesting fish in the sea. This isn't the time to start grilling him about his prospects. This is the time to attract. You'll still have plenty of time to be chaste and choosy. Right now, you are the fish who sparkles, who entices, who seems like a really good catch. Be yourself, but be the most irresistible version of yourself.

• •

CELEBS SPEAK OUT

Happy girls are the prettiest.
—AUDREY HEPBURN

• •

The best way to do this is to be open. Smile, laugh, and have fun, but don't be open in a negative, scary, or stalker way. Don't tell a lot of personal details, and don't ask questions that are too serious. Keep it light and breezy and just a little flirty but not too suggestive. The most appealing and attractive people are having fun and have their own lives. They aren't needy or grabby or braggy. They know how to enjoy themselves and they are having a good time whether they meet someone promising or not. If you give off a desperate vibe or the impression that you just have to meet somebody and you really really hope he's your soul mate, you won't attract a secure and confident person. Be secure and confident yourself, however, and watch the field of possibility expand.

Confidence is intoxicating. When you are confident, people are drawn to you. When you feel bad about yourself, people are less likely to notice you or respond to you. I've seen some girls go out feeling bad about themselves. They get ignored, and this makes them feel worse. It turns into a negative spiral that nobody wants to be around. But I've also seen girls who go out not caring who notices them. They just want to have a good time. These girls almost always appear more attractive to everybody around them. The universe hears everything, and you get what you put out there, so put out the energy you want to get back.

• •

DR. AMADOR SAYS . . .

Confidence says, "I don't need to sell myself—I'm already desirable." Arrogance has the added edge of "You'd be a fool not to want me." They are not the same. Beware of arrogance.

The research on confidence is clear—others (both men and women) see you as more attractive and desirable when you believe in yourself, and move and speak with self-confidence. If you don't feel it, find it. One way to find it is to make a list. Really! Write down those things you believe you are good at. List the ways you are physically attractive (your smile, eyes, figure, etc.) and personally attractive (intelligence, sense of humor, warmth, etc.). Keep it with you on your phone and look at it when you are feeling less confident.

—XAVIER AMADOR, PH.D., PRESIDENT,
LEAP INSTITUTE, WWW.LEAPINSTITUTE.ORG

• •

How to Get Reeled In

If you let somebody hook you, the next step is to let them reel you in just enough that you can get a feel for who you are dealing with. You don't want to get so involved that you can't get out easily until you have a chance to evaluate the person's potential and chemistry. The best way to do this is to be the one who sets the tone and pace of the relationship.

Setting the tone and pace of the relationship means controlling, at least to some degree, how often you see each other, how you communicate (for example, texting vs. phone), and the way you spend your time together. It also means establishing the basic rules and boundaries of the relationship. You want to establish these because then the guy knows who you are and where you stand. If he doesn't know that, then you can't ever know if the relationship will work.

This doesn't mean you plan all the dates. On the contrary, it can mean that you make sure *he* plans at least most of the dates, if that's what you prefer. You set the tone by how you react and respond to situations right at the beginning, like how he treats you or what kinds of things he suggests you do together. If he is rude, don't brush it off and make excuses for him. If all he wants to do is watch sports with you and you don't enjoy watching sports, speak up. It's not that you can't ever hang out and be the cool girl at a sports bar or a football game, but if you don't want to do that every time, you set the tone by creating other opportunities for you to be together. Can he handle a Friday night at a museum or a nice restaurant? If not, maybe he's not for you.

This also involves setting precedents. If you don't want a textual relationship, for example, do not respond to every text message. Encourage him to call you instead. If you want to determine who will pay for things, establish that precedent right away, too—you let him pay, or you go Dutch, or whatever makes you comfortable. This way, you can tell right from the start if money issues are going to be a problem. If you want to take it slow, don't get persuaded into bed too soon. Whatever matters to you, don't cave in to it in the beginning, or you will never get it later. Dog trainers say that you shouldn't let a puppy get away with things you wouldn't want him to do as a big dog, like sleeping on the bed or jumping on people. It's exactly the same with relationships. In the beginning, yours is a puppy, and you don't want the puppy to make the rules or you'll be living in a house full of chewed furniture and dog poop.

The next important thing to do if you want to get reeled in is to be who you really are, right from the start, but in gradually increasing doses. Not the whole you—you don't want to scare anybody off with every level of your personality all at once—but the essential you. Let him know who you are, what you want, and what you stand for. Don't conform to somebody else's idea of what they want in a girlfriend because ultimately you won't be able to keep that up. Otherwise, the person who hooked you won't know who you really are, and you won't know whether the match works.

Be beautiful and sexy in your own way, not in some way you think someone else wants. Show your sense of humor. Show your compassion and affectionate side. Show your interests and show that you can be caring and supportive. Don't be a doormat and don't give up the things you like to do because you are waiting for a call or a text. Keep on doing your life the way you always did, or even better. Let the intoxication of a new relationship fuel all your interests and make you happy and glowing, but don't be needy or selfish or neurotic or clingy. Be kind and warm and interested and a good listener, but never bend over backward or do something that makes you uncomfortable. This is the time to be gloriously you, and if the person you are interested in responds and is enchanted, then the relationship might be worth pursuing. If the person tries to control you and make you into something different from who you are, don't waste your time. Let go of the hook and move on.

But it's not *all* about you. There is a line between being a doormat and recognizing that the person you are interested in has things he wants and needs as well. If you are in a relationship with a man, it can be useful to know what kinds of things generally make men feel really good about themselves and you. Giving him those things isn't compromising yourself. It is being a good person who wants to be in a relationship and is working at it. Everybody wants to feel loved and appreciated. Most people like affection and admiration. If you can offer these to someone as well as accept them from someone, you are on the right track.

But there are some particular things that men tend to like, and it can be helpful to know them and tap into them. Although every man is different, there are two very simple things you can do to make a man feel pleasure in your presence, or just thinking about you, without compromising yourself in any way:

1. **Make him feel like a man.** Men want to feel like they are the big strong protectors and we are the little baby bunnies. Whether there is any basis in reality for this is irrelevant. Your guy could be a skinny

musician or a huge weight lifter. You could outweigh him by fifty pounds, or he could pick you up with one arm. If you make him *feel like a man*, then you've got his number. He's ten feet tall. He's Mr. Universe.

This is so easy to do, but for some reason, women think they shouldn't tell a man how good he looks, how handsome he is, how strong he is, how big he is, how safe he makes them feel. Aren't they supposed to be the ones complimenting *us*? I completely disagree with this. Men are just as susceptible to flattery as women are. The more manly and adored they feel, the more they will adore you.

This isn't about kissing a guy's ass. Don't overdo it. Too much can sound insincere, or worse, needy. You don't want to come off as clingy, subservient, or stalkerish, but a little bit of vulnerability and letting the man be the strong one goes a long way when you are first establishing a relationship. Don't be afraid to tell him that he's helping you. Don't be afraid to tell him he is strong or powerful or commanding or accomplished or whatever it is. You can even let him rescue you from the occasional emergency situation (plumbing problem, dead car battery).

There are a lot of little ways to sprinkle in this kind of sentiment. Here's a cheat sheet of things to add to a conversation when relevant (or just randomly) that are guaranteed to get a guy's juices flowing. Don't say any of these things if they don't feel like you. Pick the ones that seem natural, or find your own versions of these same sentiments:

- You're so sexy.
- You're so strong.
- You're so funny, you make me laugh!
- You're really smart.
- That's a great idea!
- You are absolutely right.
- You saved the day!
- You are so good at that.
- How do you know so much about that?
- You're my hero!

- You're really handsome.
- What would I do without you?
- Thank God you're here!
- It's so large . . .
- You're so good in bed.
- You're so hot, baby. I can't get enough of you.
- I missed you so much today.
- I'm so glad you had a good day.

You also have to mean it when you say it—at least, mostly mean it. If your guy senses any sarcasm, then forget it—your comment will have the exact opposite effect. He won't trust you.

. . . .

JUST THE TIP

Recently, a girlfriend of mine told me that her father was dating a professional girlfriend. I didn't know what that was. I thought it was some kind of hooker, but no. She said that a professional girlfriend is a girl who always looks great, who is always ready to go and do whatever you want, who is always up for anything, who is easygoing and just fun to be around all the time. She's not difficult, high-maintenance, or problematic. Obviously, most women can't be like that all the time. It sounds daunting to me. And inauthentic if you aren't really that way. However, maybe we can all take a cue from that concept. You can't be a pain in the ass every minute of every day. (I'm talking to myself here.)

. . . .

2. **Don't be easy.** Even if you just told him how much you need him, how much he is your hero, a man also has to know that if you aren't getting what you need, you'll say something, and if you aren't ever going to get it, you will walk. Do not let a man take you for granted. Whenever you show your vulnerable side, balance that out with a glimpse of your independent side. This is not only important for your own power in the relationship but also for not scaring him off be-

cause he thinks you are too needy. Most importantly, never make the conquest of you too easy.

Despite what they say (or even think), men do not like things to come easily. The hunter instinct is strong, even in the most enlightened twenty-first-century man. They want something to work on and achieve, and they don't like to win by cheating. They also want something for their effort. They are hunters and they will be immediately suspicious and even disrespectful of anything that seems to be right out there in the open, for the taking. It seems like a trap, or like that thing they thought they wanted must not be very valuable since anybody could have it. At the same time, the prize can't be so difficult to win that it isn't worth the effort. If the chase is ridiculous, a guy will get distracted and might look for someone who isn't so difficult. Part of the trick of seeming like the fish while actually controlling who catches you is to strike that balance between presenting a real challenge and being attainable. Be the enticer, not too easily won but not impossible, either. A game fish that will be a challenge but totally worth it in the end. This doesn't just mean not having sex too soon (and if you do, you'd better be pretty damn good or mind-blowingly sexy or the most interesting person he's ever met). It also means maintaining your independence and your own agenda even while you allow yourself to be pursued. If you are fun to pursue, then the game is on.

. . . .

GIRL TALK

I've made a lot of mistakes in my attempts to get a guy interested in me, and I've observed even more mistakes out there in the world. Some of these things are obvious when you see other people doing them, but you might not realize it when *you* are doing them. If you are having trouble getting a guy interested, these are some of the things you might be doing wrong:

- Talking too much. Stop dominating the conversation! You will learn more by listening.

- Talking only about yourself, especially bragging and/or being a know-it-all. Let your date discover how smart and accomplished you are. Let the truth unfold naturally.
- Not talking at all or having no opinions. Don't be a doormat.
- Being indecisive. This is so annoying. For example, you never know what you want to do, or you say "I don't care" to every question about plans, like where to eat or what to do. This is especially reprehensible if you actually do care but don't want to admit it because you are afraid you will sound demanding. Have a point of view. You don't have to control the plan, but don't be wishy-washy, or that girl who has to workshop everything to death.
- Acting subservient or helpless. Get a backbone. If your date opens doors for you or is chivalrous, that's great, but you also need to know that you can open the damn door yourself if you have to.
- Insecurity and putting yourself down constantly. It's not charming and it's not the same as modesty.
- Showing obsessive interest in your date. That makes anyone uncomfortable, and it degrades you. Don't act like a stalker.
- Talking about your exes, especially how great they were and all the things they bought you or did for you, or how psycho they were, because why would you put up with that kind of behavior?
- Being too critical. If you are constantly criticizing, nagging, or emasculating your date, you probably won't get another date. Some men do stay with naggers, but they have been snipped and also can't stand their partners.
- Taking too long to get ready or being otherwise a high-maintenance pain in the ass.
- Obsessing about every bite you eat, special-ordering everything, or yammering on about how much you worked out. Obsessive dieters and fitness people are only interesting to other obsessive dieters and fitness people.
- Being completely uninterested in sex. People who aren't into sex are eventually only interesting to other people who aren't into sex.

- Being excessively critical or cynical about everything. You might think you are being ironic or clever, but it can come off as plain negativity, and that's unpleasant to be around.
- Acting superior. You might think you are hot shit and even too good for that nice guy taking you out for dinner. You are not. Show me a hot girl and I'll show you a guy who would rather watch *Family Guy* than bang her.

Evolving

Once you've been hooked and are in a relationship that is at least somewhat established—maybe you don't call each other "boyfriend" and "girlfriend" yet, but you have standing plans on the weekends and see each other during the day sometimes—then you can also be the one to determine how and at what pace the relationship evolves.

Women usually want to see things moving forward, whereas many men are perfectly happy to let things stay exactly as they are for years on end. A lot of guys would be content to have a girlfriend for the rest of their lives and may only think about marriage because of societal pressure. Women, on the other hand, are biologically programmed to want more security than that. What that means is, if you want things to move forward, *you* have to be the one moving them forward.

The first step is to assess whether they are moving at all. Are you seeing each other as often as you want or think is necessary to maintain the relationship? Are you seeing each other with an appropriate amount of intensity? If you've been dating for six months and you still only see each other once a week, or you mostly just hang out and watch TV, that's not evolving if that's not what you want to be doing. (If you have kids, that may be all you can manage, however. All rules have exceptions.) If it's incredibly intense every time you see each other, that's not sustainable. You have the power to speed things up or slow things down. Suggest doing something different, or make plans to shake things up.

When working to evolve a relationship, sometimes you have to be a little bit stealthy about it, so you don't scare away a commitment-phobic boyfriend with good potential, and methodical, so it is clear to everyone that you are not going to waste the next five years doing exactly what you are doing now (dating on weekends only, never going away together for the weekend, not meeting each other's families, not moving in together, etc.). Don't be whiny or emotional about how things aren't going the way you want. Instead, be straight-up and frank about what you would like to see happening next. Keep the pressure off, but be clear. Think of it as negotiating a sensitive business deal. Not that relationships are a business (although if you ever get divorced, you will know that in many ways, they are), but you should both feel like you are getting most of the things you want, you should both feel just slightly out of your comfort zone, and you should both feel happy with the way the deal is going. Something has to happen for something to happen. Shake it up to get a different result.

As you work to help your relationship evolve, be careful. Sometimes when you want something badly, you might get too eager or emotional and put the pressure on. This can scare someone who is nervous about commitment. Handle with care, pay attention to reactions, and don't be emotional. Be straight-up, and if you detect the other person getting nervous or withdrawing, back off and reassess your approach. Think of the commitment-phobic guy as a wild animal. You can't rush in with your hands out or he'll run away (or bite). Enact your strategy gently, sweetly, with reassurances and support. Here's what you could try:

- Making day plans, if you only see each other at night.
- Discussing having standing weekend plans—you assume you will do something unless one of you informs the other he or she is busy. Propose this casually, not with pressure.
- Revealing something personal about yourself in a quiet private moment together, if you have been guarded about doing this.
- Pulling back just a little to encourage your partner to move forward just a little. If this doesn't work, try the opposite—be just a little more available and affectionate, to remind him you are there for him.
- Changing it up. If you always stay home, suggest getting dressed up and going out. If you always go out, suggest staying home and cooking together.

- Planning a weekend getaway (if you both feel ready for it—don't do it as a surprise, or before six weeks together).
- Proposing getting your families together for a low-key social activity.
- If it's time, maybe planting the seeds of moving in together without necessarily bringing it up directly. Point out cool apartments or areas of town to live in. Talk about your future together casually, like, "Wouldn't it be cool to live in this neighborhood?" You can also be fanciful. "I could totally see us in a cool apartment in Paris someday." This can get him thinking in that direction if he isn't, but if he gets scared, back off and reassess your approach.

In a good and evolving relationship, both parties have to be willing to step slightly outside their comfort zones for something that matters to the other person. If progressing matters to you, then the person you are with should be willing to go there with you. If not, maybe it's not the right relationship for you.

Changing Your Strategy

Sometimes, your attempts to master the situation don't work. You want to move forward, but your partner resists making new plans or trying new things, or starts trying to control you when you back away. Maybe you like each other but you keep having the same argument, or you don't like something your partner is doing—maybe he goes out with his friends more than you would like, or ogles other women, or maybe you are just in a rut. If you really like the person and you don't want to give up yet, now is the time to change your strategy. They say the definition of insanity is doing the same thing over and over again and expecting different results. Stop doing the same thing. Make a change. Here are some ideas:

- Try pulling back more, to see if he comes after you. If you've been too available, maybe you will be slightly busy for a few days. If he wants to go out with the guys, maybe you warmly and gladly support this instead of bitching about it, and then make plans to go out with your girlfriends, or even go away for a weekend. This is a time to change your approach. Be extra understanding. Give him enough rope to hang himself and see what happens. Some men run when you put a fence around them, but when you take away the fence, they suddenly don't want to go anywhere. Maybe you don't realize that you are hovering too much or giving him too much attention, and if you pull back, he'll lean in to get your interest back. Don't disappear, though. Just lean out.

- If you have been pulling back and he's pulling back, too, then this isn't working. This might be a time to lean in, but in a different way. Maybe you've been complaining a lot about what he does. Change it up by putting the emphasis on yourself. Maybe this is a time to be vulnerable and admit that you are feeling insecure or you don't feel like you are getting enough time with him. If you do this, however, you have to get in and get out. Don't turn it into a whiny-needy session. Say how you feel in a few short sentences, then stop. Give him a chance to respond. If he doesn't know what to say, give him some time. Back off and go do something else for a while, not in a passive-aggressive "you hurt me" way, but just because you have a life and you have stuff to do. Go do it.

- Sometimes if you are feeling disconnected, the answer isn't about words. You can reconnect with physical interactions, and I don't just mean sex. Try being a little more loving, a little more snuggly. He might be feeling ignored. Men can feel neglected in relationships, too.

- If you can't tell what he wants, and all your hints and analysis aren't working, try asking. Be direct. Just say something like, "Look, I'm not sure what you want exactly, but we're not spending that much time together. I like to know my relationships are evolving." Again, if you do this, get in and get out. Don't bring in every problem you have. Just ask where you stand, and let him answer or think about it. Honestly, he might be totally unprepared for a question like that and he might need a little bit of time to think about how he actually wants to respond, but if you nag and pressure, he might fight back in a way you will both regret.

The bottom line is that fishing is a sport—for the fisherman, but also for the fish. Be a good game fish, master the catch and release, and enjoy the game.

CHAPTER 4

. . . .

Don't Hate the Player,
Hate the Game

A delayed game is eventually good;
a bad game is bad forever.
—SHIGERU MIYAMOTO,
JAPANESE VIDEO GAME DESIGNER

Sometimes I hate the game. It takes effort, it involves strategy, it can be difficult to play it well, and it can result in horrible misunderstandings, hurt feelings, even breakups. Why can't relationships be straightforward, aboveboard, logical, and easy? Hold on, actually that sounds boring. Because sometimes I love the game. It's fun, it's engaging, it's entertaining, and it can be a great way to get what you need out of a relationship, jump-start a stalled relationship, break out of a rut, find out who someone else really is, put an end to bad habits, even get a commitment out of someone who is afraid to give away his heart. It's a little bit like gambling. You can win big, or you can lose big, but you know what they say about the New York lottery—you have to be in it to win it.

I've always enjoyed a good game, and I was recently in a relationship that I thought was ready to move to the next level. We were involved in a complex game of cat and mouse (I'll explain this game later in this chapter), and we were both having a lot of fun with it, but then one day I realized we had gotten to the point where neither of us was letting the other one know how we really felt. I really liked this guy, but I didn't know for sure whether he really liked me or if he was just playing. I also suspected he didn't know for sure whether or not I really liked him.

When, after a particularly great day together, he didn't call me, I thought something was wrong. I called him: "We had so much fun yesterday. You said you've never felt this way with anyone before. Why didn't you call me?"

He said, "I was testing you. I wanted to see how you would react."

Wow. That's when I realized we'd played the game for too long. He didn't even know for sure that I wanted to be with him and he was still trying to figure it out. That's when I knew I had to put the ball down and give him a little glimpse into the real me.

I told him, "Hey, I think about you a lot. I like to talk to you every day." He was totally surprised. We spent a few mellow days taking the whole thing down a notch and just being together and recognizing that our relationship could actually evolve if we could just stop playing the game for a few seconds. It was a great break—we were both happy to sit on the bench for a few innings.

So what is the game, exactly? The game is basically a set of techniques and tricks for engaging people, tweaking relationships, flirting, and testing each other. Like any game, it can be fun for all, or it can get too competitive, get too aggressive, or result in injury. Sometimes the game is a necessary evil, and sometimes the game is a force for good. At its best, the game is completely natural. In fact, you see it in nature everywhere. Courtship rituals, posturing, teasing, playing hard to get. Humans didn't make up the game.

People who are particularly experienced and adept at the game are called "players," and I've met a lot of players and played a lot of games in my day. But the game isn't about lying. It isn't about faking anything or pretending to be somebody you're not. You have to be yourself. If the other person doesn't like who you really are, it will never work out in the long run anyway. But the game is about being yourself *playing a game*. Is a football player lying when he plays quarterback or wide receiver? Of course not. He's playing a game, but he's no less himself than when he's having dinner or having a nap or having sex. The way he plays the game is an extension of who he is.

· ·

DR. AMADOR SAYS . . .

Winning is the goal of nearly all games. What does it mean to win the games of courtship and relationship building? Bethenny's right: You have to figure that one out for yourself. Is it one night of passionate sex or a lifetime of loving partnership? Is it being right when you argue? Or is it becoming happier and closer? If the object is love and partnership that is lasting, you have to survive the courtship phase.

During the first quarter, when men and women fall for each other, they become psychotic. What I mean is, they lose sight of reality, feel emotions very intensely (men hide them better, but they pop out when we act out), and have serious lapses in judgment.

The second quarter can be fraught with an adrenaline rush fallout (disillusionment, depression, and anxiety), stumbles (self-doubt and second thoughts), fouls (incidents that cause mistrust), and injuries (arguments and periods of distance). If you play the game with this temporary "psychosis" in mind and your eye on your goal (e.g., a trusting, respectful, fun, and loving relationship), you will never have regrets no matter how it ends.

—Xavier Amador, Ph.D., president,
LEAP Institute, www.leapinstitute.org

· ·

The game is about tossing the proverbial ball back and forth. Sometimes it involves passing the ball when you'd rather hog it, and sometimes it involves getting the ball back when you've inadvertently given it away. Sometimes the game is for testing the waters or taking the temperature of a relationship. The game is an opportunity for showing off the best of you, and also a chance to subvert your less desirable qualities. Sometimes the game means leaning out when you would rather lean in, or leaning in when you would rather run in the other direction screaming because you are terrified that you might be getting into something real. Played right, the game can help your relationship, or help you confirm you should be in that relationship. When your game is tight, you can accomplish anything you want in a relationship. Played wrong, the game can break hearts. A good game won't have any casualties.

If you like the idea of the occasional relationship sporting event, then let's talk. In this chapter, I'll tell you about some of the games I've seen people play and some of the games I've played myself. I'll tell you how to dip your foot in to see how far you can go before you go the full monty and get in over your head. I'll tell you what works and what doesn't, and we'll also talk about when and how to stop when the game threatens to go too far or is no longer doing anybody any good. Because when the game goes bad, it's important to remember not to hate the player. Hate the game.

• •

MAN-FORMATION

Can you recognize a man who's got game? It doesn't mean he's good-looking. It means he knows how to make a woman feel good. He knows how to give just enough but hold back just enough so you want more. He is chivalrous and polite. He has good manners and treats you well, but not in a boring or predictable way. He excites you. You feel like you are a junior-high girl waiting by your locker, hoping he'll walk down the hallway.

• •

Who's Playing?

To be a player takes a certain type of athleticism, but I don't mean physically. You need to be willing to take some risks, play just on the edge of your comfort zone, and although you shouldn't pretend to be someone other than who you are, you should be willing to stretch your boundaries and explore parts of your personality that you might not be utilizing fully. A good game player is unpredictable, but in a fun and positive way. A good game player is not a loose cannon, because you can't have game if you can't even control your own behavior. A player isn't flaky, unreliable, mean, or difficult, but someone who has game is someone you can't easily pin down. A player doesn't lie, isn't insincere, but isn't an open book, either. A real player does what he says and is responsible but isn't necessarily predictable and doesn't always say yes. Someone who's got game may only be available for plans once or twice a week, but when you are together, he is engaged, centered, and all-in. He gives you his undivided attention. He says nice things. He creates moments and memories and makes you feel good about yourself when you are with him. But treat him badly and he might just disappear forever.

You're never totally sure you have him, but you absolutely know you want him.

This can be you if you play the game right, and it should be you. Why shouldn't you be mysterious and intriguing? Why shouldn't you have your own life and interests? Why shouldn't you be totally with someone when you are with him, giving that person your attention, respect, and affection? But if he mistreats you, or manipulates you, or has all the power over you, then why should you put up with even one minute of that? There are different types of players, but they are all secretive and they all compartmentalize their lives. There could be ten other women, and you will never know, but even if the player is totally forthcoming about dating other people, or about not wanting a relationship, he still gets you eating out of his hand. He controls it. Can you turn that around?

Why shouldn't you be a player, in the best sense of the word? You don't have to be a player like a man would be a player, but you can have power. You can manipulate. You can excite and entice and get him eating out of *your* hand. You can be an ethical player—one who is intriguing and irresistible and sometimes even gently manipulative, but only in the service of a better relationship. An ethical player plays the game *with* her partner, to make the relationship more fun, exciting, and fruitful.

When to Play

The game is best played strategically, and that means knowing when the game is on and knowing when the game is over. Use it to your advantage during certain times in a relationship:

- When you are first testing the waters of a new relationship, games can be a way to flirt. This can involve a cat-and-mouse kind of game. If he texts you, "I had a great time, I really want to see you again," don't gush back about how you feel exactly the same and ask when your next date is. Instead, say something like, "I had a great time, too." Maybe add a smiley face, but don't even use an exclamation mark. Don't let him know he has you, even if he does. This can be a little bit of a tease. In the beginning, he should never be 100 percent sure you want to see him again. This is strategic. It's also a good way to discover the other person's style of communication.

- Games help you maintain your identity during the all-consuming early stages of a relationship. It's tempting at first to be all over each other every second, but it's better to recognize right from the start that you both have lives and you need to respect each other's time and responsibilities. The game can help you to enforce this. This means not being available every second. It means keeping and continuing to live your own life, even as you are auditioning a life together. It means being clear about your responsibilities and priorities (like your job or your children), and it means respecting that the other person might not want constant calls or texts while at work (or anytime). It means understanding that even if you aren't together every day or every night, it doesn't mean you don't still like each other. It means creating space, even when you don't want to in the moment (because trust me—you will want it later!).

- Games can help establish the rules of a new relationship. Remember the analogy of the jumping puppy—if he calls you at ten p.m. and wants to come over, you can say no right from the start if you don't want that to become a habit. If he only wants to text you, you can ignore the texts or say right up front, "Hey, I'm not a great texter. If you want to make plans, call me." If you're always getting asked to do things at the last minute, you can say, "I'm sorry, I already have plans. I wish you would have called earlier." Say it even if you don't have exciting plans—staying home can be your plan. Of course, even though every game has rules, some rules are meant to be broken. Once in a while, you can say, "Hey, my plans just got canceled, I can meet you after all!" Just don't make it a habit unless you want it to become a habit. You don't want to be so rigid in your game that you come off as cold or not spontaneous (or worse, make it too obvious that you are playing a game!).

- When a relationship is stale or you've hit a plateau, the game can be like jumper cables to fire up the relationship again. If you are in a rut, spending every night on the couch watching TV and eating takeout, the game can reintroduce an interesting element to shake you up. Maybe you make reservations at a nice restaurant or buy tickets to a concert. Maybe you ask him to make plans and surprise you because you feel like going out (even if you are nervous about seeming too demanding). Maybe you show up in lingerie or sexy boy shorts and a see-through tank top. Maybe you make dinner at home and have sex on the living room floor. Maybe you are the aggressor for a change, just to surprise your partner. Maybe you get a babysitter, or book a weekend out of town, or just a night at a hotel. Maybe you role-play. (See chapter 9 for more on sexy ways to ramp up your game.)

- When you are in a funk, the game can help you get your groove back. Maybe you totally stop nagging him and even encourage him to go out with his guys. Then you plan a girls' night out or weekend away, or you book a spa day. He won't know what to think, you'll suddenly seem more interesting, and you'll also get some much-needed you time.

When you aren't getting what you need, the game can get it for you. Stop being frustrated and get back into the game. (I'll talk more about how to do this later in the chapter.)

When to Call a Time-Out

The game is useful, but there are also times when the game is inappropriate. You have to know when to take a break or let it be halftime and just relax and reboot for a while like on a Sunday, after a great weekend. Sometimes you might even need to forfeit in order to rescue a relationship that matters to you. When the game gets out of control and you decide to show your hand, it's important to be confident and secure, not gushy or bitchy. The game is a wave, a rhythm, and you have to feel it and know when not to go too far. Here's when to call a time-out:

- *When a new relationship is ready to move to the next level.* If the game is keeping you from knowing how you feel about each other, it's time to call a time-out and assess where you are going next. Call a time-out by revealing something personal about yourself, as a gesture of vulnerability. That shows you are being sincere, rather than playing.
- *When the relationship is in trouble and requires honest conversation.* A friend of mine was so afraid of being vulnerable in her marriage that she was always playing the independent game. This is a game some women play, sometimes without even realizing it—it's the "I don't need you" game, and it can take the pressure off some men, but it pushes others away, and it's not really an appropriate game for marriage. My friend was addicted to this game. She never let her husband think she needed him and even convinced herself that he was a luxury but not a necessity in her life. She worked a lot and would always deflect his attempts to have emotional conversations. When he had an affair, suddenly she realized she had played herself right out of the picture. She scheduled a date for them, swallowed her pride, and instead of pointing the finger or accusing him, she apologized for shutting him out and told him that she needed him and couldn't imagine her life without him. He was so overcome with emotion when he realized that she really did feel this way about him that he told her she was the only one he had ever really loved. He completely cut off his affair, and now they are working through their problems with a level of intimacy they never had before. Never forget that men like to look tough, but inside they are insecure, needy babies.

- *When you have gotten so deep into the game that you can't remember what it's like not to play.* Sometimes when two seasoned players get together, they never stop playing and so their relationship never actually feels real. Without the occasional time-out, the relationship might be fun but it will never be fulfilling, because you won't ever have a chance to see who you really are together. Also know that some men are psychotic. They only know how to play the game and don't even know who *they* are. If they catch you, the game is over, and they don't want you anymore. Beware of these men!

- *When you feel like the game has kept you from really knowing who the other person is.* The truth will come out, and if you play the game badly and don't reveal your true self, it can be a shock when the real you finally comes out—which it will eventually. I was in a relationship with someone who did this. When I realized who he was at the core, I felt completely duped and angry at myself for not recognizing the truth sooner. But how could I have? He played a sneaky game.

- *When someone is genuinely opening up to you.* If somebody suddenly stops playing and reveals their vulnerable self, you have to stop playing, too, out of respect. Truly listen and acknowledge that person, who is showing you something important. This is often a sign that the relationship is about to advance (or implode). If you don't hold the game, they could clam up again.

- *When you realize you honestly care about someone and want to make it work for real.* You need to get on the same page and be genuine with each other. You can always break the games out again later, to shake things up again if that becomes necessary (and it will).

Work the Burners

There are two kinds of games. There is the game you play when you are playing the field, and there is the game you play when you are really in it with one person. Let's start with how to play the field. To do this, I like to play a game called the Burner Method. I didn't make it up. Most guys know exactly what this is. They've been doing it for years, even if they don't know this game by name.

The Burner Method is like cooking a big dinner. You're making multiple dishes and you have a lot of pots on the stove at once. Each one is cooking at a different temperature. Some are priority dishes, some are just side dishes, but you keep them all going because dinner is more interesting when you're having more than one dish. In dating, the Burner Method involves keeping multiple potential partners on the "burners" at all times, so you have a lot of options and you always have someone to do something with. You keep them all focused on you, but you focus on the ones you really want, giving the others just enough to stay interested. The advantage is that having multiple burners keeps you from overfocusing and becoming obsessive about the ones you really like. It helps to keep you busy and not too available to any one person. It also saves time. If you are spending time with multiple people, you will get more experience and a better idea of who is really compatible with you.

Of course, sometimes it's a one-pot supper. You meet someone, you like him, he likes you, you are fully locked and loaded right from the start, and you never need any other burners. That does happen. Some people hear about the Burner Method and they say, "What do you mean, why would I do that? I met my boyfriend, we had sex, we've been married for fifteen years." That's great if it happens to you, but you will appreciate the Burner Method if you aren't sure what you want yet, or you are just getting over a breakup or a divorce and you want to ease back in to dating but are rusty, or know you shouldn't get too serious with someone else right away, or aren't ready to settle down and want to play the field for a while. Maybe you're just not a good dater. Not everybody is great at dating, but the Burner Method gives you practice until you get better at it.

When you work the burners, there will be those "hot" burners (the people you are really attracted to) and the lukewarm burners (the ones you like as friends but probably wouldn't want to get into a serious relationship with, or the ones you're just not that into). There are the burners you've got turned off, but you still have a pot sitting there, just in case, and the burners you have to turn off when they're boiling over. If you've ever made a complicated meal, you've done this with a real stove. It's not easy to manage all the burners, but it is the only way to have a successful meal. Why not try it with dating?

Yet women hardly ever do. For many reasons, we think we aren't allowed to date more than one person at the same time, even though men do it. Also, women are wired differently. We tend to invest a lot more emotion in the early stages of a relationship, whereas men tend to be better at compartmentalizing their emotions. They can disconnect more easily. They can be amazing in the moment with one person, then turn that off and go be amazing in the moment with somebody else. And without any guilt. I knew a man once who said he never lets any part of his life mix with any other. He's got a lot of burners going, but he will never let his food touch—nobody knows about anybody else. There is no one-pot meal in his life, and that's just how he likes it.

Women, on the other hand (and some men, too—I am generalizing here), tend to feel guilty about going out with more than one person. They express their emotions early in the relationship and they think they need to worry about hurting the other person. What I want to tell these women is: The least interested party always wins. Obsessing over somebody, even internally, never works. The other person can feel it and it's a turnoff. The beauty of the Burner Method is that it helps you not to obsess because you aren't putting all your hopes and dreams on one person. This gives you a chance to calm down and make a sensible choice. How do you know what flavor you like if you've only tasted one or two?

. . . .

GIRL TALK

If you're going to use the Burner Method, just remember one rule: Do not sleep with more than one person, unless you are very sure you can handle it. Most women can't, because our hormones get us emotionally involved even when we don't intend to be. Plus, it's a bad look to sleep with a lot of guys. People find out. It's hard to erase that reputation, even if it's an unfair one.

If your burners are a platonic zone, you can relax and take your time. Once you start sleeping with somebody, turn the other burners off—or at least turn them down. If it doesn't work out or you stop sleeping with that person, you can always get back in the kitchen. Or maybe you can sleep around, guy-style, and not freak out about it, and totally pull it off. If that's you, then I salute you! That ain't me (sometimes I wish it were).

• •

The Burner Method gives you space and time to figure out what you really want in a partner, and at the same time it makes you more attractive to potential partners, who can sense without you ever saying a word that you've got more than one person interested in you. It's a good way to assess what you like and don't like, and it can even keep a fledgling relationship hot because you remain mysterious and interesting and desired, and you have a life outside that one person. Don't you always want something a little more if you know that everybody else wants it, too? Relationships are like jobs. When you have one, they all want you. When you don't have one, it's crickets chirping. Nothing happens.

The Burner Method is an excellent cure for neediness. Here's how to play.

1. **Set up your burners.** Think about all the guys in your life: flirtations, passions, friends. They can all be on the burners. You should always have something bubbling, something warm, and something that's cooling off. Here's an example of how yours might look. You might only have a few of these types of relationships, or you might have even more than I've listed here. This is just to get you thinking about who's out there and potentially on your burners:

Burner #1: This is the spot for the guy you think could really turn into something. He has potential and you have chemistry. You might be so into this guy that you can't even see straight, but the logical part of your brain knows that if you rush it or obsess over him or get too needy or seem like you have no life, you could burn it all down. All the other burners exist so you can check yourself before you wreck yourself with Mr. Might-Be-Right. Keep him on Burner #1, but be ready to turn down the heat if it starts to boil over, or to turn off all the other burners if it gets serious.

Burner #2: This might be that guy you only run into every now and then who keeps resurfacing in your life. Maybe he lives in a different city so he's an occasional fling. He's cute and you idealize him. You fantasize that he could be The One in another life, but you are well aware that he isn't. Maybe he's an old flame—and what better place for an old flame than on a burner? You have chemistry with him, and you have his number in your phone, but you know it won't ever really work because he lives far away or he is noncommital and you don't actually have that much in common. Still, he's fun to hang around with for the weekend when he's in town. He's a nice security blanket, in a fantasy kind of way.

Burner #3: This guy always had a thing for you, but you never felt quite the same about him, so you never actually had a serious relationship. Or maybe you hooked up once and he's still into you but you just don't feel it. He's good to go out to dinner with because he always makes you feel interesting. You enjoy his company, but don't sleep with him when you are feeling desperate because he likes you too much and you'll be leading him on. You know he is not the one. He might also be the guy you have to "drink pretty."

Burner #4: This guy has money, or a really interesting or unusual life. Maybe he's athletic, a snowboarding instructor, or a trainer. Maybe he's a successful businessman or a jet-setter or a little bit famous or doing something cool; maybe he's a bartender or was in the Peace Corps or he is a poet or a musician. There's just something different about him and he likes to whisk you away on fun trips or out to fancy restaurants or take you to do cool hip things you might never do on your own. He's fascinating and a true adventurer, and he looks great on paper, but when you are really honest with yourself, you can't see it ever actually working out. Maybe you are just too different, or you know he will always put his work first, or you can't see him settling down. Still, maybe you get involved. If you do, proceed with caution.

Burner #5: This might be a colleague—someone you work with, someone you are in business with, or an associate who deals with your work in some way or whom you know through some professional network. Maybe he's even your doctor, your best friend's dentist, or your (watch out!) boss. You've always had chemistry, but you aren't sure whether something more would be a career disaster or exactly what you always wanted.

Burner #6: This is a great friend you can really talk to or an ex you stayed friends with. You have a personal history or an ongoing flirtation, but this is more of a supportive relationship than a romantic one. He may or may not really like you. If he does, be careful with him. Keep him as a friend, but don't lead him on. Maybe you're both lonely, but your friendship isn't worth jeopardizing.

2. **Turn on the stove.** Once you've got your burners all set up, it's time to play. Stay in touch with all your burners. Talk to them, e-mail them, go out and have fun. Don't dwell on one pot and ignore all the others. Don't lead anybody on, but be out there in the world having fun and keeping your connections active. There can be many people in your life, and that makes you more intriguing. The Burner Method sets you free to be a girl who has a life and doesn't hover over the phone waiting for a call or text. You're too busy, even unavailable to any particular person who might want to see you on short notice. A watched pot never boils, and is the true beauty of the Burner Method.

3. **Cook your meal.** The Burner Method takes focus, attention, and vigilance. You have to be observant. If one of the people on your burners isn't working out for any reason, remove that pot and replace it with another one. If a burner is boiling over, turn down the heat and step back from the stove. Be unavailable, or take a vacation, or just chill out for a while and take some time for yourself. Or turn up the heat

on another burner so you don't get too obsessed—it's easier to step back from one relationship if you step closer to a different one.

4. **Practice kitchen safety.** If you think someone is going to get genuinely hurt, turn off that burner and remove the pot. Your burners should be full of people who can handle it, just like you have to be able to handle it. If you do it fairly and don't lead anybody on, then everyone should enjoy it. It's like juggling, especially when you find yourself having coffee with one person, then dinner with another, then drinks with another, or texting four people at one time. Don't send the wrong text to the wrong person! Be sensitive, and play at your own pace. Maybe you can only handle three burners, or maybe you've got eight. Just keep going out, meeting new people, being friendly, being yourself, and paying very close attention to which burners seem like potential flames. Never forget that every relationship is an opportunity to practice and work on yourself, even if it's not going to be a keeper. It's the only way to check out all your options and grow as a person at the same time.

Just remember that the Burner Method is a game and a temporary situation. You also probably don't want to be the person who works the burners for life. Some guys do this—the terminal bachelors, the chronic players, who can't or don't ever want to settle down. However, most people get to a point in their lives when they are ready to settle down long-term with somebody who really understands them. As soon as one person is clearly the hottest, best, most irresistible person on your burners and that person feels the same way about you, there is an unwritten emotional contract that neither one of you is playing the field anymore.

But for testing the waters or getting past a breakup or having a good time until you find the right person for you? The Burner Method just makes sense. As soon as a relationship gets serious (you are having sex, you've met his parents, you feel committed or have talked seriously about commitment), it's time to stop playing this particular game. Turn off all the other burners and focus on keeping your fledgling relationship hot. If it doesn't work, you can always play another round.

. . . .

JUST THE TIP

If you're married, obviously you aren't going to be dating a lot of different guys (unless you have that kind of marriage), but that doesn't mean you can't have any guy friends in your life. Your gay BFF, your old friend from college, your work colleague, even your brother can all be on different kinds of burners—friend burners, moral support burners, buddy burners. These are not sexual; they are purely platonic and supportive but still worth keeping at a simmer because they make you feel valued, give you things to do, help you get a guy's perspective, and expand your circle so you are more fulfilled and a more interesting partner. Your husband is Burner #1 of course, and your first priority is to keep that relationship hot, but you can consider your guy friends ways to make your life more full. I don't fully buy the notion that men and women can't be friends—although I'm willing to debate this. I think there is a limit and usually one person is a little more into the other person and feelings could cross the line. Don't have any guy friends if you wouldn't want your husband to have an equivalent type of girl friend (be honest!). However, I do know that you can't get everything you need in life from one person. Just don't spend too much time or get into dangerous territory with anybody. Your sexual and emotional commitment must be to your spouse. If you feel that you might be approaching the line with a guy friend, the game is over.

. . . .

Cat and Mouse

Cat and mouse is a game of flirtation. You play it when you meet someone new. You could also call it the Porcupine Game because in some ways, in a new relationship, both parties are like porcupines that want to mate—circling around each other, interested but being very careful because they don't want to get hurt. Cat and mouse is also a good game for relationships that need spicing up. It's a way to engage or reengage another person by teasing, enticing, and hovering just out of reach—elusive but also with the possibility that you can be caught.

Cat and mouse is a very effective way of drawing someone in and getting them hooked on you. It's easy to play. You let the other person in a little, and then you pull back. You are the mouse, baiting the cat, getting the cat fascinated with catching you. It's a dance of seduction and withdrawal, give and take, push and pull. It's a tease. When you pull back, this makes the other person come closer, like a cat peering into the mouse hole to see where that little fascinating creature disappeared to, and then you lean in a little more, letting them catch a glimpse, giving them exactly what they want—for a moment. Then you pull back again, maybe become a little less available, a little bit busy. But just a little, not so much that the cat loses interest. You go from intriguing to absent, hide and seek. You fascinate. In a good game of cat and mouse, the cat is *really into the mouse*, and the better you know the cat, the better you will be able to gauge how far you can go before the cat pounces.

I have a friend who is very good at this. When she meets a guy she thinks she might like, she does tantalizing little things, like put a hand lightly on his arm, lean in close when he talks, and look him directly in the eyes, but then she doesn't talk to him for long. She makes an excuse, like going to get a drink—but with an intriguing backward glance. Then she watches him, but not so that it's obvious. She ignores him completely when he is talking to other people, but at the moment when he is between conversations or begins to look a little lost, she'll happen to wander by and wink or say something flirtatious, and maybe the conversation starts again. It's a very effective strategy. By the end of the party, the guy she's chosen is following her around like a puppy.

When you're playing cat and mouse, you are a little bit available, but not too available. Maybe you have time to meet for a drink and an appetizer but you have a dinner you have to attend afterward, so you need to breeze away. Or maybe you can meet for a drink afterward. When the two of you are together, you are totally into it. You might be sweet and vulnerable, but only as long as the other person is locked on you. If his attention strays or eyes wander, you're gone. You've flitted away. Maybe another night, you have an intimate dinner together. You are totally engaged in everything the other person says, hanging on every word, making thoughtful, engaged comments, but then you need to leave by midnight, to go . . . who knows where? Maybe you are available for a few days, then you disappear for a few days. Something has come up, but you hope you can get together soon! Like the cat who realizes that he'll lose the mouse if he doesn't watch closely, he'll see that you've slipped out of his grasp again.

This also works with texting and phone calls (also see chapter 5). They text or call you, you answer briefly but with warmth and interest, they try to keep the conversation going, and you wait. You don't answer right away. You're busy. You have an intriguing life. They will wonder what you're doing, who you're with. You'll answer eventually—flirtatiously, sweetly—and then cut them off again.

This game does have some risks, however. You have to be a smart mouse. If you pull back for too long, the other person can see what you're doing and pull back, too. Then it's a standoff. When one person shuts down, it's not the time for the other person to shut down, it's the time to lean in a little more to see if they will let you in. When you both shut down, the relationship stops progressing. This is why some couples haven't spoken to each other in twenty years.

Cat and mouse is also totally applicable to married life. When things start to get a little dull, become the mouse. Start the tease. Wear something unexpectedly sexy. Touch him in unexpected ways, then withdraw with a sultry look. Send him a suggestive text (when appropriate—his boss doesn't need to see!). Take him on a surprise date night. Initiate a make-out session without going "all the way." If he isn't responsive at first—maybe you've both fallen into a rut—don't be offended or get irritable. That will spoil the whole mood. Be patient and keep initiating little sexy moves until he responds. When you remind each other of how it was when you first met, you can reintroduce exciting sexual tension back into your marriage.

The trick with cat and mouse is to stay alert. Watch what the other person is doing so you can gauge what you should do next. When they move in, you move back. When they move back, you move in. Dance the dance, and you'll both stay on your toes—and excited about what might happen next.

. . . .

MAN-FORMATION

This is a good time to remind you that men want to be the pursuers. They are natural hunters, so if you want to be caught, then ironically, you need to play hard to get. If you are too easy to win, you will not be as valued. This applies to everything. If you get something for free, you tend to treat it like it's worthless. If you pay a lot for something, you take better care of it. People are no different. If you have to work really hard to win someone, you value them more than if you can get them without any effort. Right or wrong, it's human nature.

So don't just play hard to get. *Be* hard to get. This can be tricky, and there is a line—you can't be too hard to get, or the cat loses interest. Be affectionate, be loving, be all-in, but also be busy, have a life, have standards, and don't compromise. You will know right away if you are on some guy's radar. You don't need to flirt with other guys to get someone's attention. You don't need to call attention to yourself or be a show-off or talk too much. The real trick, and the place to put all your effort, is not to let the other person know when he is on *your* radar. Be polite, sweet, interesting, but not *too* interested. Be there, and then disappear. Don't put up with bullshit, be willing to walk until the day you walk down the aisle, and you will be a prize he can't bear not to win.

. . . .

The Zen Game

I'm no Zen expert, but I do know it's about being in the moment, and this game is the sequel to cat and mouse. This is not only a strategy but a really good practice for all your relationships. Once you have been "caught" by the cat, you can settle into locking down the relationship, and the Zen Game is the way you do it. When you are with your partner, be fully there. Be present. Really listen, really respond. Be connected. Be together. Be a "we." Be on the same team. Be a family, if that's appropriate. Create memories and make that person feel really good being with you.

Once someone is locked down, they are yours to lose. If you play your cards right in the beginning, then no matter what you do later, the connection you are forging now will be so strong that it will be hard to screw it up. And even if you do, you are more likely to be able to get it back, because you started this way. Connection is what it's all about, and if you are constantly thinking about something else or looking at your phone, you can't connect with the person in front of you.

. . . .

MAN-FORMATION

It's a big deal to a man if you don't like his family or friends—a much bigger deal than it is for most women. Remember that men don't like drama. They also don't like negativity. They want everything to be copacetic. They want harmony. You don't have to be little miss sunshine all day every day, but getting along with his family and friends is a gift to the man you love. If you have a happy, cordial Thanksgiving weekend with his family or you go out tailgating with his friends or join in on bowling night and you have fun and everybody likes you, that means the world to a guy and it goes a long way. You don't need to be that girl who cooks everything from scratch or knows all about football or is good at bowling. You just need to be that cool chick who can hang out now and then without rolling your eyes or making sarcastic comments the whole time. Your guy will be grateful in ways you probably can't imagine, because most women don't really care if their husbands or boyfriends like their friends.

. . . .

Riding the Wave

Dating is like surfing. If you don't want to fall, you need to pay attention to the natural rhythms of your relationship. Watch the waves coming in so you know which waves to let wash over you and which waves to catch. Then you have to feel how to balance yourself on the board, which way to lean, when to ride a wave all the way into the beach, and when to bail. Once you're in the wave and you've got your balance, then you let go and enjoy it. You don't fight it. You relax into it and allow it to take you.

Riding the Wave is about risk, balance, and surrender. You take a risk when you catch a wave—when you take a chance on someone and decide to see where it will go. You learn to balance by determining when to lean out and when to lean in to a relationship. For example, last year I was at the stage with a guy I was dating where we assumed that we would do something together every night. Then we both started taking it for granted. The seas were calm, which is relaxing for a while, but I knew something needed to happen to keep the relationship energized or it might die out. I decided to leave town and spend some time in the Hamptons without him. I leaned out. This shook things up in just the right way for us. Suddenly he missed me. He wanted me around, and he leaned in and then I could lean in again, too. You don't have to skip town to get this effect. Maybe you make your own plans, but make it seem like the other person's idea: "Hey, you mentioned recently that you want to hang out with your guys more. Why not have a guys' night out next Saturday?" At first, this might seem great to him, and he'll probably do it, but he also might think, *But wait a minute . . . I thought we were going to spend the weekend together*, and before you know it, he's leaning back in.

Sometimes, you need to be the one to lean in. If you try leaning out and the other person leans out, too, thinking that you are getting distant or uninterested, lean back in so the other person feels connected to you. If you leaned out too far, the other person might still be a little bit hurt when you lean back in again. You might even get pushed away for a while, but keep leaning in. Maybe you need to be a little more loving, a little more snuggly, a little more focused on the other person, in order to re-forge that connection until the other person leans in, too.

Finally, you need to let go. When things are in sync, when it's all working, then surrender a little. Stop trying to control everything. Be easygoing and have fun. Ride the wave and see where it takes you. You're in the sweet spot, and this is the big payoff for your hard work.

GIRL TALK

Sometimes women ask me why they should have to do all the work to fix relationship problems. Why can't their boyfriends or husbands be the ones to determine that the relationship isn't satisfactory and take steps to change it? Girlfriends, if you are waiting around for the guy to, first of all, *notice* there is a problem in a relationship he has with someone he's having sex with, and second of all, devote time to sitting and thinking about it and consciously figuring out steps he could take to make the relationship better, then you need to go back and reread chapter 1. Men need to feel appreciated. They need to feel good about themselves in the relationship if they are going to be the person you want to be with. Ultimately, they want to make us happy, but they need a little help doing that because—as you now know—we are mysteries to them. If they are making an effort and we don't appreciate them and we only focus on the negative, that discourages them and then they don't want to try anymore. You are the one who can turn that situation around. It doesn't take much, but you need to instigate it. Maybe it's unfair, but it's reality. Consider it a fair trade for his having to put up with your PMS.

Truthfully, I believe that the person who has the problem has the responsibility of making it known and taking steps to fix it. If you are the one who would like something to be different, then you are the one who has to figure out how to change it. It's as simple as that. It's not about being a woman. It's about wanting a certain kind of relationship and going out and getting it. That usually means it's going to be up to you, and thank God, because the alternative is that you are completely at the mercy of someone else's whims. Take the power, take the control, and make the relationship what you need it to be.

Playing the Player

Getting into a relationship with a player is different from getting into a relationship with somebody who already knows he wants a relationship.

A player can seem ungettable. Guys who are players often talk about how they love being bachelors, and both men and women who are players often say that they will never get married. Sometimes, players really are ungettable, but most of the time, a player is only playing until the right person suddenly appears, not because he was looking to settle down, but just because it happened despite the player's best intentions to remain single. When all the conditions are right in the player's life, everything can change in a heartbeat. That means if you have your eye on a player and you see potential, it can happen. Just don't forget that you are attempting to turn a large ship around. That requires slow, gradual changes in direction, not cranking the wheel all the way to the left and hoping for the best.

You just have to play the game the right way:

- **Move slowly.** The most important thing is not to make any big motions. Getting a player to commit to a relationship is like getting a squirrel to eat out of your hand. Move forward slowly, carefully, and don't be threatening. Make no sudden, jarring moves, like, "Oh, my parents are coming to town, I want you to meet them!" or, "Hey, I booked this great trip for us!" These are panic-inducing moves that will make a player disappear from your radar. Anything big has to seem to them like it was their idea, even if it was yours. Let them think they are leading the process.
- **Don't make yourself too available.** Even though you are dying to be seen with your conquest, remember that small doses of you will be much more effective than constant contact and monopolizing his time. Have a life. Be independent, and let the player come to you. If you made plans with friends but you want to cancel because he wants to do something, don't do it! In fact, the moment when you most want to ditch all your friends for some guy is the exact moment when you most need to say you are busy.
- **Don't cling.** At a bar, a party, or any kind of social function, don't hang on a player all the time. Go talk to people on your own. Let the player go talk to his guys, hang out, do his thing, and give

him a chance to wonder where you are, miss you, come looking for you.

- **Be straightforward.** Ironically (because they are so seldom straight with others when they are playing the game), if there was ever a guy who requires straight talk, it's a player. Never be naggy or whiny with a player. Say exactly how you feel in three sentences or less, then pull back. You can still be expressive, even emotional, but be brief and direct, and then be gone, so he has time to consider what you said without you bashing him over the head with it. Give him just enough rope to hang himself. Plus, if there's one thing that entices a player, it's a woman walking in the opposite direction.

- **Lean in when it's fun, lean out when you feel needy.** Players are enchanted by someone who gives them a lot of focused attention and really listens, but when it comes to anything emotional, they get nervous. When you are out on a fun date, lean in and give a player your total attention. If he seems defeated, or doesn't know how to make you happy, or seems a little distant, lean in. As soon as you start feeling needy, however, that is the exact wrong time to start calling and texting a player. That is the time to be busy and unavailable. If you slept together a little too soon and you want to know what it all means, how he feels, whether he liked it, whether he's going to call you, then take my advice and get up and get out of there immediately (or in the morning). Don't ask when you'll see him again. Don't make any plans with him. For God's sake, don't talk about how he's your boyfriend now. Be confident—never ashamed—and *go*. Let him come to you.

- **Never compromise yourself for a player.** Don't ever give up your interests, your passions, or especially your career for a player. This is the worst possible thing you can do because players never respect somebody who caves in and gives them everything. The key to playing the player is to be as independent and interesting as possible, and that means never, ever devoting your life to him. Devote your life to you, and he will chase you forever. Give it all up for him, and he has won the game and will go look for another one because you are no longer interesting to him.

• •

*I think the modern-day woman will tell you that
women can be just as predatory as men.*
—MATT DAMON, REPORTED IN *ELLE* MAGAZINE

• •

The Ungettable

There are such things as ungettable people. You might even have one on your burner, but he is not a prospect for a long-term relationship. I have dated three different men who were completely unable to commit to a relationship, but I've also dated men who looked that way but weren't. There is a difference between someone who is basically defective and someone who is stunted but has the potential to grow. Look for signs of change or signs of a stubborn refusal to change. The ungettable guy likes the game of cat and mouse, but he loses interest if he smells that he has you, and if the relationship becomes too difficult, he'll check out and go for easier prey. He is never going to settle down. The guy with potential also likes the game, but if he's genuinely intrigued, you'll see his player behaviors slowly falling by the wayside as he focuses more and more seriously on you. Even small changes indicate the potential for progress and change. The ones who make zero change, zero adjustments to accommodate the relationship, are the truly hopeless ones. You might not always be able to tell the difference right away, but with good observation skills, the truth will become apparent after a few months.

Then there are the guys who make it seem like you've got them, but you don't. These are serial monogamists. They seem settled down, but they never actually fully commit. These are the guys who will date you or even live with you for years without evolving or proposing. If you force their hands, they might even break up with you, or let you break up with them. The most frustrating thing about these seemingly ungettable guys is that sometimes once you break up with them, six months later you will hear that they got married. There is nothing you can do about this. Somebody else was right for him, and it wasn't you. It's depressing but it's not your fault. If you are really paying attention, you won't let it get to this point. Don't be the girl who dates somebody for four months and still doesn't know where she stands. Then again, you never really know for sure—I had a one-night stand with an ungettable guy, and it turned into a yearlong relationship. The trick is not to let them know they have you until you are in a safe place with that person, but sometimes, no matter how you act, intuitively they just *know*.

For more about the timeline and how to gauge relationship progress, see chapter 7.

The Happily Married Game

Congratulations—you got married! Marriage comes with a whole new set of challenges. It doesn't mean the effort is over. It's the opposite, actually. Marriage is hard, and the game doesn't end when you get married. It just changes. The game can be quite useful to married people. For example, when you're married, it's easy to fall into a rut, take each other for granted, let yourselves go, stop having sex. A little well-intentioned game playing can throw the whole thing into reverse, breaking you out of ruts and helping you appreciate each other again.

I think this is the best way to play the game when you are married: Light a little fire under your spouse when things get dull. You've been walking around in sweatpants looking like a swamp thing? He's been working a lot and ignoring you? You've been sneaking to bed when he falls asleep on the couch so you don't have to deal with his advances? Turn it around. Show him you've still got it going on. Get decked out, or put on some lingerie. Wear perfume and sexy, flirty dresses. Start going out again—plan a girls' night out to rejuvenate you and help you get your mojo back. If something comes up, like a concert you really want to see, and your husband isn't interested, take a friend instead. You need to get out of the rut.

When you're together, try to see in your husband the man you first met. Pay more attention to him. Flirt. Put sexy notes where he'll find them, or tell him to meet you in a bar and pretend you've never met him before. Let him try to pick you up. There are a lot of ways you can do this, from subtle to obvious, but shaking things up with games can light a fire under both of you again.

If you and your husband haven't been talking about the problems under the surface, shake things up by getting verbal—not by whining or overwhelming him with a million things he does wrong that you hate, but by tackling the issues calmly and one at a time. When you and your spouse are both calm, even bored, with nothing else going on in your lives, you can initiate the game. Be calm, casual, sweet, and nonthreatening. A good environment might be over a relaxing dinner at home with no schedule and nothing you have to run off to do next. In a relaxed but straightforward way, say what you need (maybe to spend more time together, more attention, or more affection), say what you are willing to give (making time for a date night, more attention, more blow jobs), and then start the dance: sweetness, withdrawal, sexiness, pulling back, flirtation, indifference. It doesn't matter whether you've known someone for six months or sixty years. Be intriguing, and you can get back what you had in the beginning.

. . . .

GIRL TALK

You know you are with the right person if that is the person you want to hang out with doing nothing on a Sunday. You feel natural together, and you don't have to be doing things—or playing games—all the time.

. . . .

Is the Game Ever Over?

The game is never completely over, no. Sometimes you will call a time-out. Sometimes you will shut the game off when things get serious. When you feel safe and secure in a relationship, you can retire the game, reserving the right to bring it back out when you need it. Even if you've been married twenty years, you never know when you're going to need the game to resuscitate the relationship or calm your anxiety, like when you go through perimenopause and you suddenly get obsessive, or when he's going through a midlife crisis and eyeing that red Corvette because he thinks he needs something more interesting in his life. There are always uses for the game, but the closer you are and the more history you have together, the less you will need it. When your relationship is a healthy diet, the game is like French fries or ice cream. It livens things up, but it's not for every day.

But always have a little game in your game.

CHAPTER 5

· · · · · · · · · · · · · · ·

Control Yourself

I'm selfish, impatient, and a little insecure. I make
mistakes, I'm out of control, and at times hard to
handle. But if you can't handle me at my worst, then
you sure as hell don't deserve me at my best.
—MARILYN MONROE

If I've learned one thing in my life, it's that I am controlling. I want to control my environment, my situation, and what other people around me are doing. I have ideas about how things should be, and I want reality to live up to my ideal. I try very hard to force this to happen. I always have. I want everything to be perfect. There are all kinds of deep psychological explanations for this, I'm sure. For me, part of the reason is that I had so little control over many of the factors in my childhood. I went to thirteen different schools, I witnessed abuse, I rarely lived in the same place two years in a row, I never knew where my belongings were, and I couldn't predict any of the volatility in my surroundings. I'm no shrink, but the effect of this seems to have manifested itself in my need to control things.

This has come in many packages in my life: food and eating, money, organization, and especially relationships. For example, there was a time with a past boyfriend when I thought he wasn't being a teammate. I felt like I was making all the plans and controlling everything, and I didn't like it. Why wasn't he showing any initiative? It took a very frank discussion and some shutting up and listening on my part for me to discover that this person thought he was being very supportive of me and everything I had to do. He didn't want to impose himself because I seemed to have it all under control. Frankly, there is a lot that comes with having me as a girlfriend and I know that—the aftermath of my difficult divorce, for one thing. The guy I was with thought I was disrespecting all his efforts to support me, and all I saw was my idea that he wasn't participating fully in the relationship. It was a complete misunderstanding. I wasn't paying attention to the cues. I was just assuming I was right and that my worldview was the accurate one, without seeing things from his point of view.

We only see our own points of view clearly, which is why it is so important to pay attention to cues from your partner when you think something is off. It's not about controlling and forcing the other person to comply with how you think things should be. It has to be about letting go of that and allowing space for someone else's perspective in your master plan. This is really hard to do if you are like me, but it's the only way to move forward and find real intimacy.

You might have different issues—we all have our stuff—but if you have trouble relinquishing control, then let's talk. I know I'm not the only one. I know a lot of controlling women. It's a problem with us. I think part of the reason is that we are juggling so many balls and wearing so many hats all the time that if we don't exercise control, we could lose it all. We are mothers, friends, wives or girlfriends, homemakers, workers. We own businesses, run companies, or work our asses off to get whatever job we are in charge of done well and on time. To us, a loss of control can feel like an emergency. It can make us literally feel like we are going to die.

The problem with being too controlling and being a perfectionist is that life is not perfect. People are not perfect. Relationships are definitely not perfect. They are living, breathing creatures just like people, and they will never live up to the ideal of romantic movies, romance novels, or fairy tales. Trying to control them and perfect them will always lead to disappointment. Always. A big part of the reason why a relationship will never live up to the ideal is that a relationship by definition involves two people, and you cannot actually control someone else. You cannot make them act the way you think they should act. You cannot make them do and say romantic things at exactly the appropriate moment, or always know and feel exactly how you are feeling, or have even the slightest clue what you need.

You can influence someone in your relationship, but you can't control what they do, let alone what they think. If you think you can, you are wrong, or you are a bully (and also wrong). If the other person in your relationship acts, talks, or thinks in a way you don't like, there's not a lot you can do about it beyond deciding what *you* are going to do about it—discuss it, be hurt or pleased by it, leave. That's because there is one thing you can always control in this life: yourself.

There is nothing wrong with being in control of yourself and the way you live your life, but there is also such a thing as being overcontrolling to the point of personal misery. We have to harness control and use it for good, not evil. But that means giving up a certain amount of control (or what we think is control). Giving up control and not always knowing what's going to happen every second, or not always having a handle on every situation, isn't the same as being out of control. "Out of control" sounds scary and slightly insane. As often as we all know deep down that we can get that way, most of us try desperately to avoid at least the appearance of being out of control. The truth is, it's actually liberating to let go of things a little. When you really think about what you can control and what you can't control, your list of things to control gets a lot shorter and less intimidating.

Control Equality

Ideally, control should be equal. Most of the time, you make your own decisions but make mutual decisions when they impact you as a couple. However, control is rarely fifty-fifty at any given moment in the real world. Sometimes you are in a more powerful place than your partner, or vice versa. Sometimes you are in a vulnerable place and you need someone to step up and take care of things.

For example, maybe you are pregnant or you lost your job or something happened in your family and you are going through a thing and losing it a little. If your partner can step up and take control in certain areas for a while as a way to protect and care for you, then that's a kind of control you want. If you had a bad day at work or you have raging PMS, you may be a little more out of control than usual, and if your partner can step in calmly as the voice of reason, that's also the kind of control you want. Sometimes you feel a little insecure or vulnerable or emotional, and your partner can reassure you and guide the relationship temporarily.

At other times, your partner may be feeling insecure. Maybe he was reprimanded at work, or failed at something important, or is having a career crisis or family problems. At those times, you may be the one to step up and take the helm.

On an even more subtle level, control changes throughout the day. You might have it in the mornings when your partner is grumpy or not inclined to interact. Your partner might have it in the evenings when you are dead tired and your brain has turned off. Control is a wave. It's always changing. It changes with each person's feelings. Sometimes, women want to feel strong, powerful, and in charge of their own lives. Sometimes, we want to feel soft, feminine, delicate, rescued. Sometimes, men want to feel like little boys who have someone to nurture and take care of them. Other times, they want to feel big, strong, invincible. Women want a man who can handle them and be in charge, but they also don't want to be bossed around or controlled. Men want to be manhandled in just the right way, so they feel secure, but they don't ever want to feel weak or emasculated.

Part of the beauty of a truly intimate relationship is that people can do these things for each other—they can make each other feel strong and empowered but also vulnerable and sensitive. We all have all those things inside of us, and we look for people who can understand them and with whom we can share them without feeling in peril or betrayed.

Ideally, in terms of control, what you want is to balance these waves of hard and soft, strong and delicate, over the course of the relationship. This is a zero-sum game because if somebody wins, somebody else loses. It should be less of a contest and more like banter or cat-and-mouse. No one person should always be in charge, always call the shots, always tell the other what to do. There should not be manipulation, because with manipulation, there can't be real trust or intimacy. If one person is always in charge, the relationship will degrade, I guarantee it. Being in control 24/7 is often necessary when you're parenting little kids, but it should never be a part of an adult relationship. We think men are so tough, but they can actually be sensitive, even oversensitive. It's deceiving. Controlling behavior may make them give in to you, but it certainly won't be a partnership. It goes the other way too, of course. If someone else is constantly trying to control you, it feels like a dictatorship, not a relationship.

So what we're really going for here is control equality. This can go wrong in two ways: You might be a control freak and try to control everything all the time, either causing constant fights or causing your partner to give up and check out, at least emotionally, from the relationship. Or your partner might be the control freak who is always trying to tell you what to do and how to live your life, maybe because he makes more money or has a more advanced degree or a more prestigious job, or just has a more dominant personality.

Let's talk about both scenarios and what you can do to get control back in balance.

When You Are the Control Freak

If you are the one who always has to be in control and you literally freak out when you feel like you are not running the show, it's important for the health of your relationship to chill out a little and let some things go. This is harder than it sounds. I know because this is me. So how do you do it? How do you let go?

• •

DR. AMADOR SAYS . . .

Letting go of control becomes easier when you recognize that control is an illusion. If you've tried to change someone, if you've told him how you want things to be different and it's been weeks or even months of stalemate, it's time to let go. Otherwise, you are letting the relationship drag you along and you are making yourself miserable thinking about it. (He's not.)

Bethenny uses a sailing analogy in this section—one I like. Here's another: *You can't change the direction of the wind, but you can adjust your sails.* How do you do that? How do you let go, let your sails out so you don't get blown over and sink your ship? Write down those things you believe you can and cannot control or change about him. Then, every morning, meditate, or if you pray do that, and use a personalized form of the traditional Irish blessing to help you: Ask for the serenity to let go of the things you cannot control. Name them out loud during your meditation/prayer. Try it. It works if you do it every day and it works better if you do it throughout the day every time you feel angry and wanting to be in control. "Please give me the serenity to accept those things about him I cannot change, and the courage to change those things about myself that I can."

—Xavier Amador, Ph.D., president,
LEAP Institute, www.leapinstitute.org

. . . .

I don't know about you, but I'm no good at just sitting with my hands in my lap waiting for something to happen. I need something to do, something to replace my control urges with. This is like finding something to do rather than binge-eat cookies. You might learn to have an apple or go on a walk or do some yoga. Here are some of the things I have discovered make great stand-ins and much more appropriate strategies than the constant quest to control the universe.

- **Observe.** In a relationship, I have found that observation is more important than control. If you stop talking and telling people what they should be doing, and start listening to what other people say and especially watching what they do, you will be amazed at what you learn about what's really going on. I've been in situations where I thought I knew exactly what a guy I was dating was thinking or feeling, and it wasn't until I shut up and started paying attention to his nonverbal cues that I realized I was completely wrong. Observing your partner—and yourself—can really teach you things about yourself and how you operate in relationships. It's all about perspective. You can be in your own head, thinking about what's going on with the relationship from your internal point of view, or you can look more objectively at what's happening externally. You can think about all the negatives, about how your guy never picks up the garbage or didn't ask you about your day or isn't compassionate, or you can focus on the positives, like how he was there every day when your mom was sick or how he makes you laugh or how you have great sex or how he's always willing to go to whatever restaurant you want and doesn't care if you take off at a moment's notice to exercise at the gym for two hours. Think about your perspective and see if you can shift it. Sometimes, I'll look at someone I am dating and think, "I can't believe he just did that. What an asshole." But then I'll stop myself and think, "Hey, you know what, wait a minute—he is dealing with my divorce and he is amazing with my daughter and he doesn't mind that I'm essentially homeless right now and although he doesn't love that I'm on reality TV, he totally tolerates it." That's a much nicer picture.

- **Trust.** Trusting is very hard for control freaks. We want all the information all the time and we don't really believe anybody else will handle anything correctly. A girlfriend of mine once told me that her husband accused her of not trusting him because every time he told her something, she had to look it up to see if it was true, and every time he said he would do something, she had to check up on him to make sure he really did it. She totally copped to it. She said, "I don't trust you, but don't take it personally—I don't trust anybody!" Yet trust is extremely important in a relationship. You might have your trust betrayed now and then, but when your trust is rewarded, it's worth a few disappointments along the way. It might not feel like that now, but just try it. Try trusting. Try believing. Try letting your partner handle some things. You can't learn to trust if you never give anybody the opportunity to be trusted.

- **Go with the flow.** Sometimes, the path will guide you. You don't have to have a map. This is similar to trusting. Just go with what's happening and see where it ends up. Maybe it will end up somewhere better than where you would have forced it to go, or maybe you will avoid the disastrous results of being over-controlling. I like to use this strategy when I feel like a relationship has gotten ahold of me, and I want to get ahold of it. There is something very peaceful about just letting it go, not forcing it, not white-knuckling. Just seeing what is true and going with it and accepting it. When you can do that, then, in that moment, everything feels okay. It is what it is. Try letting that be true for a while and see what happens to your perception.

- **Don't let the future control your reality.** Once I was dating a guy and it was going really well, but it just so happened that our leases were both ending within a few months and we were both considering buying apartments. I got it in my head that if we were both going to buy, then we should just buy an apartment together and move in. He wasn't ready to move in together. I took this really personally, even though in truth, it was too early for us to live together. It was also too late for us to choose to live separately. It was a weird situation. I began to battle, even though somewhere deep down I knew I wasn't ready to move in with him, either. I latched on to this idea of moving in together like a dog on a bone, and I wouldn't let it go. Emotionally, I was scared. Intellectually, I got it, but my control issues wouldn't let me be rational. I wanted to know what it meant for our futures if we were investing in separate properties, even though it wasn't the right time to combine our resources. I kept wanting to talk about it until it became a very sore topic, but I wasn't recognizing his level of unreadiness. Men need to feel like they are financially established (if they are real men, not still boys). They need to have an identity when it comes to money. They want to be self-sufficient and capable of being providers, and he wasn't in this place yet. But all I could see was my perception of his rejection of me. I tried so hard to control the situation with constant harping and unproductive, angry conversations that

I was doing damage to the relationship to the point where no one would want to live with me anyway. I could barely live with myself. Finally, I realized what I was doing. The future cannot govern the present. Relationship shifts have to be right for both of you right now, not in some nebulous "someday." When I let it go and let it breathe, we both calmed down and we could come together again. We didn't end up moving in together, and that was right for us. Rushing it would have been a mistake. Sometimes you just need to leave it alone.

- **Try vulnerability.** Being vulnerable can be even scarier than trusting for people with control issues. Vulnerability can feel like standing naked in the street. However, vulnerability can result in leaps forward for a relationship that is stuck. A friend of mine once said to me, "Shared intimacy equals shared vulnerability." Sometimes when you are both battling for control, going head to head, and your egos are clashing, a moment of vulnerability can stop the runaway train. What if you just said, "Hey, the truth is, I miss you every day when we aren't together and right now I'm feeling a little needy and insecure that you might not feel the same way." Maybe you say, "I'm worried that because you make more money than I do, you are better than me." Maybe you say, "I'm feeling really alone because we haven't physically connected in a while, and I need that." Maybe you say, "I'm worried about aging and the fact that I'm older than you." Maybe you say, "I'm worried that because I don't have a job, you'll get bored of me." Maybe you say, "This baby weight makes me feel fat and insecure. I need you to tell me I'm still sexy to you." Ultimately, being willing to show your vulnerability is a sign of security, not in your own power but in the power of the relationship.

. . . .

DR. AMADOR SAYS . . .

Expressing vulnerability works almost every time. Pardon the dog analogy, but do you want to be the snarling dog baring her teeth, or the one on her back showing her underbelly, completely vulnerable but clearly asking to have her belly scratched? Studies of self-disclosure of vulnerability find that the person being trusted with the display of vulnerability nearly always returns the same level of trust and vulnerability. The payoff is usually within moments, not days or weeks. That's a good return on your vulnerability investment.

—Xavier Amador, Ph.D., president,
LEAP Institute, www.leapinstitute.org

• •

- **Step off.** Sometimes you just need to back up and get out of the way. Other people aren't always willing to deal with an issue the second that you are. People can be moody. Sometimes they just don't want to deal with something difficult. A guy I once dated could be in a bad mood for a week and I wouldn't see him for days at a time. I had to learn to just have a glass of wine and chill out and call my girlfriends instead of badgering him. I had to realize that 1) it wasn't about me and 2) he wasn't right for me. His stuff, his retreats, his moods had nothing to do with me. They were his. When women get scared, many of us tend to go into battle mode. If we aren't getting exactly what we need at that moment, we decide that we are gone. Then our men panic. It's like poking a bear in its cave. We are standing in front of the cave badgering the bear: "What's going on?" "What's happening with us?" "How do I need to think about this now?" And the men just want to roar at us. It doesn't work because when a man is in his cave, he needs to be there, and we need to see that and leave him alone and wait until he comes back out into the light. Sometimes you just have to let that happen and recognize that you can't control it, and furthermore, that it has nothing to do with you.
- **Recognize that oftentimes, things have nothing to do with you.** Yes, it's true. Sometimes people will snap at you, yell at you, ignore you, or not pick up the phone when you call, for reasons that have absolutely nothing to do with you or anything you said or

did. This is really hard for a lot of women to understand, myself included, but it's true. Your partner not only isn't necessarily thinking about you at every moment, but isn't always going to be on the same page with whatever you are going through. He is not a mind reader. He is not in your brain. He has his own shit. How often have you thought or even said out loud something like, "I had a really bad day yesterday, and you didn't even care. You weren't even compassionate!" He had his own day, and it might have been crappy, too. He wasn't at your job with you. He didn't see what that person said to you or feel how it made you feel. He was probably too busy dealing with whatever was happening to him (like we all are). Just like you can't assume somebody else's bad mood is about you, you also have to take ownership for your own feelings and recognize that your bad mood is about you, not about somebody else's failure to perceive it. If you need support, you need to ask for it. Directly. When you realize that it's not all about you, you also realize that there is no point in controlling every single thing in the universe. It suddenly becomes much easier to give some of that up.

. . . .

GIRL TALK

Women and men both get emotional in different ways, but what I find curious is that even though women are so smart and we always know what to do, in relationships, we let our emotions get the best of us and all that goes out the window. We overthink everything and convince ourselves that what we have concocted in our brains is true. Meanwhile, men just *act*. It's more instinctual. We should try this more often.

. . . .

- **Recognize your significant attention requirements.** We all do it— we want attention. Even people who say they are shy or intro- verted have roundabout ways of getting the attention they need. Humans are social creatures and we want to know that other people know we are here. That's fine unless we take it too far, and I know a lot of women, myself included, who take it too far on a daily basis. Here's what I've figured out: The universe will not implode if nobody is paying attention to you for two seconds. A lot of women need a fairly significant amount of attention and they expect to get it all from their relationships, but that's just not realistic. Spread the wonder that is you around to multiple friends and willing family members as well as your partner, so you can get what you need without putting too much of the burden on one person. Because yes, despite how wonderful we are, our needs can be a burden when we pile them all in one spot.

· ·

CELEBS SPEAK OUT

I had the rapper Ice Cube on my talk show once, and when he answered my question about who has the control or "runs the show" in his twenty-plus-year marriage, he said: "It's a partnership, you know? It's a true partnership. I respect my wife and she respects me." I had never thought about trying to control someone else as a sign of disrespect, but that's exactly what it is.

· ·

Control Yourself

Ironically, if you learn to control your own actions, words, and even thoughts, you will end up having more control over the actions, words, and even thoughts of other people because we are all connected and we respond to each other's energy. To step back and look at the big picture, controlling yourself is also really important for getting along with a partner. If you are constantly out of control or trying to control others but not control yourself, then you aren't really in the right mental space for the give-and-take of a healthy relationship. You know that saying about the blind leading the blind? Figure out your own issues first before you start jumping all over everybody else to get them to change and adhere to your standards.

I have a guy friend who has this problem. He feels like his own issues are so complicated and so intimidating that he can't possibly tackle them, so instead, he focuses all his energy on his wife and how she can best live her life. He says he can see so clearly what her problems are and how to fix them, but he has no idea how to fix his own, so he goes with what is easier. Sometimes his wife appreciates the constant attention, and sometimes she resents it because he gets too controlling. It really can be unpleasant to be the total focus of someone else because they can't focus on themselves. It's a lot of pressure.

So get your shit together first. Nobody is ever totally together and you don't have to be perfect to be in a relationship, obviously, but you should at least know your issues and be working on them. You have to know yourself and be self-conscious in this way. Know that you tend to control or manipulate. Know that you tend to cave and be a doormat. Know that you tend to drop everything for your man or refuse to admit for one second that you need anybody. When you know yourself, only then can you really know someone else.

. . . .

DR. AMADOR SAYS . . .

A few words about controlling yourself: *Pain is never an option. Misery always is.* What I mean is that you cannot control what you feel. Expect to feel unwanted, unexpected, and painful feelings. What you do with your feelings determines if you choose happiness versus misery.

Letting go of those things you're angry or sad about that you cannot change is one important technique we've already discussed. The other is simple acceptance. You're going to feel a lot when you're in a relationship. You can't help what you feel, but you can change your thought about it. The irony is that by changing your thoughts (letting go of things you cannot control, deciding not to rent him space between your ears, going over and over how he hurt or disappointed you, etc.), your emotions can calm down all on their own. More importantly, by knowing your emotional life well, you can make better decisions about how you act or don't act based on your emotions. This looks and feels a lot like having control without actually being controlling.

—Xavier Amador, Ph.D., president,
LEAP Institute, www.leapinstitute.org

. . . .

Here's how this could work in real life. If you're having an argument, or feeling like somebody else is doing something wrong or something you don't like, or if you are just angry or frustrated, stop for a minute. What is making you upset? Pinpoint it. Really nail it down. Is it because your partner isn't doing something the way you think it should be done? Is it because your partner isn't acting the way you think someone should act? Is it because anybody else did anything? This is the time to turn the ship around. Forget what the other person is doing and look at yourself. Why does that behavior make you angry? Is it because of how it looks to others? Is it because you feel it's not "good enough" for you? Is it because you feel neglected or unimportant? These are things you can do something about because they involve your attitude. How will you choose to view this situation? What is the best way to get a good result? Nagging and forcing and threatening obviously don't get good results, so why are you doing that? Really break this down logically. How will *you* respond? What will *you* say? How will *you* feel?

When you turn it around to focus on your own reactions, everything looks different, like the world in a mirror. You can even take this further. What specifically bothers you? See if, in actuality, the thing that bothers you in somebody else is what really bothers you about yourself. Let's say your partner doesn't help out around the house enough. What if you ask yourself, "Do I help out around the house enough?" Maybe your first answer is, "Yes! I do everything and he does nothing!" But take it further. Do you help around the house too much? Do you let anyone help, or do you criticize whenever anybody does something differently than you would? Do you honestly think you would like it if your partner did more around the house? What if he started cleaning everything and making the dinner plans and telling you what to do all the time? Sometimes it's nice to be the Mom everybody needs. What if he started doing all the play-dates and making all the snacks and getting all the snuggles? How would you feel about that? When it comes to housework, what if he didn't do it the way you think it should be done? Or do you actually not do that much and you think someone else should because you work so hard? Ask your-self all these questions, focusing on *you*.

Your partner may have serious issues about helping out around the house, or maybe they are actually your issues. Or both. If you talk about it, focus on your issues, and your partner will feel less attacked and more able to bring up his own issues in an intimate and vulnerable way.

Here's another example. Maybe you think your partner doesn't earn enough money, or has a job that isn't prestigious enough, or just isn't good enough at something, in your opinion. Why do you care so much what somebody else does for a living? What is it about money that triggers you? (See chapter 8.) What are your preconceptions about, for example, how a husband is supposed to be? Would you really honestly like it if your hus-band made all the money, or would you feel weak and threatened? Would you really honestly like it if your husband's job was so prestigious that everybody gave him respect and treated you like arm candy? What if he had a big job but no more free time to spend with you? If you were both in high-powered careers, would you butt heads and compete too much?

If you are better or more competent at something, you may have to lower your standards about that one thing a little bit, or you will make the other person feel useless. Instead, think about what he is doing that you don't do very well. We are all good at some things and bad at some things. In your more irritable moments you might think that you are better at everything, but I bet if you really think about it, you'll realize that's not true. Women with power can be just as judgmental and holier-than-thou as men with power. Give credit where credit is due, and recognize that it is unreasonable to demand perfection. Don't punish people for being less good at something than you are, like making money or keeping an orga-nized house or whatever it is. And don't forget to take a look in the mirror. What bothers you about others is very likely to be what bothers you about yourself.

Maybe your partner just did something stupid, like got too drunk and acted ridiculous. Think about whether *you* get too drunk and act ridiculous sometimes, and are you really angry at yourself? Or have you stopped yourself from doing this now so you think he should, too? Or do you do something else ridiculous? Are you taking out feelings you have about yourself on your partner?

Maybe you want more public displays of affection and he doesn't. Why do you want that? Do you doubt his love for you, or are you just needy or insecure so you want everybody else to see how much he loves you?

There are a lot of ways to do this, but I find there is almost always something I'm actually angry at myself about, and I'm taking it out on somebody else. Your issues are almost always about you. It's extremely difficult, but try not to project yourself onto your partner. But even if that's not the case, try asking yourself the questions. What is it about *you* that makes you have a problem with what anybody else is doing, and how can you work on this for yourself? Again, when you discuss the issue with your partner, say how you feel about yourself, not about what anybody else should be doing. Be vulnerable. Say, "I don't know why I get so weird about these conventional roles when I love having a power career and that isn't as important to you. I don't know why I get distracted by this and why I don't just focus on all the great things you do in your life." Say, "I know logically that we have enough money and money isn't that important, but I still have this issue, which is something I need to work on, where I cave in to this stereotype that the man is supposed to make more money." Whatever it is that you are feeling about yourself and your own problems dealing with something, say that. Think about that. Work on that, and suddenly you are controlling yourself. Because maybe it's your noise, not his.

• •

GIRL TALK

Sometimes the best way to control yourself is to get back in touch with yourself. Maybe you are feeling too emotional, PMS-y, unattractive, insecure, and you don't like your own behavior but you can't seem to snap out of it. When this happens, the answer isn't necessarily to let your partner take control. This is a time to take care of yourself. Do some yoga or go for a walk. Move. Breathe fresh air. Buy a new dress or some lingerie. Get your hair blown out. Have a spa day. Meditate. Replenish your stores so you feel like yourself again, and remind yourself that you are capable of giving yourself exactly what you need.

Regaining Control

What about the opposite situation? If you have a controlling partner, life can be miserable, or it can be incredibly easy but totally unfulfilling. Women tend to respond in one of two ways to a controlling partner: They either cave and allow their partners to run the show, feeling lucky sometimes but totally worthless at other times, or they fight and try to control right back.

Ironically, the *worst* way to try to regain control from a controlling person is to be a controlling person. When you get strict, harsh, lecture-y, condescending, or parental with your partner, you might feel strong for a minute, but you will actually lose even more control. You might win battles but you are losing the war. Don't confuse put-downs and criticism with having the reins. I've had times in relationships where I got irritable or annoyed and became abrasive or demanding, and it usually had the effect of either driving the person away from me or beating the person down. You might sometimes get someone to do what you want with this method, but it won't feel like a victory. It's a zero-sum game. If somebody wins, somebody loses.

On the other side are the men who just walk away from controlling behavior. They're not having it. Suddenly it becomes a good day to play golf or go out with the guys—in other words, a good day to get away from you because you aren't being nice and they don't want to be around someone who is acting that way. This is just a further way to control you, by ceding control. They might give in to you in the moment, but either they are just humoring you or the relationship will deteriorate.

When your partner is acting controlling because he's feeling like he isn't getting enough attention, focus, or affection from you, the best way to handle the controlling behavior is to give your partner exactly what he needs. This can be difficult if you are more inclined to punish bad behavior, but in this case, controlling behavior is a cry for help. When you recognize that bad behavior comes from a lack of attention, swallow your pride and give your partner what he needs. Lavish attention. Soften. Say things like, "I'm there for you," "I love you so much," "What do you need from me right now?" Give your partner a massage or oral sex or cook a really nice dinner, and you will quickly regain control. This kind of behavior simultaneously makes your partner feel acknowledged, which is often what controlling behavior seeks. Remember, all men really want is to have a good day. Most men are really just little boys inside, and this kind of behavior also makes them feel like you are taking care of them. I once gave my boyfriend breakfast in bed, and it made his life. That puts you back in charge.

If this doesn't work, the controlling behavior might be coming from a place of stress or oversaturation. Introverted people often need to withdraw, and controlling behavior might be a way to try to push you way. When you suspect this is the case, you can regain control by relinquishing control. Nothing will drive an introverted person away like controlling behavior. Remember that the least interested party always wins. If you let go and stop trying to manhandle a situation, if you detach yourself, then the other person might recognize your retreat, feel relieved, replenish his energy, and then try to regain your interest. By doing nothing, you end up controlling the situation instead of suffocating it.

You can also shake things up. Just like with diets or shampoos, sometimes you need to change what you are doing to get a good result. Suggest your partner spend some time with his other friends. Say, "Let's go out next weekend. This weekend, go ahead and have your guy time," or whatever you think your partner needs. This shakes the other person up and puts you back in control because if you've been particularly needy and suddenly you aren't, the game changes.

The exception to all of this is people who are abusively controlling. When there is continual physical, verbal, or emotional abuse, nothing you can do will change that situation because it is a defect in the other person.

You cannot achieve control equality with an abuser. The behavior of that person is not your fault and has nothing to do with you, aside from the fact that you are being targeted. In this kind of situation, you need to step away from the relationship. Seek help from friends and professionals if you can't do it on your own. All the strategies in the world won't help you. It's a losing battle and you need to get out before you get hurt any further.

HOW TO LOSE CONTROL	HOW TO GAIN CONTROL
You will lose control when you act like this:	You will gain control when you act like this:
Controlling	Willing to share control
Insulting	Complimentary (sincerely)
Demanding	Easygoing
Condescending	Encouraging
Aggressive	Straightforward
Passive-aggressive	Patient
Irritated	Kind, compassionate
Mean	Supportive
Petty	Laid-back
Crazy	Confident
Annoyed	Empathetic
Annoying	Soft
Insecure	Loving
Critical	Calm
Bossy	Attentive
Negative	Positive

Control-Issue Red Flags

Maybe your relationship pattern is so ingrained that you aren't really sure whether the control dynamic is natural or dysfunctional. You might suspect it's dysfunctional but you might not be exactly sure how. Is it you? Is it your partner? Is it a mutual battle? These are things some people who tend to be controlling do. Watch out for these and get control over the other person's attempts at control. Here are the issues I've personally witnessed and heard about that are major control red flags.

The Manager

Does your partner always determine what you will do in your free time together? Or is it you? Does one person always make the reservations, choose the restaurants, plan the vacations, dictate the hobbies, decide on the fitness activities, choose the dinner menu? This can lead to resentment, so find a way to shake it up. Ask the other person to take the opposite role at least some of the time. Say, "Can you choose the restaurant tonight?" or "Let me surprise you with dinner this time," or "Let's brainstorm the best plan for our next vacation." If one person is good at making plans and the other person usually genuinely doesn't care what they do, where they go, or what they eat, then that's okay, but it's still a good idea to tip the balance once in a while. When you're the one who decides everything all the time, if your boyfriend makes you dinner or your husband buys you flowers, that can make a huge difference in how you feel about always having to make plans.

This can become an even more extreme situation when one person always decides how the other person will dress, look, and talk. One person might decide how to parent, what sports the kids will play, and who your friends are. This is an even more controlling person than the one who makes all the plans. If someone determines all the aspects of your life, or if you do that to someone else, that can be dangerously controlling behavior. Or it might just be the way your relationship dynamic has evolved (dysfunctionally). Maybe one person is passive and lets the other person determine everything, while the other person tends to have strong opinions and likes it that way. If one person is only happy when the other person is doing what they want, that's a problem.

If this is the case and you recognize it, shake things up. Take ownership of the things that really matter to you, and delegate the other ones to your partner. Maybe you can agree to dress and present yourselves according to certain mutually agreed-upon standards but with individual freedom. Maybe your husband will agree not to look like a homeless person when he goes out in public, or you'll agree to wear something sexier than sweatpants and a ratty T-shirt once in a while. If this can be about a mutual attempt to help each other be better and help the marriage rather than one person's megamaniacal attempt to control the other, then it could work. Maybe you handle kid activities like playdates and your partner agrees to handle social plans, within reason—but you should still get to see your friends and he should still spend time with the kids. Maybe you agree on a set of mutual friends, but you each reserve the right to have one day every week, two weeks, or month when you each make your own plans. Living with a very controlling person can require a bit of bravery, and there aren't clear lines between assertiveness, aggressiveness, and abusiveness. It's a spectrum, so be careful. If the control isn't malicious, then the controlling partner might actually be relieved to have the other person step up and take on some of the responsibility. Maybe the control comes from defensiveness, or a competitive spirit, or even fear. If you find yourself completely unable to take any control back, then seek professional help. You might be in an abusive situation and you need to get out.

· ·

JUST THE TIP

A lot of times when people get divorced, women report that their ex-husband has suddenly become Super Dad, doing everything. Maybe he never took care of the kids before and now he's doing it all—picking them up, taking them to activities, playing with them. This can make some women really upset. Why is he such an amazing dad now? Why couldn't he have done those things before? Some women assume this is because he is trying to get back at them or prove he's a good father in a custody case, but part of the reason might be that in a troubled marriage, husbands and wives don't always let each other function to the best of their potential. If this has happened to you, consider whether you might not have given your ex-husband the freedom and confidence to be the dad he had the potential to be. Maybe you emasculated him and controlled him so much that he couldn't be his own version of a dad. Now he's free to do that. It's one of those sad realizations about divorce, and a good lesson to learn for next time.

· ·

The Spy

Do you steal your partner's phone to check the texts and e-mails? Does your new love interest stalk you on the computer or monitor your computer activity when you're in the bathroom? This is a sign of someone who not only is controlling but also has serious trust issues. Are they deserved or not? If they are (one of you has cheated), then you need to work through the problem and slowly regain trust. Trust is the foundation of a relationship and distrust is a cancer that will destroy a relationship. If the suspicious behavior is totally unwarranted, then you need to get it out in the open and either cut it off or get out of the relationship before it gets worse. And if this is you? Stop it. No stalking. No checking his phone when he goes to get a beer. Don't be that girl.

The Know-It-All

Some people have a very high opinion of their own intelligence, and this can result in control issues when that person never lets the other person talk, always has to be right, undermines the other person's confidence by questioning his intelligence, puts the other person down in front of other people, and always has to be right. You cannot win an argument with somebody who is in this mode, and what it signals is a basic lack of respect. People who know everything seek out relationships (consciously or not) with people who lack the confidence that they know enough. These people are easy to control. If you are in a relationship with a know-it-all, you need to either grow some balls and stand up for yourself or set some ground rules. Or just ignore it, realize it's based on insecurity, and let them ramble. If your partner really *does* seem to know it all, well then, it's nice to have a brilliant and intelligent partner, but you also deserve someone who makes you feel special, not less-than. Some people don't want an equal in a relationship. They want someone they can boss around, and if you find yourself in this situation (on either side of it), you might need to make some changes. You might need counseling, or you might need to leave. If it's you, you might need to practice holding your tongue and learning how to respect your partner more. Most people deserve it.

. . . .

JUST THE TIP

One of the most challenging situations for controlling women is to have a husband or boyfriend who is a stay-at-home dad or house-husband. Theoretically, I think this is an honorable thing to do, and I know it makes sense for many couples when the mom has a better and/or more lucrative job than the dad. What I'm going to say might be controversial, but I have never met a woman who truly embraces her husband being a stay-at-home dad in its entirety. They feel compelled to justify it. For one thing, men have enough trouble as it is dealing with making less money than a woman. It is fundamentally contradictory to who and what a man is. When they become entirely financially dependent on a woman and spend the day cleaning house and taking care of the kids, it does something to them. It saps confidence and self-esteem and it is emasculating. As for the woman, it's great to have a job and make money and I know many women wish their husbands would do more kid stuff, but the fact is that when a man is doing all the child care and the woman is making all the money, it can become a turnoff. The woman becomes too hard and resentful and the man becomes too soft and resentful, and all that will show up in the bedroom. All the moms think it's so sweet to have the dad at the playdate, but I don't think most women ultimately want a husband who is doing this. Of course there are exceptions to every rule and I might end up seeing lots of examples of families doing this successfully, but I think that if it does work, it is unusual and difficult, and it would take two very confident and unique people.

. . . .

The Jealous Lover

A little jealousy can energize a relationship, but chronic jealousy can tear it apart. If you or your partner is always jealous, first consider: Is the jealousy warranted? This can be linked to trust issues if one person has cheated, and you'll need to work that out or end the relationship if you can't.

A dash of jealousy can be nice, a fun way to keep things exciting. You can say cute things like, "Hey, that hot girl better not come near my man!" but if you or your partner gets obsessive about it, your relationship will stall. Jealousy is a dangerous game. If you try to invoke it, it could work to rekindle things (like the toy on the playground a child doesn't want until another kid picks it up), but you have to be very careful with it because it can easily backfire.

If your man glances at another woman, no big deal. What girl doesn't notice a good-looking man? But if your guy turns his head and looks her up and down like a dog eyeing a juicy steak, that's a problem. When the person you're with is slobbering over or monopolizing the attention of another woman, it will probably make you feel jealous, but not in a good way. You won't feel motivated to win your man back. You'll just be pissed off at him.

If you want to make your guy jealous, a little goes a long way, and be careful because it can backfire. Men don't want to hear about the guys you've been with before. They don't want to know the details. They don't want to know anything. Let them figure it out for themselves. They will notice if a guy is flirting with you and will respect that somebody else wants you but that you walked away from it, rather than getting engaged in the flirtation. If you are obviously coveted but respond by moving closer to your guy, that makes him feel not just better but a stronger sense of loyalty to you. Be extra nice to your guy when other guys are trying to flirt with you. If he knows everybody wants you but you choose him, the dividends will be huge.

If, however, jealousy is just a random constant problem in your relationship, that is a serious red flag. You need to either stop it by distracting yourself until you get out of the habit or call out your guy about it before it turns ugly (because it often does). An unreasonably jealous person can turn into an extremely controlling person, and an extremely controlling person can turn into a violent person. If the jealousy is incurable, get out now.

One final point about jealousy: If you are married or if you've been with someone for a long time and you are not habitually a jealous person, and you suddenly feel like something is off and you have strange feelings of jealousy about someone your partner knows, listen to that intuition. Women have a sixth sense about these things. You probably have it for a reason. Your partner might not have actually done anything yet, but people who know each other well can sense when something changes. Trust it and say something. Don't be jealous solely based on suspicion due to past behavior. People who cheated aren't always going to do it again. Is Tiger Woods going to cheat again? Maybe not. An isolated incident could be the result of a particular relationship dynamic. But habitual cheaters cheat in every relationship they've been in. Think about whether your suspicion is based on assumptions or on a real feeling that something has changed and something is off. If it's the latter, then trust it.

Years ago I was lying in bed with a former boyfriend and the phone rang at three a.m. Some girl said, "Can I speak to my *boyfriend?*" Alarmed, I hung up the phone and then lay awake for two hours. Finally at five a.m., I *69ed the number (that's old-fashioned caller ID—shows you how old I am!) and she and I had a long conversation. It turns out he was having an affair with her. Hey, it happens to the best of us.

. . . .

JUST THE TIP

Another mistake some women make when playing the jealousy game is remaining friends with their exes. This might seem harmless to you. You might not even realize you are playing a game, but you are. This is incredibly threatening to most men, and a lot of women, too. If you get along so well now, they wonder, then why did you break up? We see the complexity of our past relationships and we know exactly why they didn't work. We might think, *He was a horrible husband/boyfriend, but he's a great friend.*

That's all fine for you, but for your current relationship, it's a disaster. You don't have to pretend to hate your ex if you legitimately like him now that you aren't together. However, minimize the contact and don't talk about him all the time. Disengage. You ended that relationship for a reason, so stop hanging on in ways that aren't necessary, for example, parenting your kids. Also consider whether there is still some small part of you that longs for that past relationship. You might never act on it, but if there is still a tiny torch there somewhere, your current guy can sense it. If you have kids, there will be necessary contact, but it shouldn't appear enjoyable to you. Whether you think this is idiotic or not, and whether you think your past relationship should be irrelevant to your current one, it isn't irrelevant. It matters, and if you really want to invest in your current relationship, you need to let the past one go. You should not be emotionally invested in that person anymore. Every now and then you will meet a couple who still socialize with one or both of their exes, but this is extremely rare and you shouldn't expect your guy to be cool with it. If he is, you got lucky. If he's not, he's normal. Respect him enough to understand this.

. . . .

The Textual Person

If your partner only likes to communicate via text, recognize that this is a bad habit, even addictive, and also a way to control you. You might prefer texts too, just because they feel safer. A text doesn't come with facial expressions (emoticons or emojis or whatever we call them now don't count). It doesn't come with intonation, and there are many ways to subtly manipulate a person just by the way you do or do not answer a text, or how long you take to answer a text. The problem with texts is that they don't give you a real sense of the other person. They delay and even destroy real intimacy. When a relationship is new, you have the opportunity to establish good habits and lay down the ground rules, and texting is one very common area where this will be necessary since people communicate this way so often now. Things always end up the way they started. If it starts with texting, that's probably how the breakup will happen. And nobody wants to be broken up with by text.

Personally, I think texting sucks in many ways. Sure, it has its uses. Sometimes it's convenient, I know. You can exchange information quickly. But for relationship growth, the text zone is a dead zone. When you are in the text zone, you are always like a fish with a hook in its lip. You are being pulled along, waiting for a response to your text, trying to evaluate and analyze what somebody really meant by a text, what the tone was supposed to be, whether those CAPS meant the person was yelling at you or had the CAPS LOCK key stuck on or was just excited. When I am texting, I feel a lot of anxiety. When I stop texting, I feel calm.

This also goes for e-mail and Facetime or Skype or other forms of video chatting and anything technological beyond an actual telephone. I have found that the people who are obsessed with texting or other forms of technology for human communication tend to have intimacy issues. For a disconnected person, texting is a dream. In a text, you don't have to look someone in the eye or deal with the immediate reaction to what you say. There is a safe zone that happens between texts, for those who fear a real connection. They can get the immediate gratification of a relationship without the accountability for their behavior or having to try very hard to make contact (they don't even have to get dressed).

I have a girlfriend who met a guy at a party, and they connected over a bottle of wine. The next day, he video-chatted with her from his bedroom, and almost without her realizing it, this became their main method of communication. At first, this seemed novel and fun. He got her all set up with the video-chat program, which she had never used before. However, the more she tried to get him to call or go out with her, the more she realized that he never wanted to leave his house or socialize with people he didn't know. She didn't realize the full extent of the situation until it was very difficult to extricate herself.

Be a sexual person, but don't be a textual person. Here are my simple rules for a healthy textual relationship:

1. At the beginning of a relationship, if you give someone your number, just say something simple, like "Give me a call." If you get a text, you could text back briefly a few times but don't let it go too far. Text back: "Why don't you give me a call?" This sets a precedent right up front. If it continues, shut it down. Start ignoring the texts completely. Once, a guy who was interested in me wanted to text all the time. When I told him I wasn't a "texting person" and wanted to speak to him on the phone, he fell off the grid. I could have wasted six months sending him texts and hoping it would turn into something more. I'm glad I shut it down early. At the beginning of a more

recent relationship, I admitted I wasn't a great texter. I did that in the beginning because, later, I knew I could fall back on that if he started texting me too much. He could always say, "You're not really great at this texting thing," and I could say, "I told you!"

2. Once you've received a phone call, only use texting for the exchange of brief information, like confirming details or locations. "See you at 8, I drive a Volvo," or "In the corner booth wearing the blue shirt."

3. Once you've been out on an actual date, texting is okay for brief flirtation or anticipation. "Had a great time." "You looked so sexy last night." "Really looking forward to tonight!" But be sure the anchor of your communication remains in-person or phone conversations. Don't get sucked into an hours-long textual exchange, as romantic as that may seem to you. Keep it brief. Save the intimate exchanges and playful banter for in person or at least on the telephone, where you can hear each other's voices.

4. Once you are in a long-term relationship, you don't have to be quite so careful, unless you start to get lazy and sloppy and you stop connecting in person. If you share a life together, especially if you live together, texting does become convenient. "Can you pick up something for dinner?" "This meeting is boring! Thinking of you." "I have a surprise for tonight . . . ;-)." The goal is to eventually have more but briefer texts and fewer but longer phone calls. It's texting with a side of phone. This is also convenient when either or both of you are at work. Unlike a phone call, a text can be read when it's convenient.

5. Never, ever, ever have emotional conversations, arguments, or important discussions by text. The potential for misunderstanding is just too great. Don't be one of those people who never looks up from her phone. Connect with real people. It feels so much better.

6. Cheaters use text. Just know that. His wife could be in the room while he's texting you.

If you find yourself in the text zone, you need a text-ervention. Just stop texting back. Or wait to text back for a while. Instant responses mean you're too available anyway. Answer a basic question like "When are we meeting?" but don't answer questions like "Hey, what are you doing?"

or even worse, "Hey . . ." (Translation: booty call.) Refusal to live in the text zone will separate you from the booty-call girls.

If texting has become an ingrained habit for both of you, you might also consider doing a cleanse. Agree to do it so you each know the other isn't ignoring you. Even one day of not texting each other at all can make the biggest difference in the world, if that is how you have become used to communicating.

• •

JUST THE TIP

If you've been in a relationship for a while, there is nothing wrong with a little harmless sexting (sex over text, in case you didn't figure that out). It's like phone sex but with more typing. With Facetime, e-foreplay can get even more interesting. However, sexting should be about foreplay or connecting in a fun way when you are far apart and can't meet. If you start sexting more than actually having sex, things are going in the wrong direction. Turn off the phone and have a real date.

• •

Control is complex, ever changing, frustrating, exhilarating, and a natural unavoidable part of any relationship, but never forget that control is, above all, about self-control. A girlfriend once told me, "Don't annihilate your relationship." This is what control can do. When something bothers you, sometimes you have to be vulnerable. Sometimes you have to talk about it. Sometimes you have to step back and let it breathe, or you'll cause damage. Sometimes this is extremely difficult, but it will never be as difficult as trying to control somebody else. When it comes to control, it's all about you.

CHAPTER 6

. . . .

Get a Life

*We live in an era of globalization and the era of
the woman. Never in the history of the world have
women been more in control of their destiny.*
—Oscar de la Renta

Something happens to a woman who gets into a relationship. She changes. A switch goes off, and suddenly, the relationship becomes *everything*. The interesting, independent life she had becomes a distant memory. Suddenly, she doesn't do anything alone. She stops focusing on her own interests and makes her partner's interests her own. She transforms from "independent woman" to "girlfriend." Later, she might change again. She might become "wife." When she becomes "Mommy," the person she was might seem so far away that she doesn't recognize herself anymore.

It happens gradually, this loss of ourselves, and it doesn't happen to everyone, but it's shockingly common, especially with girls in their twenties. I find that women in their thirties and forties who have been in a long-term relationship or who have been married and have kids tend to circle back and regain their fun identity once their relationships feel settled and secure. Younger girls, and also women who just got divorced and are panicking about being alone, are more susceptible to losing themselves. We've all seen it (even if we aren't quite ready to totally admit we've done it). The girl who doesn't know what her plans are until her boyfriend tells her what they are. The girl who won't decide what she's doing that weekend until she knows what he's doing, who doesn't know what she wants to eat or what she should wear or what she should listen to or believe until he sets the tone. Some people are just easily and quickly consumed by a romance. It can happen to the strongest and most successful people, and they themselves don't even necessarily see it or understand what is happening to them. But this is what is happening: a loss of identity and self.

DR. AMADOR SAYS . . .

I see a loss of identity in my clinical practice over and over. I've also written about this in my book *Being Single in a Couples' World*. This loss of identity, the loss of the now smaller "me" to the larger "US" or "HIM," will not only lead to resentment on your part but will also ultimately make you less attractive. Keep a sharp eye out for this and listen carefully when friends and family complain that they never hear from you anymore. Some immersion into the couples' world is natural, but should not happen at the cost of your identity.
—Xavier Amador, Ph.D., president,
LEAP Institute, www.leapinstitute.org

As much as I like to consider myself a strong, independent woman, this has totally happened to me, too. I remember once I had a fun trip to Florida planned with a group of girlfriends. We were all really excited, and then I met a guy. I told him about the trip and he made other plans, but then his plans got canceled. He would be home alone! Without me! I actually canceled on my friends and didn't take the trip, just so I could hang around with him that weekend. We didn't even have any plans. I've always regretted doing that. Clearly, I needed to get a life. Maybe it's biological, but it's real. Once you become a "girlfriend," everything becomes conditional. You love to go out with your friends . . . *if he's busy doing something with his friends.* Or you'll do it . . . *to get back at him because he went out without you.* You'll go to the gym . . . *if he's busy.* You're happy to meet your sister for coffee . . . *if he's busy*. You'll be there for family Thanksgiving . . . *unless he wants to go to his family Thanksgiving*. You might have great ideas and great plans . . . *but you cancel them because you want to be with him*. You stop noticing other men. Dates? Giving hot guys your phone number? Boy talk? You no longer know what that is. If you don't have enough time together, or if you lose time together you could have had, you obsess about it. When you don't get the attention and romance you fantasize about, you might even flirt with other guys to get back at him or elicit a reaction, or post fake Facebook statuses about the fascinating things you are doing just to make him jealous—when in reality you're sitting at home waiting for the phone to ring, the text to pop up on your phone.

If this isn't you at all, you can skip this chapter. However, infatuation can happen to anyone, at any age, and when it does, you won't recognize yourself. So maybe *don't* skip this chapter. And if you know, even a little bit, what I'm talking about, then read on, because you need to get a life.

· ·

MAN-FORMATION

It is my personal opinion that men do not perceive time in the same way women do. Specifically, they don't value relationship time the way we do. They think of us as always there, somehow, even when they are on a guys' weekend or a bachelor party or playing golf. They don't think about how many times they've seen you this week, or how many hours, or which hours, or why the way we do. They live in the moment. Having a girlfriend means having a girlfriend, whether she is physically present or not. For some women, if their boyfriend isn't with them, it's like he might never come back! A woman will think, *Okay, so I've got this business trip. If I don't see him tonight, I won't see him for four whole days! I better cancel my girls' night out tonight.* A guy would never think that. He would never calculate the cost in time together of a guys' night out before a business trip. Women tend to take this very personally because they assume men see time the way they do, and men tend to think women are crazy because who cares if it's been four days, they're ready to see you right now, so what's the problem? It's just one of those gender-bending differences that interfere with sane communication.

. . . .

Signs That You've Lost Yourself

I get it. I've been there. I've lost myself in a relationship. It's so easy to do, and we slip into this mode so effortlessly, that you might not even realize it's happened. Here are some signs:

- You hover over your phone, waiting for texts or phone calls.
- You aren't seeing your friends. You don't even think about them because you are obsessing about him.
- You don't make plans with your friends or family until after you know whether you have plans with him.
- You stop doing things you used to enjoy because he doesn't do them or because you might miss a call if you're not home.
- You're home a lot—even if he's not.
- You want to be with him all the time, and when you aren't to-gether because of something he has to do, your feelings get hurt.
- You get irritated or angry when he wants to do something with-out you or if you are apart for a while.
- You want answers *now* about commitment and how he feels about you.
- You get a little bit paranoid, needy, jealous.
- You will delay an important call or interrupt work or family plans for this person.
- You are so preoccupied by the relationship that it interferes with getting your work done.
- You talk constantly about him to your friends.
- You think about him all the time, more than you think about anything else.
- You aren't getting any alone time to recharge and stay in touch with yourself.
- You are feeling obsessive, extreme, or out of control.

- You feel like you are forcing it.
- You are terrified of losing him.
- It even crosses your mind to drive by his house when you can't reach him.
- When you are together, you hang on his every word.
- The relationship has become your identity.

If you checked even one of these boxes, and especially if you checked more than three, then we have some work to do. If you know you are this person right now in your life, you need to take a deep breath and start being very deliberate about what you say and do. It's time to get ahold of yourself. If you call or text and you don't get an immediate answer, you need to stop yourself from doing it again and again. You need to remind yourself that maybe the other person has something else going on, or is on the phone, or is sleeping. Also remember that men process things differently from women. I know you feel insecure. You wonder why that person didn't call you back, but your behavior is smothering. You have to control yourself. (See chapter 5.) Say what you need to say, but stay on high alert for your own personal crazy, because it's just under the surface right now.

. . . .

DR. AMADOR SAYS . . .

If you have lost yourself, it is time to reclaim yourself. Women are socialized to put relationships first above almost everything else. This often results in morphing their identify into that of the man's. This training starts when you are a toddler. There's a lot of research on this but you don't have to read it to know its wisdom. Just listen to yourself, friends, and relatives talk to little girls and boys and see what gets rewarded. Girls are praised for being sweet, kind, smart, and pretty (read: attractive for the purpose of attracting) while boys are rewarded for action and doing things well ("good throw!"). If you have drifted away from friends and family, it's time to reconnect. Make a

new schedule that includes people you saw and things you did before the relationship. Make room for your independent and separate
self so you can become *interdependent*: Two people enjoying being a
couple but also remaining individuals.
                    —Xavier Amador, Ph.D., president,
        LEAP Institute, www.leapinstitute.org

. . . .

Men tend to try to live about the same as they did before the relationship, and this can really upset us. We want to say, "Look, I changed
all these things and made you the main focus of my life. Why aren't you
doing that, too?" But why should anybody do that? You are both individuals with lives, and it's time to get yours back. Make a coffee date with a
friend. Organize your closet. Cook something. Go for a walk. Get lost
in a book or a movie. Whatever it takes, you have to start distracting
yourself so you don't wreck the whole relationship with your obsessive
behavior.

Once you detach and let go a little, you will begin to feel more secure
in yourself. It's like a cleanse—the first two days suck, but when you get
to the third day, you feel clearer and easier and you realize you can do it.
Getting your identity from a relationship will only make you feel insecure because you are handing your personal power over to someone else.
When you get it back, when you allow yourself to reclaim your own life,
your friends, and your interests, you will feel free.

Your relationship will get better, too. No matter how he acts or what
he says, no matter how mopey he gets when you are busy, a man wants a
woman to have a life beyond him and the relationship. He might not even
consciously recognize it, but it's true. Men respect independent women
with their own personalities, opinions, and interests. Otherwise, they will
begin to feel suffocated. They will lose respect for you, and eventually,
they will break up with you. If you want your relationship to work, you
need to get a life. Even more importantly, if you want to be personally
happy, get a life. If you want to keep your options open until you have a
commitment (and you should), get a life. And if you want to respect yourself, get a life.

Get Your Balance

A new relationship, especially a really passionate one, really can sweep you off your feet, and that's fun and exciting. It's not necessarily bad that this happens. For many of us, it's inevitable. You're in love! (Or extreme like. Or lust. Or whatever it is that hijacks your brain.) Enjoy it. It's part of what makes life fun. I would never deny you that human pleasure. At some point, however, you have to get back on your feet. You can't live like that any more than you can survive on candy.

But getting back to yourself can be difficult. Especially in a new relationship, it can take a little time to get reacquainted with yourself and regain your identity, interests, and balance. You also tend to forget your own worth. You don't remember how cute you are anymore. You don't know if guys even like you or think you are pretty. If you feel a pull in that obsessive direction, it's time to get dressed and go do something without him. Get back to who you are. It's hard if you are a homebody who hoped to get a boyfriend so you'd never have to go out again, but this isn't good for you because you will lose yourself if you don't interact with other people besides your new love interest.

Once you start giving up things you want to do because someone else doesn't want to do them, you are headed into dangerous territory—identity-losing territory, resentment territory, doormat territory. You don't have to be extreme about it, and you haven't ruined everything if you've done this already. You can repair the situation. Trickle your life back into your existence. Don't do it spitefully. Do it for yourself. The first step is recognizing that you need it, then the second step is to white-knuckle it a little bit. Hold on and don't blow up at him or yourself for losing touch with your life BR (before relationship). Do something on your own or just for yourself at least once a week. If something fun comes up, like a concert or a show you want to see, and your partner isn't interested, go anyway, with someone else. It doesn't have to be intense. Go to the mall. A cooking class. A movie.

Don't be that girl who thinks (or says), *Never mind, I don't need to go because you don't want to* or *I won't go without you.* Don't blame him or say things like, "I canceled this for you!" Nobody asked you to do that. This is all on you. Only you can make yourself happy. If you have simply made the mistake of thinking that was somebody else's job, now you know the truth. Now you can get down to the business of taking care of yourself.

. . . .

JUST THE TIP

There are definite advantages to going out on your own. You will be more likely to meet interesting people. It can be a relief to go out when you aren't trying to hook up with someone, too. You can actually enjoy the event and the company of friends. You'll feel like the focus is on you, not on you as part of a couple, and that can build your self-esteem. It will also help keep your partner on his toes. If he knows you have a life and he doesn't have control over everything you do, he will have to be a better partner to you or you might meet somebody better. He'll have to jump in and make a move if he wants to get on your calendar. This is the position you want to be in. It's good for both of you and it keeps the relationship alive, active, and exciting. It also puts you both back on equal footing, which is where you should be.

. . . .

Get a Relationship . . . with Yourself

The next thing you need to do if you have slipped into "get a life" territory is to get reacquainted with yourself. Men need alone time, and maybe you don't think you do, but you might be surprised at how good it can feel to just be with yourself for a while. Women love to be social and many women are afraid to spend too much time alone, but sometimes you need to spend some time with that girl in the mirror, just relaxing and contemplating the big questions: Who are you? Where are you going in your life? Who do you want to become, as you evolve, beyond your relationships to other people?

You can't fully become who you are without spending some time alone every now and then. You might not need much of it—alone time is exhausting, if fruitful, for extroverts—but you should be getting at least some. If you never take the time to really think about these questions, without anybody else's input, you will remain undeveloped. You don't have to sit at home if that drives you crazy. Go for a walk. Go to the gym. Get in your car and take a drive. Maybe you're the type of person who would love to spend the whole day at the library by herself, browsing the stacks and finding new things to read. Or maybe a massage or a spa day is more your speed. You could curl up in bed and have a nice nap, then a movie marathon. Do some yoga, shop online, even masturbate. Make yourself happy, and it takes a lot of pressure off the relationship.

Socializing beyond your relationships is also extremely important. This gives your partner space, which everyone needs, but it also gives you space to pursue your own interests and social relationships. Maybe you blew off all your friends for the first few months of a new relationship. Is it time to reclaim them? So let your guy go out golfing all day. You've got a spa appointment with your best friend, or coffee, or shopping, or an outdoor concert, or a game of tennis. Maybe you've got a yoga retreat and your partner is going to have to figure out what to do with *his* time.

This is all about getting back in touch with your personality and getting your mojo back. This is about reminding yourself that you are in control of your own happiness. This isn't about acting busy. It's about being busy. It isn't about acting independent. It's about being independent. Anybody can be busy. Even if you don't have a full-time job, there are always things to do, at home and out in the world. Organize old pictures. Clean the garage. Start an exercise program or a book club.

Nobody wants to be anybody's everything. How often do you really need to hear from a person for him to prove he likes you? Maybe not as often as you think. You're busy. *Be busy.* And don't be annoyed that he's busy, too. Even when you are truly madly deeply, take a few days apart to miss someone and get refocused every so often. You don't have to be together all the time. You *shouldn't* be together all the time.

If you're married or in a long-term relationship and you've gotten into a funk and you never do anything but you always do it together, then you can shake it up, too. You can get a man on his toes again. Go do something interesting, and if he doesn't want to do it, go do it yourself. He will take notice. That doesn't mean you should stop being sweet or letting him know you need him and love him, but a woman who has her own interests and makes her own plans and changes and grows is more attractive than a woman who becomes an appendage to a man. You don't have to grandstand about it, though, or brag about what you are doing so he'll pay attention. Be light and breezy about it. "I thought I'd go try trapeze classes." "I'm taking up windsurfing." "I'm planning a girls' weekend to Florida. I'll miss you!" After you get back, throw on some lingerie. That should wake things right up.

. . . .

JUST THE TIP

We've all heard stories about those couples who do everything together all the time, and we've also heard stories of couples who are away from each other for weeks at a time, or even live on separate coasts. These stories are interesting, but they are not the norm. Most of us wouldn't thrive that way and most couples who have too much or too little proximity eventually don't work out. This isn't always true, but it often is. These are the exceptions, not the rules. The best relationships are usually a balance between these two extremes.

. . . .

Needy Is as Needy Does

The hardest part of reclaiming your individuality in a relationship is that feeling of neediness we all get. I think it comes from a biological impulse to be with another human. We fear that it's not going to happen, that it won't last, that we *need* it, and neediness is the overreaction we tend to have. Even the most strong, independent, self-sufficient women can get needy. It happens to everyone.

Maybe you have a good reason—all the same things that make us feel insecure or temporarily crazy can make us feel needy in a relationship. You were fired from your job, so you get needier in the relationship because your self-esteem is damaged. You just had a baby and you feel fat and your husband is still hot. You're older or much younger than your partner. You feel like your partner values his family or friends more than you. Maybe you're feeling needy because you're going through a divorce and just starting to date, and the stress compels you to try to get a premature commitment from someone else. Maybe you just have PMS.

There are many different reasons why you might feel needier during certain times in your life, and that's normal. If this is you and you trust your partner, then cop to it. Especially when you are in a long-term relationship/married, you should be able to say to your partner, "Hey, I'm feeling a little insecure right now. I know it's not rational, but it is what it is." See if he can deal with you. Because I guarantee that at some point, your partner will be feeling insecure, too. If you can both help each other through the needy times, then your relationship will be stronger. Occasional neediness isn't a crime, and you can ask for understanding without being demanding or whiny.

It's the chronic neediness that erodes your connection—the kind where you are *always* the needy one and your partner is *always* running away from the neediness. Just like jealousy, neediness is okay in small doses but destructive when it's going on all the time. They have a word for relationships where one person constantly bends to please or accommodate the other person all the time, and the other person allows and even encourages it. It's "codependent." Don't be that girl. The danger is that you could become a doormat by letting your partner take advantage of your neediness, or lose all your self-esteem because your partner doesn't know how to give you what you want (or just won't). Chronic neediness is a relationship killer. It's like a chronic disease—it's always in the background and it's really hard to cure.

If you've gone too far in the direction of chronic neediness, you can repair the situation. Change something you are doing now so you can break out of the cycle and get your life and your personality back. Needy is as needy does, meaning that if you act needy, you are needy. If you stop acting needy, then you will stop being needy.

· ·

GIRL TALK

Here's a very important thing I have learned: You have to really intellectually understand that winning and getting what you want is never as important as knowing the truth of the situation. Ultimately, needs and wants based on something untrue will never be met. Maybe something feels true in the moment, but you know it isn't actually true. You will not die without that other person. You might be very sad for a while, but you won't die. You don't need that person, and you have to recognize this and act on it. If it's hard, then fake it until you make it, but you definitely have to make it.

If a relationship really is right and it works, then it's right and it works. If it's not right and you're trying to force it and you're terrified that you might lose it, you have to face the truth that it's not right and it's okay to lose it. Sometimes I ask myself whether love is really enough. I don't think it is. How do you face the fact that you are in love with somebody and it still might not work out? Should love be enough when you aren't compatible or going in the same direction as someone else? And on the other side, is compatibility enough without passion? Should you be with somebody you can live well and easily with but whom you don't love? How far do you take this? Is the relationship worth fixing?

I think you take it back to the truth. You might want it desperately, but maybe the person you are in a relationship with right now isn't the right one because the truth is also that the two of you can't make it work. Neither of you can sustain a life trying to be anything other than who you really are. If you are a person who always feels longing, who is basically needier than average, then you may not do well with somebody who is superconfident or very independent, even if you have gotten very good at pretending it doesn't bother you. You may need somebody who can be needy with you. If you are independent and can't stand clinginess, you might have to let go of that needy person, even if you love him, just because you can't keep pretending to be needier than you really are. If your relationship constantly gives you a bad feeling in the pit of your stomach, that may be a sign to move on from it. But you can also ask for what you want in a nondesperate way, and you just might get it. Then again, you might not. If you can't sort it out, that's what therapy is for. I just want you to know that whether your relationship lasts or not, it is also true that you will be okay. You have to know that, and when you realize this for yourself, your lack of need will radiate as confidence, independence, a woman who has a life. And that's the sexiest thing of all. It just might save your relationship in the end.

• •

Here's an example of one way to head off the needy impulse. Let's say you just had an especially great night of romance. It was all perfect—the perfume and the lingerie, the candles and the music, and he was so romantic! It was amazing and the earth moved. Great. Lucky you. Now, what do you do the next morning? Do you cling? Do you want to cuddle for hours? Do you want him to skip work and do it all again? Do you want to talk about the future? Even if the earth moved for him too, this kind of behavior from you is a guy's worst nightmare. Instead, if it's early in the relationship, get out in the morning. Don't hang around all day waiting for more. Get on with your life and let him be the one to come after you for more. If you've been together for a while and you hang out in the morning, that's great too, but let it be mutual and breezy and pleasant, not clingy and full of grasping. Remember, men need to be the pursuers. When you pursue, cling, and try to force commitment issues, he'll run in the other direction.

You might feel it, but if you don't act on those feelings, after a while, they will go away. Distract yourself. When you are feeling needy or you feel bad about your relationship, you feel gross and you might even look gross. I've been in that place—I post pictures on Twitter of myself in sweatpants with curlers in my hair. You have to get it together. Stop wallowing and go get a facial. Get your hair blown out. Put on something nice and get out in public.

Most importantly, *maintain radio silence* if you're going to be a mope or a whiner and you know it. Or maybe you don't know it. As soon as you hear that tone in your voice, end the conversation and go do something else. You could say something like, "Hey, I don't have much to add to the conversation right now, I'm in a bad mood. I'll be fine, I'm just cranky. Get back to me later." Don't cave in to the temptation to send fake-casual texts that solicit a response because you are desperate to hear from him: "Just thinking about you, are you okay?" When you need your mojo back, remember this rule: *You have no fingers. You cannot dial your phone. You cannot text. You are incapable. And your car is incapable of going in the direction of his home or workplace.* A friend of mine likes to say, "How can you miss them if they never go away?" Go away and let yourself be missed a little bit. Depending on where you are in your relationship, that radio silence might be a few days (early in the relationship) or just a few hours you can take to calm down and get centered (if the relationship is advanced).

. . . .

GIRL TALK

One of the most important things *not* to do when you are feeling needy, insecure, and obsessive is to have a relationship conversation. If you detect the seeds of an argument (even if your partner starts it), don't engage. Don't be a moper or a whiner, either. Intervene in your own behavior. Don't escalate things that don't need to be escalated, even if you are feeling like you need to prove your point. When you are feeling needy (or PMS-y), definitely don't say things like, "So, when are we getting engaged?" or "Shouldn't we be moving in together by now?" Those might be totally legitimate questions to discuss when you are both in a calm, neutral place, but trying to discuss them when you are emotionally charged is a huge mistake. When you get emotionally charged, he probably won't be able to hear what you are saying.

. . . .

Women are thinkers and often overthinking gets us into trouble. We convince ourselves we need to act on something that actually just requires a little more time to cook in our heads. Or we create whole scenarios based on a long, intricate, convoluted thought process, but we forget that the other person wasn't there inside our heads and has no idea what we are talking about.

The Needy Wife

This all changes a bit when you are married, but married people can definitely still deal with neediness, especially when it becomes a marital pattern. You cling, he withdraws, you cling harder, he withdraws more. This is a frustrating cycle, and you can't just leave or be mysteriously unavailable or not answer texts if you're married. You live together and you have joint responsibilities. However, you can still shake it up. Don't be a sack all day. Get up and go do something. You've gotten your night of romance. Now get back to your life. Get back to work, whatever that is for you. Get back to you. Put it in perspective—it was great, but so are all the other things you get to do with your day. You're a hot passionate wife—and also so much more. Do something that has nothing to do with your husband or kids. Do what needs to be done. You don't have to neglect your family, but focus on getting your confidence back for a while. Do something you enjoy, something outside of the house. It's amazing how much better you'll feel.

Sometimes you have to be okay with not talking because men (and some women) need to retreat, and you can benefit from it, too. When you are really having a problem and you know the neediness and fighting have to flush out, step back and let it be for a while without any intervention. I know this is impossible. No, not impossible, but hard. We panic. We don't understand how he can go out and play golf after a fight and not want to talk about every aspect of a disagreement, but men are different beings. You have to give them a break. Let them work things out in their own way. Let it breathe. You can't always impose a discussion just because you feel like having it at that moment.

I know this is harder than I'm making it sound. There is always that fear that if you don't cling, if you don't put your plans on hold, he might disappear. You might think that the person who loved you yesterday won't love you today if you take a break from each other. There is always that feeling that the romance was *so good* that you are addicted and you don't want to miss the chance to get more. What if you act like that mind-blowing night was no big deal? Will he think you're not really interested and move on to someone else?

Of course not. There is nothing more intriguing and addictive to a guy than a girl who breezes out after a great night, like it was no big deal. He won't understand why you aren't following him around, and his next move will be to follow you around to figure you out. Men love a good mystery and a woman who isn't too easy to manipulate or understand. Men also need space, and if you give it to them, they will be even more head over heels about you.

And if he does blow you off, what you need to understand is that you don't want him. You are the fisher, not the fish, and if he's not a good catch because he doesn't value you enough, then you need to throw him back. If he's really interested in cultivating something with you, he will be more interested, not less interested, when you get up, get out, and get busy with your interesting life.

Get the neediness under control, get yourself back, and *then* you can look around and see who's still interested—in the woman you really are, not the needy, clingy woman you temporarily became.

Look, you are an interesting and complex and independent woman. You don't actually *need* a relationship. You *want* a relationship, and those are two totally different things. Now, here's the important part: If you act like you *need it*, like you can't live without it, then you will be much less likely to get what you want. Scared money never wins. If you really *want it*, you must act like you don't need it. It sounds counterintuitive, but it's true, and it works. Fake it till you make it. Act like you don't need what you want, and you'll get what you want.

· ·

JUST THE TIP

I have a philosophy about relationships: Even the ones that probably won't last are worth working on because it is about *you*. Even in the wrong relationship that you are staying in for whatever personal reason, you can workshop it. A challenging relationship is an opportunity to work on yourself so that down the line, in the next relationship, you won't keep having this same issue. When a relationship feels uncomfortable, make it about you. Dive in and really figure out what's happening. Get to the bottom of the insecurity, the jealousy, the boredom, the disrespect. Try to work through it because you will be better for it later, with or without that relationship in your life.

. . . .

Find Your Passion (Apart from Your Relationship)

Going out with your friends more is great, but it's also important to feel like you have a purpose apart from your relationship. If you live for your husband and children, for example, you might be just fine, or you might eventually start to wonder what your purpose is and even get depressed. This is very common with wives of rich men who don't have to work and end up not doing very much, or with anyone who doesn't have to have a career or a purpose and isn't particularly driven toward any one direction. They lose themselves because they don't go out and seek something just for themselves that drives them and that they feel passionate about. Why do you think all those 1950s housewives were on Valium? They were expected to be fulfilled by housework and parenting, but it's the twenty-first century now. We have options.

However, some women still feel like it's selfish to do things for themselves. This is not true at all. Having a purpose and something you love to do, whether it's a job or a hobby or a volunteer situation, makes you a happier and more interesting person. Everybody always talks about how men need to have a career to be fulfilled. I don't believe anybody can be truly happy if they don't have something for themselves. It's not a gender issue. Everybody needs to have a sense of self-worth and accomplishment, not just men. Whatever that thing is doesn't matter. It could be your career, but it doesn't have to be. Even if it's going to the gym or running or doing yoga or learning Italian or training for a marathon or painting or volunteering or doing some kind of charity work or blogging or travel or your book club, if you are passionate about it, it will feed your soul. Only then will you be able to stop demanding (out loud or just in your head) an unreasonable amount of time, attention, and validation

from your partner. (Just to be clear: You absolutely should get time, attention, and validation from your partner, but it can't be his whole reason for
living. He has to have a life, too.)

The secret is to be passionate about something. Find it, and go and
do that thing. If you don't know what it is at first, experiment. Try lots of
things and see what sparks your interest. Get more invested in your career,
or take up a hobby, or do something social. If your guy is maintaining his
guy connections and you're sitting at home all the time waiting for him to
get back from his guys' night out, ask yourself why you aren't doing something with your life. You are not a product of someone else's love. Being
a doormat with no personality (or a suppressed personality) is one of the
least attractive qualities a person can have. You are your own person, so
think back and remember who that is, and get out and be that person. You
will have a much better life, whether you are in a relationship or not.

Getting a Life: Special Circumstances

There are a few situations where getting a life can be particularly difficult and especially necessary. If you are an empty nester or your kids are
teenagers and they have their own lives and don't need you that much
anymore, you can start to feel really depressed or just lost. A lot of moms
make their children their purpose in life, even unintentionally, and when
that purpose is winding down, it can be confusing. This is a very important time to take up something new. Maybe this is when you finally plan
that trip to Europe, or write that novel, or start that business, or take up
some kind of art or craft. Maybe it's time to remodel the house or finally
volunteer at the animal shelter or the food bank, or maybe it's just time
to reassess and experiment. Take some classes and figure out what your
next great passion can be, but find one, because even though your kids
will always need you to some extent, you have a lot more life to live. Don't
waste it on feeling lonely and worthless. That's not you.

Another situation where it's really hard to get out and be someone
confident and strong is after a breakup or divorce. Even in the friendliest
of breakups, there are bruised egos and hurt feelings. When it's nasty, it
can really take a toll on your confidence and self-esteem. I know this first-

hand. I'm still recovering from my divorce, and I may not ever be quite the same. It's a brutal experience and it injures you, even if you were the one who wanted it.

Recognize after a breakup that you do need a period of mourning, just like you would if a friend or family member passed away. Your relationship or your marriage has passed away, and that takes some time to get over. Be patient with yourself and focus more at first on self-care. That doesn't mean you don't go out and booze it up a little with your friends, but be mindful that booze, sugar, caffeine, red meat, and lack of sleep will all make you more emotional. Nothing will make you feel more focused than exercise, a good night's sleep, and a break from the highs and lows of sugar and alcohol.

Also work on being calm and tolerant of your own mood swings and bad feelings. The only way for them to pass is to experience them. If you stuff all the feelings down inside, they'll only come out later, bigger, and nastier, so go through it. Dr. Amador says, "Don't let negativity rent space between your ears." Things only matter when you let them matter. You are broken-hearted, but that doesn't mean you have to get mired in it. Enlist friends to help you if you need them (and you probably do, even if you don't think you do), but also spend time by yourself just processing, thinking about what went wrong. You're a different person now, and you need time to acknowledge this. Just know that everything is as it should be right now in this moment. Even if you have screwed things up, just know it was supposed to happen, and don't relive the past and torture yourself about what should have happened. But do learn from your mistakes. Look at what actually happened so you can avoid making the same mistakes next time. You should understand why your relationship ended and then you can start there and move forward. For more on breakups, see chapter 7.

It feels really good to get back to yourself after you've been swept away by a relationship, and when you do, you'll love what happens next: Your relationship can get deeper, more interesting, more intimate, and more meaningful. When two people who know themselves and know each other choose to go in the same direction together on equal footing, that's the stuff long-term relationships are made of. Nobody else can save you. Only *you* can save you. Only when you save yourself can you find contentment in your relationship.

CHAPTER 7:

. . . .

Trust Your Gut

You can't connect the dots looking forward; you can
only connect them looking backwards. So you have to
trust that the dots will somehow connect in your future.
You have to trust in something—your gut, destiny,
life, karma, whatever. This approach has never let me
down, and it has made all the difference in my life.
—STEVE JOBS

My gut has always spoken to me loudly and clearly, but that doesn't mean I listen. I get easily swept up in the moment, in the romance, in my expectations, or in the game. I have a goal in mind, like marriage or commitment or whatever it is, and I don't see the obvious red flags right in front of me. I don't hear my gut yelling that maybe I should take a step back. For example, I was dating somebody when Jessica Simpson and Nick Lachey got divorced, and I remember that he said to me, "They're getting divorced? He should take half of everything she has." I ignored it, but like Julia Roberts said in *Pretty Woman*, "Big mistake. Huge." I should have paid closer attention to that comment because I remember having a gut feeling about it that made me very uncomfortable. Yet I ignored it because I wanted to believe the best in him. Let's just say this ended up costing me hugely, in many different ways.

Your gut is a reliable barometer of everything you do, and I don't know why people don't pay more attention to it. Especially when it comes to relationships, your gut will always tell you the truth, and you need this information because most of the time, the way people get into relationships is relatively random. People get into relationships for a million different reasons, and in most cases, it isn't some perfect scenario where you see each other across a crowded room and you know you've finally met "the one." More often, you strike up a conversation at a bar or a party or at work or get hooked up on a blind date or meet someone on a dating site. Maybe you went out with someone because he thought you were hot, but you don't know him at all yet. Maybe you approached someone with dark brooding good looks, but you have no idea if he's a good person or compatible with you in any way. Maybe you just want to have your first one-night stand. As long as you are clear about it and pay attention to what happens next, you will be okay. To know what you should do—to know whether a new relationship is something to pursue or something to ditch, to know whether to hold 'em or fold 'em, you have to tune in to your own intuition. You have to listen to your inner voice. You have to trust your gut.

Yet so many women I know, myself included, are terrible at this. Even when our guts are jumping up and down waving red flags, we will do just about anything to ignore them if we like the idea of a certain person or we just want a boyfriend. I read something once about how a woman will defend her husband passionately, right up until the moment she leaves him. This is what we do. We try so hard to convince ourselves that something is right even when we know it's not. We don't trust our guts, or we simply don't listen to them. So let's talk about this. Let's look at the signs and teach ourselves to listen to ourselves, because your gut knows what's right and what's not right. There isn't a huge mystery to it. The answer isn't in your horoscope or with a psychic or in the collective opinions of all your friends and family. The answer lies within.

• •

DR. AMADOR SAYS . . .

What is your gut? I will share a little story from my own dating life as an example. I was dating someone who, when we would eat out, was incredibly rude and even cruel to the servers. It was so bad that

I refused to go out to dinner with her unless she let me handle the ordering. I told her it made me uncomfortable, not only because we seemed to have different values but also because I thought it was only a matter of time until she treated me the same unforgiving, judgmental, and spiteful way. She was adamant that it was just a difference in the way we were raised and that she was happy to let me be the spokesperson for us both when we ate out. She reassured me she would never treat me that way.

My gut told me she was lying to me, to herself, or both. I ignored it. I saw her mistreat a friend in the same way and spoke to her about it from a perspective of concern for her friend and for her. She listened to my advice and reconciled with her friend, whom she had treated like dirt (there's no easier way to describe her spiteful behavior). With me, she remained kind, supportive, loving, playful, sexy, devoted, and fun. But my gut kept telling me this relationship would never work out.

After we became more committed and I proposed marriage, my gut was proven right. Almost overnight she became as nasty, judgmental, and cruel with me as she had with the others. I should have listened to my gut because although I asked her to go to therapy and she did, it didn't help.

So what is your gut? Listen to that nagging feeling about the way your partner behaves. If you have a recurring suspicion or worry that won't go away for months or years, even when you've had a reasonable conversation with your partner about it, I believe you should trust your gut.

—XAVIER AMADOR, PH.D., PRESIDENT,
LEAP INSTITUTE, WWW.LEAPINSTITUTE.ORG

. . . .

Early Warning Signs

The first stages of a new relationship are so much fun—the excitement, the butterflies, the passion, the obsession. So much fun, in fact, that you can completely ignore the early warning signs that a relationship is not the one you want. It's easy to get misled. Sometimes, someone looks great on paper, but when you're with him, it just doesn't feel right. Or sometimes somebody looks bad on paper, but your physical connection is so strong that you don't see the problem, or don't let yourself see. This is when you risk getting too deep into something that is totally wrong for you. No relationship is even close to perfect. You might convince yourself that yours is made in heaven at the beginning, but you will soon see how untrue this is. Do you have an instinctive negative reaction—for example, you worry about how he treats other people—but you try to ignore it? Do you have a feeling of foreboding, like you've been here before and it didn't turn out well last time, but you are comfortable in your pattern so you try to ignore that, too? Remember what I always say about the definition of insanity—it is doing the same thing over and over and expecting different results. Are you repeating your old pattern? Never let your head or your heart convince you to ignore what your gut knows to be true. The truth will set you free, so you might as well face it. It might be good news or bad news but it's going to come out sooner or later. The sooner, the better.

Maybe you have unrealistic expectations. Do you get excited about each new relationship until the person proves he is human after all? Maybe your gut tells you that you are addicted to drama, the highs and the lows, and that maybe you need to be more realistic or just calm in your relationships instead of seeking out the extremes of feeling. You shouldn't settle for someone who isn't good for you or who doesn't excite you, but there is a difference between lowering your standards to the point of being realistic, and settling for something less than you need and deserve. If the person you are with has issues but is growing and has potential, you can work with that. If the person is so set in his ways that the relationship is immovable, that's not promising. People change sometimes. I've seen it happen. I've done it myself. You can't ever know the future for sure or know what will happen in your relationship, but your gut is a good indicator, so listen.

You need your gut, which factors in the head and the heart and adds a dose of instinct. Your gut will help guide you and train you to listen to your inner voice. Here are some general scenarios that I've experienced personally or witnessed firsthand that don't bode well for a relationship. If any of them sound like your relationship, ask yourself if you don't already know, deep down, that there is a problem:

- Something feels off from the beginning, even if you can't quite verbalize it yet. Certain things the person does or says make you uncomfortable, rub you the wrong way, or just feel wrong somehow. This isn't the same as the uncomfortable feeling of excitement at not knowing someone yet. I mean a negative instinct about someone's character or morals.

- You often don't understand what the other person is saying. It's not that the talk is above you or below you and I'm not talking about an accent. I mean when the person says things and you legitimately don't understand their point of view or why that person would say or even think such a thing. This is a sign that you are not connecting.

- You are repeating a pattern that hasn't worked for you in the past. Do you go for the bad boys, and then you are always disappointed when they don't turn out to be upstanding citizens? Do you always go for the nice guys, and then you get bored? Whatever your pattern, your gut will tell you if you are repeating it. The relationship will feel familiar but also wrong. You might even have a feeling of foreboding that you can't pin down. That's because you've been here before, my friend!

- If someone has fundamentally different morals, beliefs, or values than you. This might be exciting at first because you are experiencing something new and completely out of the realm of your experience, but this won't usually work out in the long run. There are exceptions, but if one person is very religious, for example, and the other is an atheist, that will probably be a problem. If one is very ambitious and the other one thinks that ambition is a negative quality, that's going to be a problem. If one of you is a strict rule follower and the other thinks it's fun to bend or break the rules, or even the law, that's going to be a problem. Have your fling if you must, but move on to somebody with the same kinds of priorities and values as you have for your long-term relationship.

- If you are desperate for a relationship. This is a red flag even if the other person seems to be everything you want, because when you are desperate, you are blind. Great potential partners are likely to run from desperation. They are attracted to people who are not looking, who are confident and happy as they are. If you are desperately searching, that is the smell of blood in the water. You cannot possibly make a good decision about a relationship if you feel like you desperately need a relationship. Desperation is palpable, and people who prey on those who are desperate and vulnerable have a radar looking for *you*. These kinds of people are very good at manipulation and acting like just the person you want. But even if you find a great person, desperation will wreck the relationship eventually. If this sounds like you, the most important thing to do is hold off on all relationships until you get your shit together and get a life. See chapter 6; then we'll talk.

Your inner voice knows. You can feel it in your gut when something isn't right, and the time to really listen is early in a relationship. When your gut talks, listen, and then say something to figure out if it's real or if it can be fixed. If not, move on. Life is too short to be in an unhappy relationship, and you don't want to get stuck there.

Read the Signs

Once you're in it with someone for a while, you may want to use your gut to determine how the relationship is going. Is he really into you? Is there commitment in your future, or is this just for fun? Are you walking on a similar path? There are a lot of subtle ways to tell what someone thinks about you and how someone is trying to fit you into the future without ever actually asking. Part of it is knowing the person you are with, paying attention, listening a lot, and feeling the energy around what that person says, cares about, and does. I was only dating a guy for two weeks, and he wanted to spend New Year's Eve with me in Florida. To me, that was a sign that he was potentially serious. To some people, this might not be a big deal, but my gut told me it meant something to him.

Your instincts will be different because your relationship is different, but maybe he mentions his parents or wants you to meet his boss, or he changes his behavior and starts acting more polite around you than he did at first. Store that. It means something. Here are some more signs that you are being seriously considered for a long-term relationship, or even a marriage proposal. Nobody will do all of these things, but any of them are good signs that the person you are interested in is thinking about you in future terms:

Signs That You Have a Future Together

- You hear secondhand that he has been telling other people about you or bragging about you to his friends.
- He wants to spend weekends and important holidays with you or assumes you will spend them together.
- You don't only see each other at night. You have daytime plans.
- He makes plans with you for more than two weeks in the future.
- When you tell a story, he looks you in the eye and comments on the details of what you said. He seems genuinely interested in what you are saying. In other words, he's listening.
- He holds your hand.
- He wants to spend Saturdays with you.
- He acts proud of how you look.
- He acts protective, putting his arm around you and shielding you, maybe unconsciously, from the environment when things get loud, rough, or crowded.
- He is passionate about you. He is obviously happy to be in your company.
- He changed his Facebook status to "In a relationship."
- He calls you the next day after every date.
- He is comfortable with your toiletry items and with you leaving some things at his house.
- He cares about you—he acts like the world revolves around you.

- Sometimes he gets a little nervous around you, as if he is amazed that somebody like you is with somebody like him.
- He makes an effort to be particularly nice to your parents and friends.
- He takes you to work events and trusts you around his colleagues.
- He opens doors for you and pulls out your chair.
- In restaurants, he lets you order (or orders for you with your permission) before ordering for himself.
- He gives you compliments (but not unrealistic ones or in excess).
- He confides his weaknesses, secrets, or other personal information to you, or is vulnerable around you.
- Your friends tell you that he adores you, or his friends tell you that you are different from his past girlfriends, and that he is different with you than he has been before.
- His parents connect with you and act like you're going to be around for awhile. They care what you think.
- He acts caring and respectful of you in front of his friends.
- He shows you affection in front of other people.
- His friends know about you.
- He refers to the future, even in subtle ways, like "Someday we should go to Fiji," or "Wouldn't it be great if we lived in the mountains?"
- He always checks in with you when you are out.
- He makes you feel safe.
- He handles things or fixes problems for you.
- He stops dating other people.
- He appreciates your quirks.
- He misses you when you go away.

There are also signs that he isn't serious, that's he's just having fun with you and has no intention of ever committing to you. If that's what you want too, then no problem, but if you are in the market for something more permanent, watch out for these signs that he's not in it for the long haul:

Signs That You Don't Have a Future Together

- You meet his friends and they don't seem to know about you.
- His eyes wander when you tell a story longer than thirty seconds.
- He spends weekends and holidays without you.
- You've been together six months or more and he hasn't introduced you to his family.
- He introduces you as his "friend."
- He booty-calls you.
- He can go for days without speaking to you.
- He can take or leave being with you.
- He doesn't listen to you when you talk.
- He compartmentalizes you. You are not integrated into the other parts of his life.
- He is not passionate about you, or the relationship isn't passionate. (This is only okay if you both genuinely prefer it that way.)
- He goes out on Saturday nights with his friends and only hangs around with you on Sundays or other days when he is hungover or needs an ego boost or has nothing better to do.
- He doesn't make day plans with you. Your dates are evenings only.
- He blows you off sometimes, often at the last minute, and you are stuck with nothing to do because you canceled your other plans.
- He is habitually late to meet you or pick you up.
- He rushes out in the morning before breakfast.
- He doesn't change his Facebook status.
- He never takes you to work events.
- He is still dating other people after six months.
- He is disrespectful of you in any way, putting you down or belittling you or the things you do.
- He says harsh or mean things to you, even if he apologizes. I once had a guy call me a piece of shit. He apologized, but that was definitely a sign that the relationship was not going to work.
- His family members misbehave, even if he doesn't. This isn't necessarily a red flag, unless it gives you a bad feeling. If several

family members are involved in illegal activities, are in jail, or are violent or bigoted or chauvinistic, be careful.

- He abuses drugs or alcohol, or does other things in excess, like gambling.
- He is violent in any way.

These are just a few of the signs that things aren't going well, but anything could be a sign. Every person is different, so pay attention and listen to your gut. If you think something he says or does implies he is not interested in building a future with you—even if whatever he did or said wouldn't mean anything coming from somebody else—investigate that feeling. Your gut is probably correct. Whatever it was, no matter how seemingly innocent, may be a harbinger of things to come if it hit you in the gut.

JUST THE TIP

Some guys are good at acting like the world revolves around you and you are everything, just to get what they want. The next day they completely forget about you. Run as fast as you can away from these guys—there is something wrong with them.

Evaluating Your Progress

One of the things that I think confuses women more than anything is knowing when the relationship is progressing in a satisfactory way and when it has stalled. How do you know if you are demanding a commitment prematurely or if you have waited way too long to hint that you are ready for the ring? This is tricky and it depends on a lot of variables. It's all too easy to obsess about getting the ring before you are really ready or know the relationship is right, and it's just as easy to get lulled into complacency and end up still being the weekend girlfriend years into the relationship without ever getting anything more. There is no question that plenty of women are jumping the gun or have missed the boat.

I have often gotten this wrong, and in retrospect, I have seen that in most cases, there is a rational and reasonable timeline for relationship progression. This may not sound like trusting your gut, but when it comes to the timeline question, that can be really difficult to do. There are always ways to tweak this timeline according to your situation and that's where you can listen to your gut. It will tell you when the date on your calendar really isn't the right date to demand a commitment. These aren't rules, just guidelines for when you might expect these milestones if they are what you want. However, in my opinion, it should usually go something like this:

At three months: After three months of dating, you should know you are taking this in the right direction. This doesn't mean married, it doesn't mean engaged, it doesn't even mean a commitment or being exclusive, necessarily, but it could and possibly should mean, "Hey, you and I, we're really doing this." Three months is not too soon to expect some level of commitment, like making an assumption that you will do something on the weekends or that you will talk on the phone most evenings. If you don't want that yet, that's totally fine. Keep being casual. But three months is not premature to bring up the topic: "So, are we a thing? Are you my boyfriend/girlfriend? Are we still dating other people, or is that seeming less attractive to both of us at this point?" If you've invested three months, especially if you are over thirty, you have the right to take the temperature of the relationship.

If, at the three-month mark, you are "a thing" by mutual agreement, and you live in the same city and you have a mutual understanding that the relationship is progressing, you should have met at least one to a few members of his inner-circle friends. This is as much an indication to them that you're important to him as it is to you. If he already wants you to meet his parents and you don't feel ready, make sure you are on the same page about the relationship. This could be a little bit too soon for family vetting. In general, consider three months to be a good time to define whether the relationship is serious or casual. You should both be in agreement.

• •

JUST THE TIP

If you have been sleeping together for three months, I think it's a good idea to have some sort of guideline for going forward, even if it is only that neither of you is having sex with anybody else. You need to be able to respect yourself. For more about sex, see chapter 9.

• •

At six months: By the six-month mark, you should definitely know where you stand. That's half a year we're talking about. How old you are matters, of course—six months in your twenties isn't as high-stakes as six months in your forties, if you are looking for a commitment. The word "boyfriend" might be scary for some people, but you should at least know you are going in the same direction and are on the same page. Do you both still want to be able to see other people, or does one or both of you want to be exclusive? Are you moving too fast, or too slow, or just right? Do you both want to stay in the metaphorical car with each other, or does one of you want to get out? If somebody wants out, this is the time to get out.

By this point, you should probably be spending most nights together unless one of you travels a lot. You should also have met the people he works with. This is an indication not only that it is serious, but that he trusts you to represent him when it matters. If he still keeps his job separate from you, six months is not an unreasonable time to ask why, or to ask to meet some of those people. If you get stonewalled, this is a good time to consider whether the relationship really has potential or if you are both just biding your time until something better comes along. By six months, you should also pretty much know all of his local friends (although keep in mind that friends with kids are harder to pin down, especially if neither of you has kids).

Six months is kind of a big deal in my opinion. It's the point where you reassess. It's the point where you have given a relationship a reasonable and respectable amount of time to work, and you need to decide whether you want to keep going with it or if it's really not going the way you want it to. You're in it by now, but you're not in so deep that you can't get out with minimal pain and suffering. Think seriously about this at six months, because where you go next matters.

At eight months: If things aren't going well by now, it's time to cut your losses. (I'll talk more about breaking up at the end of this chapter.) By this point, you should be integrated into each other's lives, not 24/7 but enough that you can both assume you have weekend plans and several weeknight plans, and you are probably sleeping over with each other frequently. The mood is more relaxed, you are more comfortable together, and you both know you want each other in your lives.

By this point, you should meet his parents, if you haven't already, assuming they live within a reasonable proximity to you. This varies in different situations, however. If the two of you are of different races or religions, that can prolong the timetable for meeting the parents. When that is the case, be patient and understanding. It could be a difficult meeting.

. . . .

JUST THE TIP

Introducing someone to your parents speaks volumes. If you are ready, however, go for it. You can get a lot of intel from the mom. Someone I was dating had me meet his mother two months in (granted, she was a fan from TV, but still). She told me after a few drinks that he had never felt this way about someone and that she thought this was love. I honestly had no idea, prior to hearing this from her. When you do meet the parents, no matter when it happens in the timeline, pay attention. Family dynamics say a lot about a person.

. . . .

Once you have a commitment from someone—you are officially a couple—then you might find yourself wondering when you should expect something even greater. Maybe you are committed . . . but not *really committed*. Maybe you want marriage. In general, I think this depends a lot on how old you are and what stage of your life you are both in. How long should you wait out a period of no growth in a relationship? In general, I believe in the 3-2-1 Rules.

The 3-2-1 Rules are good guidelines for how long to stay in a relation-ship without seeing real signs of a serious commitment (marriage or what-ever you need). Unless you don't care about a commitment and you are happy with your relationship exactly the way it is, the maximum time you should stay in a relationship without this movement is:

- In your twenties: no longer than three years
- In your thirties: no longer than two years
- In your forties: no longer than one year

Of course, all rules have exceptions, and if two people are very differ-ent ages, you may need to find a way to meet in the middle. A guy in his thirties with a girl in her forties may not be ready for a commitment as soon as she is. A guy in his fifties might want to settle down more quickly than a girl in her forties just getting over a divorce. Otherwise, consider the 3-2-1 Rules loose guidelines for bringing up the conversation about needing more than you are getting. Your relationship should be what it is, but when you feel really lost, the above timeline can help give your cha-otic thinking some structure.

• •

CELEBS SPEAK OUT

Maria Menounos on dating:

As far as dating goes and finding a partner, remember you have to spend the rest of your life, potentially, with this person. My rule is to marry your best friend. When it's all said and done, and you're both middle-aged, it's the best friend you'll be counting on, not your lover. Whoever you end up with must be your choice and not your friends' or family's. Judge them also not by their looks or finances, but rather by their heart. And by "heart" I mean they must have such traits as in-tegrity, honesty, loyalty, sensitivity, supportive, and a strong work ethic.

Kev was in terrible shape when I met him. He was having some ca-reer and financial difficulties. On top of that, he wasn't Greek. For all of the above reasons, he was shunned by my family and, for sticking by his side, so was I. My dad stopped paying for my college and even speaking to me. Yet what my family failed to see was the fact Kev had heart—the likes of which I've yet to see from anyone. He had spent the previous two years providing round-the-clock hospice care for his dying father. At the time I met him, he was working three jobs, seven days a week, paying off his debts. And soon he was paying off mine while putting me through my college. He believed in me and my lofty career goals when no one else did and said he wouldn't stop till I achieved them.

And though my family insulted and harassed him, and me, he never fought back. He felt our focus should remain on our goals and that engaging my family would only perpetuate matters. He also believed over time, if he didn't fight back and add gas to the fire, my family would see the truth and come to their senses. It took a couple of years but come to their senses they did. When they saw how committed we were to each other, how hard we were working, and how successful we had become, they realized the error of their ways. Today, my parents are his parents and he is their son. We joke they like him better than me. Lastly, when dating, do not share intimate details of your relationship with anyone. When you get into fights, etc., make best efforts to keep that to yourself. When you blab to friends and family they'll take your side. Later when you and your partner resolve the issue and move on, friends and family may not. They'll certainly always remember the negative. It's not fair to your partner and only leads to trouble. If you are being abused or victimized, of course, this does not apply.

On the marriage front, Kev and I wanted to early on but with the family drama it wouldn't have been a pleasant event. Later, we got slammed with work, but whenever things slow down, I'm sure we will marry. The bottom line is that we are married in our hearts. As far as children go, they are a whole other subject. I know I want children but I'm grateful I waited till my midthirties to consider it. Personally, I liked having my twenties and half my thirties to work, grow, travel, save, and live. According to my friends who have children, they all say it's the most amazing experience in the world and the best thing to ever happen to them. However, they also state emphatically that their lives are no longer their own and advise me to wait as long as possible before doing so. I recommend having pets while you wait. It is a great warm-up, as other moms have confided. And on the example of pets, dogs in particular; I have had as many as five. And while, like children, Kev and I adored each and every one of them, we always felt we didn't have enough hands to pat them and laps to sit them on. It was hard to give that many babies the required attention. Based on that, I think it is awfully hard to handle more than three children close in age. I think two is a great number to strive for, even from a financial perspective. That is strictly my opinion, and one I admit I do not have enough experience to base it on.

—MARIA MENOUNOS, HOST OF E's *UNTOLD*

Should You Get Married?

Marriage isn't for everybody, even though most women still seem to think, at least when they are in their twenties and often into their thirties, that this is something they are supposed to do. It's never too late to get married—people do it in their eighties—and yet it's also totally unnecessary today for women who can financially support themselves, especially if they don't want children. Katharine Hepburn famously said, "If you want to sacrifice the admiration of many men for the criticism of one, go ahead, get married." At this point in my life, I can't help appreciating that sentiment.

Still, maybe you want to do it. I know I wanted to, many times. The idea of marriage is seductive: someone who will always be there for you, to grow old with, to share your life experiences with. The idea of having a partner forever is very romantic. Maybe you want to have kids and raise them in a two-parent home. Maybe you just love somebody like crazy and you want to make it official.

Sometimes it ends up like this and sometimes it doesn't. I never got it right, and at this point in my life, I'm not sure I ever want to do it again.

But maybe you do. Nothing is a sure thing, and the divorce rate (depending on where you look) is up to 60 percent (higher for every subsequent marriage).

· ·

DR. AMADOR SAYS . . .

In my research I've found that women are choosing not to marry, or remarry, in greater numbers than at any time in history. Some choose to stay single, others choose serial monogamy, while others choose lifelong partnerships without the complications that a marriage certificate brings.

The point is, if you don't want to get married, you have plenty of good company. Don't succumb to the stigma that still exists for unmarried women (less so for unmarried men). If you still feel like an outsider, I suggest you check out the nonprofit organization "Unmarried Equality" for resources, support, and education about this choice.

—Xavier Amador, Ph.D., president,
LEAP Institute, www.leapinstitute.org

· ·

Many women today find themselves faced with a decision, if not a marriage proposal: *Should I do it? Should I get him to propose? Should I say yes?* The idea of having a partner forever is very romantic, but is it right for you, right now, with this person? Of course only you can answer these questions, but here are a few things to consider that I wish I would have thought harder about before I walked down the aisle:

- Why do I want to get married? You should definitely know the answer to this question, and be honest about it.
- Where will we both want to be in five years? In ten years?
- Are we on the same page? Are we going in the same direction?
- Do I envision being on a park bench with this person when we are ninety years old?

- How will we work out problems?
- How will we handle our finances? Will we share? Keep our accounts separate? Do we have the same financial goals? Do either of us have credit issues or a large debt?
- Who will have what household responsibilities?
- How will we communicate with each other when something goes wrong (which it will)?
- What will we actually be promising each other?
- Are we a good partnership? A good team?
- Have we lived together yet? Are our living styles compatible?
- Can I imagine living without this person for the rest of my life and being happy, or can I only imagine a future that involves both of us?

These are hard questions, and a flighty sense of romance or the thrill of getting to plan a wedding are not reasons to overlook them. Have some frank discussions about these questions before you set a date. If you both feel good about it in your guts—if you know deep inside that this is the right thing for you to do—then go for it. A solid long-term commitment is something to be proud of, and it can give you security and confidence to go through life with someone you love and trust. And congratulations.

• •

EXPERT ADVICE

A prenuptial agreement—sometimes called an antenuptial agreement or premarital agreement—is a written contract created and executed by two people before they are legally married. It usually spells out how assets will be distributed in the event of divorce or death. Contrary to popular opinion, prenups are not just for the rich. They are often used as a financial planning tool that can help resolve many issues regarding property ownership, resolution of debts, division of business interests, spousal support, and other asset-based issues that arise in the event of a divorce.

Prenups have been in existence for thousands of years, dating back to the royal families in Europe—and in other cultures. If you decide not to enter into a prenuptial agreement, the laws of your specific state will determine how property, other assets, debts, and spousal support will be calculated in the event of your marriage ending—through divorce or death. When you marry, the court views the union like a contract where automatic property rights exist for each spouse. Determining what your specific rights and responsibilities are, relative to assets acquired before the union and after, can be a very important step in asset protection in the event of divorce or death.

If you fall into any of these categories, you should consider consulting with an expert in family law:

1. You own a business.
2. You own real estate.
3. You have received—or may receive—an inheritance.
4. You earn much more than your partner.
5. Your net worth is much higher than your partner's.
6. You have children from a previous relationship.
7. You have elderly parents who depend on you for financial support.
8. One partner has accumulated a great deal of debt before marriage.
9. You want to leave your assets to others and not only to your partner.

Prenuptial agreements can encompass many other topics. If any of these categories apply, you should seek a consultation with a family law attorney to learn if a prenup would be in your best interest.

—VIKKI ZIEGLER, CELEBRITY FAMILY LAW ATTORNEY,
CEO OF DIVORCEDATING.COM, AND HOST OF BRAVO'S
UNTYING THE KNOT (WWW.VIKKIZIEGLER.COM)

. . . .

Should You Get Out?

Maybe the relationship is just getting started, and you are getting that bad feeling, like you've eaten something that doesn't agree with you. You are feeling you need to get out before you get too involved. I know this feeling well. I once dated a successful, good-looking man who was in his fifties. On our third date, on a Sunday night, he took a pill and offered one to me. I was like, "Um, no, I'm forty-three, and that's not my deal." He was a loser, successful or not. And by the way, drugs on a Sunday? Isn't that supposed to be the day of rest?

Maybe you've been involved for a while but it just keeps getting crazier and you're starting to think, *Stop the ride, I want to get off.* Maybe it's all too tumultuous. Maybe you're even committed, but you're miserable and not getting the love and treatment you deserve and no matter what you try, it's not getting any better.

It's hard to know which relationships will work and which ones won't. Nobody has a crystal ball, and those 1-900-number psychics know less about your relationship than you do. We all make mistakes and we screw it up. There have been many times when I have gotten involved with someone who seemed like he would be great in so many ways, but then there were problems that we couldn't overcome. If someone travels all the time and you never get a chance to spend enough time together to grow the relationship, that can be a problem. If someone never pays attention to you, that's a problem. If someone says one thing but does another and proves himself a chronic liar, that's a problem. If someone disregards you, doesn't listen to you, doesn't respect you, that's a problem. Physical and/or emotional abuse of you, parents, friends, or employees is definitely a problem, as is substance abuse. If you get emotionally attached to someone despite all the signals that the relationship isn't for you, or you are lonely and willing to take anybody who will have you no matter how they treat you, that's a problem. Remember that everybody is on their best behavior at the beginning of a relationship. It may take some time for the problems to reveal themselves.

However, the existence of a problem is not necessarily a reason to get out. There will always be problems, but are they insurmountable?

Maybe your partner is insecure and afraid. Maybe he doesn't know how you feel. Maybe he doesn't know how to express himself very well. Maybe he means well but he has bad habits or he just isn't sure how to move forward.

Sometimes, these problems can be resolved. I was involved with a guy who wasn't spending enough time with me. We'd been together about a month, and although that isn't very long, I wanted to know the relationship was moving forward, or I didn't want to waste my time. I was very direct with him. I told him that I needed to hear from him after a date, that I needed to be involved in his life, and that we needed to be evolving. If he just wanted to have fun, that was fine, we didn't need to be exclusive, but I needed to know what it was. I wasn't desperate about it, just matter-of-fact. I knew what I needed to know.

His response was to involve me in his life more, to start calling me after dates, to move forward. He might have done that anyway if I hadn't been clear to him about what I needed, but because I was direct, it guaranteed that he understood and was willing to give me what I wanted. You should never allow yourself to be treated like shit, but at the same time, you can't expect anyone to be perfect. It's better to say something and see if you can fix the problem. Then you know the truth.

· ·

GIRL TALK

In my experience, and in the experience of many of my friends, this is the anatomy of a typical relationship fight: The guy does something thoughtless. The woman gets emotional, terrified, and scared. She cries, yells, and/or says things she doesn't totally mean. This paralyzes the man, who has no idea how to react to extreme emotion. The result is that he doesn't react at all. He shuts down. This makes the woman so angry that she feels like she could walk out the door and be ready to end it. That's when the guy realizes he really wants her and tries to get her back. He says he will change, she takes him back, and then it all starts over again.

· ·

Be a Straight Shooter

The way you bring up a problem can have a major impact on how successfully you can resolve it. If you know what you want, and it's a deal breaker, and if you are genuinely willing to walk if you don't get it, then that is not being insecure. That is about doing what it takes to get it, by either receiving it from the person you are with or opening up a space in your life to find someone new. If something is a deal breaker, be straightforward about it. Get in and get out of the conversation.

But if something isn't a deal breaker, you can't threaten to walk when you know you will miss the person and be willing to compromise when your threat doesn't work. That's not being a straight shooter. Don't throw out the divorce card or the breakup card just because you think it will manipulate the other person when you don't really mean it or intend to follow through. Instead, be calm, be direct, and ask: "How can we fix this?" Then listen. If the other person doesn't feel heard, doesn't think that you understand them and value their perspective, or thinks you aren't willing to consider what they want, then you won't get anywhere. Whenever there is a problem, both people almost always have equally compelling perspectives.

Delivery is important—you can't detract from the issue with all your other issues. Remember, one subject at a time, briefly stated with confidence. That's the best way for the other person to hear you, to get an answer, and to determine the truth.

You also have to mean what you say. If you have a major issue and you decide it's time to bring it up, you better mean it if you say that it is intolerable to you. You have to be willing to back it up, within reason. If you tell someone you will never be able to deal with a certain behavior or issue, and they won't bend, and you walk away from the relationship, you can't just decide you can deal with it because you miss the person. You can say you will move a little on it if they also move a little on it. You can't be totally inflexible in a give-and-take relationship, but you also shouldn't be Silly Putty. If you always have to be the one to change everything and your partner never has to change anything, then you have lost control and have no power in the relationship, and that's a dangerous place to be.

Reasons to Stick with It

Discomfort isn't always a reason to get out of a relationship. Sometimes, discomfort can grow a relationship, or energize it, or pop it out of a rut. Here are some examples:

- Your new relationship is a diamond in the rough. People evolve in a relationship, and maybe the one you are in has potential to turn into exactly what you want. If the relationship keeps moving forward and you see positive signs of change, give it a chance. Even if the progress is slow, even if he has a long way to go, it's the movement that counts. It means he's not stubborn, that he is willing to change himself to be with you or that he's willing to grow. That's worth something.

- Your new relationship is a little bit intimidating. I draw certain parallels between a new relationship and a new business deal. It's a little exciting, full of possibility, but risky, too. A new relationship should never feel too comfortable, in my opinion, but it also shouldn't feel like you are getting away with something. If you get too comfortable too soon, you might get careless or inconsiderate or you might disrespect the other person. Discomfort can keep everyone sharp. For example, maybe your guy goes out every night, and you don't love that, but it gets you out more than you would go out on your own and keeps you taking good care of yourself so you can hold his attention. Maybe he thinks your clothes are too sexy or your girlfriends are too much, but he becomes more protective and attentive to you to be sure he keeps your attention. As long as you both feel good about the relationship, these minor tensions can build the passion and keep the relationship moving forward.

- In a new relationship, you feel like the other person is out of your league, or you don't quite understand the other person yet. Maybe you like him too much and you aren't sure it's mutual. Maybe it's all just new. Women tend to do crazy things like overcommunicate, ask for things prematurely, or want to know the future, or we end it preemptively because we are afraid the other person is going to break up with us. Don't make that mistake. If it's all just unfamiliar and new, breathe through it and ride it out. You don't know what you're doing yet, so you're not in a position to make a decision. Don't jump to conclusions until you know what you're actually dealing with. Unless you have that bad feeling, give it a chance and see what happens. A new relationship is like a sauce. If you add too much salt or burn it, it's very hard to go back, but if you start with something bland and add a little salt here, a little heat there, you can gradually get it to the place where you love it. It's always better to be able to add more than try to take back something you already did. Don't give too much too fast. Tread lightly and taste often.

- You don't feel like you really "have" the other person. Especially at first, you can be into someone without totally having them or letting them totally have you. This is a better way to proceed than throwing yourself fully into something before you really know who the other person is. You can always lean in and pull back, but the ability to be hot, then cold and keep them guessing can be fun and exciting to a point. When everybody feels good and excited but not totally secure, you're in the right zone.

- Your expectations are too high. Women expect a lot from their partners. Is your list of necessary qualifications or your deal-breaker list realistic or fantasy? Are you always nitpicking? You can't forget you are dealing with an imperfect human being. Yes, men can be animals, and women can be crazy, but you have to pick your issues. What's really important, and what really isn't such a big deal? (Evaluate this when you *don't* have PMS.) Hold out for sexual chemistry, sure. Hold out for a good person, but a good, true, loyal, morally upright guy with supermodel looks and an eight-figure annual income? Good luck with that.

- Your relationship gets temporarily unequal. Maybe you've been a stay-at-home mom and you go back to work and he feels a little insecure that you have your power back. Maybe he got in shape and is looking hot and you just had a baby and feel fat and don't have your sex drive back yet. Maybe he just got fired and you just got promoted or vice versa. Maybe he's making money now and you feel insecure because you were with him back when he had nothing. These kinds of discomforts can grow a relationship and are not worth ending it over. He might need to step it up to keep up with you. You might get inspired to get in shape so you can feel as hot as he looks. If you're in a good place and he's in a bad place, or vice versa, these kinds of discomforts can be opportunities to reach across the aisle and help each other.

JUST THE TIP

What do you do when you really, genuinely fuck up and do something unforgivable? When you know it's totally your fault, and the person you love says he will never speak to you again or you feel them shut down? When this happens, it really sucks, but if you want to fix things, you have two choices: Either you put your tail between your legs and beg, or you write a letter or leave a detailed phone message in which you apologize in a loving and caring way without shifting the blame to anyone else. Or you apologize in person, if you can. The method you choose depends on your personality and your partner. Which is more likely to work? The point is to sit them down and get them to remember the good things so they don't just think you are a piece of shit. It might not work, but if the relationship is strong enough, you can rebuild. Even the unforgivable is often forgivable.

Don't Make Decisions out of Fear

Before you make the decision to end a relationship, make sure you aren't acting out of fear. Factor into your decision that fear is never a reason to end a relationship or a reason to stay in a bad relationship. The only kind of fear that is worth considering is fear for your personal safety or the safety and well-being of your children. The kinds of fear you should never let control you include:

Fears that makes you stay in a destructive relationship

- Fear of being alone
- Fear of failure
- Fear that you can't financially afford to be on your own
- Fear of having to figure out how to move all your stuff
- Fear that breaking up will be too much trouble, or you just can't deal with it right now.
- Fear that you won't ever be able to meet anyone else because you like to stay home
- Fear of being alone on a holiday, your birthday, an upcoming wedding, over the weekends, etc.
- Fear of going through the pain of a breakup
- Fear that you will never find anyone better
- Fear that you will never get married or have kids if you don't stick with this person because you've already wasted too much time
- Fear that you are too unattractive/fat/neurotic/screwed up/ "damaged" to have a good relationship
- Fear of having to confront yourself or really look at yourself
- Fear that nobody else will ever love you
- Fear of somebody else being with your partner
- Fear that you aren't good enough for a healthy relationship or you don't deserve happiness
- Fear that you might be leaving a relationship worth fixing
- Fear that nobody will ever really understand you so you might as well just stick with what you have
- Fear of the stigma of divorce; fear of what people will think
- Fear of ruining your kids' lives, or making them sad, or making them hate you or blame you (children do best when their parents are happy and in healthy relationships, and staying in a destructive or unhappy relationship is doing them no favors)
- Fear of hurting your partner
- Fear that the other person couldn't make it without you/ codependency issues
- The belief that you are responsible for someone else's happiness and therefore owe it to them to stay with them

- Fear of losing your partner's family
- Fear of regretting it later
- Fear that staying is the only way you will ever learn how to commit to someone
- Fear that you are too old to start over

Fears that can make you leave a good relationship or a relationship worth fixing

- Fear of commitment—fear that you "just can't do this marriage thing"
- Fear that you are missing out on something better
- Fear that your past will rear its ugly head
- Fear that you have settled for less than perfection and that the perfect person must be out there somewhere
- Fear that you are missing out on somebody better
- Fear of getting old (read: midlife crisis)
- Fear of not being able to control every aspect of your life
- Fear that someone will find out how crazy you are
- Fear that someone else might not do everything exactly like you think it should be done
- Fear of compromise
- Fear that you have wasted your life (instead of just living your life right now!)

Fear distracts you from the truth, and you will never truly know your decision was the right one if you made it out of fear. The only way to make a decision is out of truth, and the only way to feel the truth is to tune in to your gut. Fear will drive you to do the wrong thing every time. You get afraid, so you reject someone before they can reject you. You get afraid, so you stay with someone who doesn't let you be who you really are.

I get scared a lot, and I've made plenty of relationship decisions out of fear. Suddenly I will think, *What am I doing, why am I here? I don't want to be here!* And then I run. I fear discomfort, I fear being controlled, I fear being out of control, I fear that I am wasting time, I fear I am making bad choices. I fear abandonment. I fear being hurt. I fear going through the pain. I fear not having good sex. I fear that nobody is ever going to love me again. Maybe you fear that you will never have kids, or you fear the pain of a breakup, or you fear that you will miss out on your soul mate and settle for someone less than who you could have had, so you are always looking over your shoulder for the next perfect guy. None of these reasons has ever been a good reason to begin, stay in, or end a relationship, and it's been very difficult for me to see and internalize that truth.

If you are calm and clear in your mind, you will open up to the truth. This can be hard to do, but there are ways to make it easier. Get more sleep. Do some yoga. Eat healthy food. Rest more. Be calm. Limit caffeine and sugar. Work out. Go to the beach. Notice what makes you emotional and avoid those things while you are trying to make a decision. Notice what makes you calm and do more of those things. When you don't take care of yourself, when you're eating poorly and not moving enough, you will be more likely to feel depressed or bad about yourself. Only when you are breathing and feeling calm can you actually think straight. That's when the decisions become clear.

I don't want you to act out of fear, as I have at certain times in my life. I don't want you to run when you could really benefit from staying put, and I don't want you to stay put when you really should run, but the only way to know for sure is to move past the fear and listen to your gut instinct.

In many cases, people who look beyond the fear and really step back to objectively evaluate their situation without reactivity discover that they genuinely don't want to end their relationship at all. In other cases, people realize that they really do need to end it.

So what if you really do need to end it?

· ·

EXPERT ADVICE

Deciding to end a relationship can be a gut-wrenching experience. Staying in a bad relationship can be just as difficult. It's time to leave if there is physical and/or emotional abuse. Ongoing resentment, hostility, or complete indifference are toxic to relationships and can also signal that it's time to exit.

—JANET TAYLOR, PSYCHIATRIST FROM
NEW YORK CITY, WWW.DRJANET.TV

. . . .

The Separation

Sometimes, when you really aren't sure about the status of a relationship, it can be beneficial to take some time apart. This can be official, as in when a married couple decides to live separately for a while to see how it goes, or it can be unofficial, like when two people who are dating just drift apart for a while and take more time for themselves. The separation isn't without risk. The two of you might come to totally different conclusions—one of you wants to keep going and the other one becomes sure it's over. However, it can also give you room to think and breathe and calm down. A separation gives you more perspective. Do you feel relieved to be away and free from the person, or do you realize you really miss him and that you don't like the way your life looks without him in it? You have to get past the loneliness stage in order to be truly discerning about this. What is the truth? Do you like being apart, or don't you?

Separations are easy for some people and extremely difficult for other people. It's hard to break communication with somebody who has been in your life for a long time, and sometimes you don't know what you've got until it's gone. But you can't immediately start harassing the other person. How will they know whether they miss you if you never go away? You have to stop calling, stop texting, and let the other person feel and process what life is really like when you aren't in it. Don't bust his balls. Give him space. Let him process his own feelings, rather than telling him what his feelings should be.

Also stay away from his friends and his family. Don't text them. Don't ask his mom what she thinks. And don't drink too much. Concentrate on getting your own life back in order while you wait to see how it all shakes out. Really disconnect. Truly separate.

Many couples who separate say that one of the things they realize they don't want to give up is the family aspect. What if you feel like that person is family to you, even if you don't want to be romantically involved anymore? What if your extended families are intertwined? What if you are in business together? Some couples find they can transition into a more familial or a more work-related relationship and let the romantic part go. For many others, however, this is nearly impossible.

Consider all these things when you separate. Really use that time for contemplation, and set a date to reassess. Maybe it will be in a week, maybe in a month, maybe in three months, maybe even six months or a year, depending on your situation. However long it is, keep that date and then be open and honest about the experience. On *Sex and the City: The Movie*, Miranda tried this with her husband Steve. They separated and then they said that whoever wanted the relationship to work would meet at a certain day and time on the Brooklyn Bridge. They both showed up. But what if one of them hadn't? Sometimes the truth is a wonderful surprise, and sometimes the truth is a slap in the face, but you need to know the truth so you can rip off the Band-Aid and get on with your life.

So how do you both feel now? This isn't usually an easy conversation and some people have a hard time delivering bad news. You might need to ask directly: "Just tell me the truth right now. Are you done?" This is something you need to know. And don't just talk. Also listen. Is there still a spark between you? Do you both feel like it is worthwhile to work on your issues? Is one of you ready to let it go? Maybe you both are but sometimes you can feel done when it's actually just fear. Breathe and make sure you are thinking straight before you say something you aren't sure is true.

. . . .

JUST THE TIP

Sometimes you can be pretty sure you want to end a relationship, but when it gets right down to it, you realize that you really don't want to end it and that the relationship really is worth saving. At this point, you have to fight for it. You might already have done damage, and that damage may take some time to repair, but if you know it's worth the effort, then go for it. Men can be weak in this area. If they think you are leaving them, they tend to shut down rather than fight for the girl. If that happens, you have to make your case. You could say something like, "What we have is rare, and I don't want to do any more damage to it. I want to save this. I don't want to lose you. Can we backtrack and fix this and make a new commitment to be good to each other?" It might not work because the other person might have already decided it's too late, but if you don't try, you might always wonder if you could have gotten him back.

. . . .

How to Get Out

If there is no evolution, if there is no change, if you sense trouble or have that bad intuition about a new relationship, or if you know in your gut that a long-term relationship really is coming to an end, then how do you actually get out? How do you make that happen?

First of all, you have to consider timing. Even if you know you need to break up, you won't always be ready to do it. Sometimes you just can't handle it emotionally because you have other things going on, like a lot of stress from work, a sick family member, or financial issues. Maybe you make your plans but you wait to execute them. When you feel strong and calm and ready, that's when you make your move. If you have been separated, this is easier. You've already done the hardest part.

Next, you need to make a promise to yourself to break up amicably, no matter what. Breaking up is never fun, even if you want the breakup. There can be a feeling of calm before the storm or a scared, shaky numbness when you sense the end is near. This is when you have to be gentle on yourself and gentle on the other person. High emotions make it easy to lose your temper or get overly emotional and say things you don't mean. Say only what you mean in a calm, gentle, and direct way. Don't add insult to injury by throwing in everything the other person did wrong. If you have decided to end it, that won't help anything. You don't need to fix the person you're about to break up with. Just say it's okay. Say you're going to be all right. Tell the other person to find their smile.

And if you know it has to end, you have to cold-turkey it, no matter how hard it is. Don't throw a relationship in the trash and then keep fishing it out. Dramatics and insults and "I'll find someone better than you!" and "You'll regret this!" and then "I want you back!" are all just theater. You can't convince someone to love you, and you can't force yourself to love someone. Do you want the last thing your partner remembers about your relationship to be you acting insane or saying you hate him? Do you want him to think of you as a crazy bitch when he remembers your relationship, or do you want him to think of you as mature and cool? Think of breaking up as dissolving a business partnership. If you screw over your business partner in the end, it's a bad look and you will feel guilty later. Go out in a classy way. Leave on a high note.

I know a girl who was in a relationship and was not an assertive person. People thought of her as a doormat for her entire relationship, but when she finally broke up with her boyfriend, she did it in such an admirable way that even he talks about how classy it was. She told him that she knew he wasn't into the relationship, and that it was obviously not working, so she wanted to end on a positive note. She told him not to call her or text her unless he legitimately changed his mind and said she would be fine. He really respected it. It was calm and rational and they each parted with good feelings about the other person.

This also helps you when you look back over the relationship. If you leave on a calm note, then you can think about the relationship in a calm way, looking back to discover what you learned rather than ranting to yourself or hating yourself for the way you acted.

The hardest situation of all is when you genuinely love the person, but you know it's not going to work, or when the connection is strong and mutual but your lives simply won't blend, for whatever reason. Real love and connection are hard to find, and it can be heartbreaking to have them and have to give them up. But if you know it's over, then make a clean break and move on.

Or not. The clean break is one way to do it, but how the breakup goes depends on how long you've been together and the nature of your relationship. Here are some methods that I have found work pretty well for ending a relationship:

The Slow Fade

If things aren't going well and you haven't met the parents yet and he hasn't bought the ring, you don't have to be drastic. Be subtle. Step back a little and take stock of the situation. Maybe withdraw a bit. All of a sudden, you have other plans. You're not as available. Let it fade out. It's hard, but it's less hurtful than cutting someone off or having a big scene. Maybe he's also feeling that it isn't right, and when you step back, he'll step back and you can both just let it go gradually. You don't have to call attention to it or say you are doing it. Just start to be more independent. Give yourself a chance to breathe and think.

Taking a Break

This might be one of the least effective strategies. Taking a Break can be an excuse to break up without hurting the other person too much by falsely leading them on and thinking there is a chance. Don't do this if you don't really mean it. It is not kinder to lead someone on. However, if you both agree that you need some time apart, this strategy can work and you might decide to try it. If you do, set a date to reconvene and reevaluate—in two weeks, a month, two months. Then follow through. Use that time to seriously look at yourself and the relationship. Can you get what you want, or probably not? The risk is that when you do this, you might not both come to the same conclusion. Don't blow off the reevaluation. Get together. Meet. Talk. Is it over, or not yet? Sometimes you need to have a break from someone to miss them. If you don't miss them, that is a sign that either the break wasn't long enough or, more likely, the relationship will never be right. If you do miss the person, you can say, "Look, I will change, but I need you to do some things, too." That can be the grounds for a discussion about moving forward.

Anything other than a consensus to keep going is grounds for the Cold Turkey, but you both might realize you really miss being together and it's worth working out. Or that it isn't.

The Cold Turkey

If none of the gradual methods work, then Cold Turkey it is! End it directly and kindly, then get out and don't come back. It's not working and you're sorry but it's over. Don't make it sound like there is hope if there is no hope. Don't do the Cold Turkey unless you know you can actually go cold turkey and you genuinely want out of the relationship forever. The Cold Turkey is most appropriate if you know the other person is going to be heartbroken. You need to let that person get over you. Cut it off. If you are the one who has been broken up with, you can still do the Cold Turkey. No texting. No calling. For God's sake, no begging. Be good to yourself as you move forward and don't ever look back.

Most importantly, no matter how you decide the breakup has to happen, or no matter how it happens to you in spite of your wishes, be kind. Don't tell someone all the details of your internal dialogue, because your emotions may make you believe you are changing your mind back and forth, over and over, when in reality it is over. This can be a confusing time, but the kindest thing to do is not subject your partner to your moods and an emotional roller coaster, especially when you are confused yourself. What you say can stick when it wasn't really what you meant. This is a very hard thing to do, but if you remove yourself from the situation, it will be easier. I've had many times when I wanted to be a bitch, but then I said to myself, "Just be kind." Even though I might have to say or text something I don't really feel at the moment—or *not* say or text what I really did feel at the moment—I know it is always better to be kind. This can be hard for me because I'm usually so honest and straightforward about how I feel in the moment, but I also know from experience that how I feel in the moment isn't necessarily how I really feel. Bottom line: If you are breaking up, for any reason, yours or his, be kind. If you are trying to get back together, also be kind. It's a rule that should always apply, whether a relationship is on or off or somewhere in between.

HOW TO GET SOMEBODY BACK

What if it ends, either because of you or not because of you, and you realize it was a mistake? What if you are on the verge of relationship implosion, and you want to save it? There are ways to do this. They won't always work, and some of them are risky, but they can be very effective. If you have nothing to lose, and you are sure you want the relationship, give these a try:

- Change it up. Get happy. Be your own person again. Get confident and don't be needy. Start living your life again. It's the best way to make yourself attractive (and also happy), and actions speak louder than words.
- Stop yelling, nagging, whining, and complaining. Pull back, observe, and see what happens. If he's been tuning you out, he'll soon realize there is nothing to tune out anymore, and he might turn around and come back for you.
- Fire up the burners again (see chapter 4).
- Say something. This is very important. Too many relationships end because nobody ever admitted they wanted to stay together. The worst thing in the world is to lie awake at night blaming yourself because you never spoke up and said, "I love you and I still want you."
- But don't say *everything* you are thinking. Most men can't handle that.

. . . .

The Divorce

If you are married and you want to end it, the whole breakup question gets a lot bigger. It turns into a divorce question. I'm not going to tell you that you should end your marriage, and I'm not going to tell you that you shouldn't. Only you can determine this very important, personal, heart-wrenching answer for yourself, possibly with the help of marriage therapy. If you aren't sure, if you keep changing your mind, then I suggest you sit still in your relationship until you know, and get some professional help so you can sort it out more effectively.

What I mean by that is that you do not rush to a conclusion, you do not force a decision, and you do not ignore the question. You wait to take action but you pay very close attention to what is happening in your relationship when you stop reacting to every little thing that happens out of misery or frustration. Take a step back. Ask yourself how you would feel without that person in your life. You might be angry, be irritated, be frustrated, or even feel betrayed, but how would you feel if that person were completely and totally gone? Would you breathe a huge sigh of relief? Would you be free? Or would you feel like you lost a part of yourself?

Maybe right now you think you know the answer, but unless you give it time to breathe, unless you give yourself a quiet space in which to really contemplate all the ramifications of this question, you won't know for sure. Do you have kids together? How will it affect them? The answer to that question also isn't always clear. Kids can suffer just as much from a dysfunctional parental relationship as from a divorce, but you have to assess your own situation to know what will be best for them. What about your spouse? Will he be able to make it without you? How important is it to you if the answer is no? Or is your spouse more resilient than you think and you will recognize that if you step back and give the relationship some space?

With a marriage, sometimes you can feel like you already swam halfway from Florida to Cuba, and now you don't know whether to keep going all the way there or turn around and swim all the way back. This can require some serious soul-searching.

. . . .

DR. AMADOR SAYS . . .

When she says that a marriage can feel like you already swam halfway from Florida to Cuba, Bethenny makes a great analogy. My mother escaped from Cuba with my brothers, sister, and me, and her decision about whether or not to complete her escape from Cuba and the dangers she faced when she decided to finish what she started are exactly like what I see women, with whom I have worked in individual and couples' therapy, experiencing when they are on the brink of divorce.

My advice is to get counseling, even if you feel certain you are going to turn back. Counseling is almost always the right thing to do, especially when there are children involved. Some of the couples I have worked with have divorced and some have stayed together, but the focus of the couples' therapy was always to bring peace to a warring household, build bridges of trust and kindness, and create a safe haven for any children involved. This is a solid foundation for both marriage and divorce. Don't go it alone—get help.

—XAVIER AMADOR, PH.D., PRESIDENT,
LEAP INSTITUTE, WWW.LEAPINSTITUTE.ORG

. . . .

Every relationship sucks in some way. That's just the truth, even with the most apparently happily married couples. Relationships are about compromise, and I'm sorry if nobody told you that going in. In the best cases, the compromise is totally worth the benefits you get from being in a marriage, but sometimes it doesn't feel worth it. Marriage is not about 24/7 passion and having fun. Nobody else is ever going to do or be or act exactly the way you want all the time, and even if they did, you probably wouldn't like them or respect them. Maybe a serious heart-to-heart is in order. Maybe counseling will help you clarify how you really feel, since we all know how much our feelings can change. You can hate somebody one minute and love them the next. Welcome to marriage.

In many cases, even if you are seriously thinking about divorce, you may feel unsure. You might feel one way one day and another way the next day. In some cases, the answer actually is clear-cut. There are good no-compromise reasons to get out of a marriage. If there is physical or mental abuse, get out (or get treatment, or both). If there is major drug or alcohol abuse and your spouse refuses help and you can't live with it another day, get out. If there is habitual cheating, get out.

An affair isn't necessarily a reason to get out, if you are both committed to repairing the relationship. Sometimes, what you think is a deal breaker turns out not to be a deal breaker because you love the person enough to work it out. In the case of a single affair, there is usually some fault in both parties. I know a couple who dealt with cheating. He had an affair, but she had funneled all her energy into the kids and the only way she ever reacted to her husband was in a cold, naggy, bitchy way.

He looked for emotional support elsewhere, and it turned into an affair. Once they realized what had happened in counseling, however, they both shifted their priorities and they didn't get a divorce.

· ·

EXPERT ADVICE

Lots of women—and men, too—commit what they consider to be "small" acts of financial infidelity, like hiding money or keeping purchases secret every now and then from your partner. In many cases, people do this just to "keep the peace."

But cheating on your mate—financially, that is—is never a good thing. And it could lead to huge problems. The National Endowment for Financial Education (NEFE) released a 2014 study that found that financial infidelity is on the rise when it comes to the joint finances of couples. One-third of people with combined accounts said they've committed a financial deception, like lying about their income or debts or keeping certain accounts secret. Even more disturbing: Financial infidelity has enormous consequences. NEFE's study showed that 76 percent of people polled said that when financial deception occurred, there's been an impact on the relationship—anything from big arguments to divorce. So beware that financial infidelity can be just as devastating as physical or emotional infidelity.

—JANET TAYLOR, PSYCHIATRIST,
NEW YORK CITY, WWW.DRJANET.TV

· ·

It's important to recognize that cheating doesn't happen in isolation. If you are a nagging bitch who constantly tears her husband down and never says anything nice, who doesn't care about her appearance, and who makes everything difficult, your husband might meet some fun, light, bright, sexy girl at a bar or at the market or on a business trip and think, *Wow, she's so easy, she's so fun, what a difference!* This is totally unfair, I know, because that is a false impression. That girl is a false advertisement. She doesn't have to take the kids to school and clean the house and work at some crappy job and try to scrape by and keep everything together, and she doesn't know all your husband's annoying qualities. Still, the point stands: When you are the best person you can be with your partner, instead of the worst person you can be, then your partner will be more inspired to be better, too, rather than wandering away looking for greener pastures. That's not to say the woman is to blame for a man's infidelity. Absolutely not! But both are involved. Infidelity is a sign of a breakdown.

Infidelity might not necessarily be a reason for divorce.

. . . .

EXPERT ADVICE

People often ask me about dating after divorce. Giving yourself time to both breathe and grieve the loss of the relationship is important. Divorce is a transition and opportunity to examine your will, motivation, values, and sources of happiness in a very deep and real way. Moving forward to the passivity of a new relationship should provide the opportunity for more growth. Avoid looking for the familiar and be open to dates that honor your own truth and real self. Have fun, explore, and stay in the moment.

—Lynnette Khalfani-Cox, The Money Coach,
www.askthemoneycoach.com

. . . .

A lot of problems can be fixed or worked through, but you have to know in your heart that it is better to work through them than to end it. Maybe you will be willing to do that work, and maybe you won't. Some people can't do that work at the drop of a hat. They have to be ready. It's hard to work on a relationship when you are going through something else like a bankruptcy or getting fired or having a death in the family. You have to be ready.

But it isn't just about you. Maybe your spouse doesn't want to work through your issues and you don't have a choice in the matter. If you do, however, then try this. Step back. Don't react. Don't discuss. Just let it be for a few weeks and see what the relationship—and your spouse—does without your direct and constant interference. The answer will likely be illuminating. I have a friend who tried this. She was married to a guy who was very emotional, who had dramatic ups and downs all the time. Sometimes he was cruel and derisive to her. Other times, he was helpless and totally irresponsible and saying he couldn't live without her. She was always reacting to him according to her own mood swings. The relationship was volatile to say the least, and they would get in huge blowout fights that didn't involve physical violence but involved a lot of emotional abuse on both sides. They had a high level of passion fueled by all this emotional energy, but most of the time she felt like she hated him and she wanted to punish him for being so unstable and mean to her. Yet she didn't feel like she could leave him because when he wasn't having an "episode," he seemed incapable of making it on his own. She felt responsible for him.

One day, she couldn't take it anymore. She had no energy left to fight, so she just stood back and looked at her situation as if she were an outside party. She stopped engaging with him and reacting to him, and she decided just to watch to see what would happen if she dropped out of the interaction. As soon as she did this, he didn't know what to do. He was used to being fueled by her reactivity and when she stopped reacting, at first he seemed to calm down, but then he really let loose. He started fighting all by himself. She told me that she was stunned by how truly unstable he was and that she was incapable of fixing him. Then it all became clear. She had always felt like she shared half the blame for the issue, but she finally saw the situation for what it was and realized he was abusive and she couldn't fix him. She filed for divorce, and her sense of relief and freedom was almost immediate. She never regretted her decision, and he turned out to be just fine, pulling himself together on his own when he no longer had her as a safety net. Another friend had a similar situation but the opposite result. She and her husband argued constantly and he often accused her of picking fights and being difficult. She accused him of being unreasonable and having opinions that were stupid. They would both yell a lot and they both felt miserable and confused about how to fix what was obviously an unhappy marriage. This friend decided to try the same strategy. One day, she vowed to go an entire day without negatively reacting to anything her husband did. She decided she would only say positive or totally neutral things to him and around him.

This was really hard to do at first. Whenever he did something that irritated her or that she thought was wrong, she wanted to say something and had to keep biting her tongue. After just a few hours, however, she realized that the things she kept wanting to say, the things that she was holding back, were all trivial and petty: that he was doing something the wrong way, or saying something the wrong way, or that he should fix his hair or wear a different shirt. She realized she had been totally micromanaging everything about him.

For his part, her husband visibly relaxed. After just a few hours, he began to smile more. He seemed calmer. He said nice things to her. They had a wonderful day, and she realized that she had been nitpicking him to death because she was feeling insecure in the relationship. She began to look at her own issues, and she also recognized that she was still feeling some commitment issues with the whole notion of marriage. She told her husband that she wanted to get some counseling to help her work out some personal issues, and he was warm and supportive about this without ever blaming her or saying something she admits she might have said, like, "Good, because you need it!" The moment of clarity that came from temporarily disengaging from the relationship resulted in the realization that she was the one tearing the marriage apart, and maybe she could fix her issues and that could help to repair the marriage. Maybe your situation isn't as dramatic as either one of these examples, but taking even one day to step back and not react to someone you are having issues with might just provide you with some answers.

There are many things to consider when considering divorce. Sometimes, a less-than-ideal marriage is good enough and you stay together for the sake of the kids. Sometimes, the unhappiness is there but it's hard to define and you're just not sure how to fix it. I would never judge anybody else who got divorced. People think they know someone else's relationship by witnessing it from the outside, but even if you were on a reality show that broadcast the details of your relationship to the world, nobody but you and your partner would know the truth of it. Every relationship has secrets and indefinable energies and inner dynamics. When it comes right down to it, nobody but you can ever know what your relationship is really made of and what your heart is telling you that you have to do to remain true to yourself. Everyone's priorities are different. For me, passion, love, and connection are the priorities, and when I am having great sex with somebody, I'm really proud of that. For someone else, passion and a lot of sex might feel too tumultuous and unsustainable, and compatibility and friendship are more important. Know yourself and know that one size does not fit all. Never judge your marriage based on anybody else's marriage. Judge it on what you need and what works for you. That is the only way to make the right decision about your future.

If you do this, and the conclusion you come to in a calm, rational state is that the marriage you got is not the marriage you want, the pain and unhappiness are too great, the betrayals are too unforgivable, or the differences are irreconcilable, then you have a tough but valuable road ahead. You are going to have to be ready to be alone for a while, for loneliness, for the deep emptiness and soul searching you will experience as you heal. A divorce is like a death in the family that you chose. It can feel like the end of the world, and you will probably spend sleepless nights blaming yourself and other sleepless nights feeling angry at your ex. It will pass. It will get better, but it's going to hurt.

Just be sure you own your stuff. Recognize it. Be aware of it, because make no mistake, if you don't recognize it, you will take the same stuff to your next relationship. If you aren't happy in Chicago, moving to New York is not going to make you happy. Not even moving to Hawaii, because you will bring the unhappiness with you. If you are acting out and doing things you've done before, it doesn't mean it's all your fault, but working on yourself will make your future prospects much brighter. Do you want to bring that same heavy bag of bullshit into the next relationship? If you don't want to wreck another relationship, you have to clean up your side of the street so the next one is better.

Divorce can also be a financial and legal mess. I'm not going to pretty it up for you. If you have mutual debt, mutual property, and especially mutual children, the mess just gets exponentially bigger. You really do need to determine whether it will be worth it, or if you would rather work it out than put yourself through all that. In the case of genuine personal irresolvable misery, however, the answer is likely yes, it is worth it. The pain of divorce can be severe, but it fades with time and you will come out on the other side.

EXPERT ADVICE

When you tie the knot, your credit report doesn't automatically merge with your mate's. Nor does one party's credit score impact the other person's score. But that doesn't mean you shouldn't be *ultra* careful in managing your credit. For starters, every woman should have at least one credit card in her own name. Also, realize that if you co-sign for joint accounts, such as a mortgage or car note, you'll both be on the hook for those debts, even if you divorce down the road. Many women mistakenly think they're in the clear financially if their divorce decree says their ex-husband was supposed to pay all the old bills. But that divorce agreement only dictates what happens between the former couple. From a legal standpoint, a creditor or bill collector can come after *either* party—individually or jointly—based on who co-signed for the debt. And a court judgment for an old debt could ruin your credit.

Also consider a prenup. There's been a big jump in the number of couples seeking prenuptial agreements, divorce attorneys say. In fact, a recent survey of American Academy of Matrimonial Lawyer members found that 63 percent of divorce lawyers report an uptick in prenups from their clients. Furthermore, 46 percent of attorneys surveyed revealed that women were the ones *initiating* the prenup request—because more women are now the breadwinners!

But don't think a prenup is automatically an iron-clad agreement. Although prenups are helpful, especially when you're the higher wage-earner, they can sometimes be partially or wholly voided by a judge. The courts only do this if there was fraud involved, if the contract was entered into under duress, or if the agreement is deemed as "unfair" or "unconscionable" toward one of the parties.

—LYNNETTE KHALFANI-COX, THE MONEY COACH,
WWW.ASKTHEMONEYCOACH.COM

• •

The Aftermath

One of the hardest times in life is the aftermath of a breakup, especially of a long-term committed relationship, including a marriage. It's hard to recover from a breakup, even if you were the one to end it.

The first three days after a breakup can be torture. You can't even see straight. You want to throw up. You cry for hours. You are in hell. It's like doing a juice fast. The first day is the worst, the second day really sucks, but by the third day, you're not hungry anymore and you feel like you can juice-fast forever. By the third day after a breakup, you suddenly start to cope. One good week with no contact, and you can fly, so ride it out. There is light at the end.

Recovering from a divorce will take much longer than three days, of course. There can be so much to resolve that the process can feel excruciating. To help you get through it, here are some survival-guide-type strategies I have learned really do help:

Post-Breakup "Don't-Do" List

- Don't cut your hair.
- Don't start eating ice cream (because you won't stop).
- Don't give in and call or text the person. If he doesn't answer, you'll feel worse. If he does, you will just be opening the wound again.
- If you panic or get hysterical, do not make contact under any circumstances. Work through it with a girlfriend.
- Don't cave in to the fear or you will be back at square one. Let it process. If you go back due to fear, you will do even more damage.

If you do any of these things, don't beat yourself up. Take a deep breath and get back on track with your own life.

Post-Breakup "To-Do" List

- Do something cleansing, like drinking green juice or doing a sugar cleanse or training to run a 5K or even a marathon. Exercise more. Do a little something every day if you can.
- Do yoga, or even go on a yoga retreat with other singles. Anything spiritual will help you to get back in touch with yourself.
- Hug your friends, hug your kids, hug your family. Physical contact helps.
- Open the window. Breathe fresh air.
- Step away from the phone. Put it away for increasingly long periods of time, or put limits on how often you can check it. First an hour, then two, then three. Leave it at home when you go out. Physically disconnecting yourself from your phone can be liberating.
- Take your ex's name out of your phone contacts.
- Stay busy.
- Watch your intake of alcohol or drugs, which will make you feel worse.
- Get enough sleep. Sleep deprivation exacerbates everything.
- Remember your truth. Keep reminding yourself. Never forget the core issues that led you to the decision to end it. Write them down and look at them often if it helps.
- Be strong. It gets better.
- Do the best you can.

Sometimes, you can't resolve an issue. Sometimes, you will get your heart broken, or you will break someone else's heart, because humans are social animals and we keep trying to come together even when it's all wrong. We can't always see the big picture. We can't always see the *little* picture or what's right in front of us. We don't always appreciate the good, and we tend to gloss over the bad in an effort to forestall loneliness. Sometimes, it's amazing that people come together at all or that it ever works.

But sometimes it does work, and the number one predictor of success is your gut. So pay attention. Tune in. Let it inform you and let it influence your rational side. If the relationship is right for you, or right for you right now, make it work. If it's wrong for you, get out so you can find one that is right for you. Ideally, you will move forward, one way or the other, based on a joint decision—a cue from your gut, followed by an analysis by your head. This two-party system can actually be very effective, if you let it. And when it tells you to go ahead? Then go ahead. You might have everything to lose, but true love is worth it.

CHAPTER 8

. . . .

Manage Your Money (Noise)

Money cannot buy peace of mind. It cannot heal ruptured
relationships, or build meaning into a life that has none.
—RICH DEVOS (COFOUNDER OF AMWAY)

Money has always been a volatile issue for me. I remember growing up with six cars in the driveway one week, and the next week having no furniture in the house and having to eat dinner off a card table. This was the life of a gambler's daughter—life at the racetrack. I remember times when we lived like big shots and times when my stepfather was asking if he could borrow money out of my piggy bank. I also grew up being told that I would never have to worry about money because I would always be taken care of, but then I went on to spend my whole life worrying about money anyway because the man who told me not to worry lost everything he had. I've tried to find someone to take care of me, but then I was never comfortable with that because I never really believed that the money was secure. I might wake up the next morning and—as it so often happened in my childhood—all that money, or the man who had it, would be gone. If I wasn't worrying about it, who would? If I didn't have that piggy bank, what would happen to me?

Money has been an issue in many of my relationships. When I didn't have any and was dependent on a man who did, I felt stifled and suffocated and controlled, even when the man I was with wasn't consciously trying to control me. I've also been in a relationship with someone who didn't make as much money as I did. That was a real struggle, too. I wanted us both to contribute to our lives together, not equally but proportionally to our income. I felt that he really struggled with paying for things, and this was a sign of things to come because later, it came back to bite me in the ass. I should have dealt with this problem, or at least been more aware of it, right from the beginning. I didn't expect him to equal my paycheck, but I also didn't expect him to live off me and try to take from me all he could.

If you think for one second that money issues won't matter in your relationship, you are wrong. Money is power. Money is security. Money is certainty. Money is confidence. Money is prestige and social acceptance. But most importantly, money equals control. To make money is to have control, in your personal relationships as well as in the world, and the more you make, the more control you have. A friend of mine always says, "He who makes the gold makes the rules." Consequently, to rely on someone else to make money is to give up a certain degree of relationship influence. Right or wrong, this is how it almost always is. Being the breadwinner or being the financially dependent person might work best in your relationship, but if you aren't prepared for what that will mean in your relationship, the situation can cause a lot of friction. Money brings out all kinds of hidden emotions. Money triggers issues about balance, control, and self-worth. Money matters.

• •

DR. AMADOR SAYS . . .

Money can be used for control, and it often is. However, let me offer a different point of view. I know lots of people with loads of money who have control of very little in their lives. Money sometimes equals control in relationships, but it can also be the currency of respect and love.

Money is inherently and interpersonally a symbol. Paper currency, the account balance you see on the ATM screen, even a $100 bill is worthless. What it symbolizes, however, has value. What money symbolizes for you comes mostly from your childhood and how you first experienced money. Was it a reward for good behavior, an expression of love, a source of tension, or a meaningless stand-in for the love you wanted but never got?

Knowing what money symbolized for you in your first love relationships—the one with your parents or caregivers—will help you gain control over how you deal with money in your current love relationship. Does giving money symbolize giving love? Does receiving money symbolize receiving love? Or is money standing in for something much different? Love and money can both be controlling, and can both be given freely, or with strings attached.

We all know money can't buy you love, but what we often forget is that money only has the power you give it or allow it to have over you.

—Xavier Amador, Ph.D., president,
LEAP Institute, www.leapinstitute.org

. . . .

If money were simply a bartering or transaction tool we all used in society, it probably wouldn't have as much influence as it does. However, most people have what I call money noise. Money noise is what I call an emotional reaction to money, which usually results in an unhealthy relationship with money. I don't know anybody who doesn't have some degree of money noise because money is such a powerful influence in our culture. It's almost impossible to escape. Money makes people do crazy things. It makes the people who have it look down on the people who don't have it, and it makes the people who don't have it look up to the people who do. It makes people brag and show off and say things they would never say about any other subject. Money puts pressure on people to keep up with the Joneses. It embarrasses people. It makes people feel inferior. It causes people to lie about what they have and what they don't have. It makes people all show and no go. It makes people act cheap—often, people without money are more generous than people with a lot of money (depending on how they grew up). I've found that people who know what it's like to live off tips, like servers and hairstylists, tend to be more generous than wealthy people.

Today, with women being more and more likely to have money, make money, and make *more* money than the men they are with, it causes even more relationship troubles than it once did. It is one of the most common reasons people cite for why their relationships fell apart. I see this a lot on *Housewives*. This is a franchise that took affluent, privileged couples and gave the women fame and money and power they didn't have before. In many cases, couples who had been married for years with an unchanging dynamic in which the man made more than the woman were thrown into chaos. Now the kids were grown or getting close and suddenly the woman becomes famous and is making money and oftentimes becomes the breadwinner. The men can't handle it. They get jealous of the fame and power and money, and they resent their wives for suddenly making more than they do. Sometimes they start talking badly about their spouses to the press, or taking money from their wives. It's a power struggle they didn't expect and had never encountered before. The men try to get the control back by trying to steal the spotlight as well as the resources and they might get their 15 minutes of fame, but in the end the relationships don't always survive. I see this happening, not just on *Housewives* but in every reality show franchise in which the women are the stars.

Money is powerful, no doubt about it. It must be handled with care, especially in your relationship. We have to deal with financial transactions every day, and the money situation in your relationship is what it is. Money is always in motion; you might have it and then not have it and then have it again. Both people in any relationship have to learn how to deal with that if they don't want money to interfere with the relationship's quality and stability.

One of the biggest problems I've both experienced and witnessed is confusing the relationship dynamic by throwing money noise into the middle of it. Money is usually a sore topic. How many times have you been in an argument about something else, and somebody has said something like, "And *another thing*—when are you going to get a job/get a better job/make more money/take more financial responsibility/get our accounts in order/follow the budget/stop being such a penny-pincher/stop wasting all our [or worse, *my*] money!" Maybe one of these comments is totally justified in your relationship, but when you throw it into fights about something else, it will slowly tear the relationship apart.

Some people are surprisingly secure about money. I dated a guy who grew up not having to worry about money. It just wasn't a big issue in his household, so he's very generous and doesn't have a lot of money noise. I've also been with a guy who was very uncomfortable spending his own money on anything but didn't seem to have any problem spending mine. Nobody feels sorry for rich people, but having money definitely comes with its own problems. For one thing, people think that if you have money, you should pay for everything and you won't know the difference. This is definitely not true. Wealthy people who made their own money are hyperaware of every dime that gets spent. I had a friend who was dating a very wealthy guy. He bought her very expensive presents—Chanel, Hermès, Gucci. She said, "He doesn't care what he spends on me!" But when she left a $7,000 pair of leopard pony pants at work, I couldn't believe how she was taking his money for granted. He was letting her act like that, but for how long? And why wouldn't she just take the $7,000 and save it? It's a huge turnoff to be careless with or disrespectful of somebody else's money. Eventually, the person making the money will resent that kind of disrespect. People who make a lot of money notice every penny. In fact, any man who's ever made a dollar notices this.

And by the way, men love a girl with no debt. Debt can be a deal breaker.

EXPERT ADVICE

Here's a question for a first date: "What's your credit score?" I'm only half kidding. No, it's not a romantic topic . . . unless you consider good credit *sexy* like I do! But knowing about your mate's credit standing before saying "I do" is crucial to getting off to a good financial start together. So if you're serious about someone (i.e., dating a long time, living together—or even already engaged or married), you should know each other's credit scores. If neither of you knows your score, take time to get them together. You can obtain your free credit reports—from Equifax, TransUnion, and Experian—free of charge online at annualcreditreport.com. You have to pay for your FICO score. It's available at myfico.com. But some credit card issuers and banks will give you a FICO score or other credit scores free. A good credit score is 700 or better.

Getting your credit reports/scores allows you to *honestly* see each other's debts and credit rating. Whatever you find, whether the person has been responsible or reckless, don't judge. Instead, carefully discuss the issues, find out what problems or setbacks may have occurred, and ask if they learned anything from their credit/debt setbacks. Doing this—and using the five tips mentioned above—will be good preparation for a healthy marriage filled with financial harmony for you both!

—LYNNETTE KHALFANI-COX, THE MONEY COACH,
WWW.ASKTHEMONEYCOACH.COM

• •

Most of the time, money is a sensitive issue, whether you have it or you don't have it or you are somewhere in the middle. Who makes it and who doesn't make it and how people spend it can be an issue. Family and who gets what and where the money comes from can be an issue. It can make paying during group dinners awkward, and it can make friends as well as romantic partners jealous when one person makes a lot more than everybody else.

If you make it even more of an issue in the beginning, then every time money is involved in your life (which is all the time), it will be a sore topic. Instead, figure out your dynamic early, or find a way to work on it constructively if it's already established. Know your money issue, and vow to keep it in its own box, let it be its own discussion, and never confuse it with your emotions about anything else in your relationship. How do you feel about money? Be honest with yourself. Is it important that you earn your own and are you more comfortable being the one with financial control? Do you think your partner should earn the money and support you? Or do you think all money and money issues should be equal in a relationship? There is a cultural expectation that the man is supposed to be the provider, and I do think men need to make money, but what if they can't possibly compete with how much money you have? It's a different world out there. I don't expect someone I'm interested in to make what I make because that's just not realistic most of the time, but I'm not interested in dating a freeloader, either. Let's look at some scenarios so you can figure out what applies to you.

⋯⋯⋯⋯⋯⋯⋯⋯⋯⋯⋯⋯⋯⋯⋯⋯⋯⋯⋯⋯⋯⋯⋯⋯⋯

EXPERT ADVICE

Believe it or not, nearly half of all women in the United States are the primary breadwinners in their homes. According to a 2014 survey from Prudential, 44 percent of all women in America are out-earning their spouses or live-in partners. Don't be afraid to acknowledge and *use* your earning power, whether it's taking charge of the day-to-day finances in your household, investing, or having a larger say in how money is handled in your relationship.

—Lynnette Khalfani-Cox, The Money Coach,
www.askthemoneycoach.com

⋯⋯⋯⋯⋯⋯⋯⋯⋯⋯⋯⋯⋯⋯⋯⋯⋯⋯⋯⋯⋯⋯⋯⋯⋯

When You Make More

Once upon a time, the woman almost never made more money than the man. However, that's all changing fast. According to a recent article in the *New York Times*, 40 percent of women are the breadwinners of the family (including single moms), and 26 percent of married women are the sole earners or make more money than their husbands.

If you are the breadwinner, this can cast your relationship into a weird light that neither of you may know how to handle. You might like having financial control, but a part of you still feels like the man is supposed to be the provider, so there must be something wrong with him or he's just not doing his part. This situation is also very difficult for a man. If he isn't the breadwinner and is instead financially dependent on you, he is already feeling unbalanced and unmanly about it, whether he admits it or not. For a woman who feels resentful, it's tempting to stick the knife in and turn it with comments like, "I guess I'll pick up the tab *again*." If you really care about someone, you will stop yourself from doing this. It's hard when you get angry or annoyed because it's such an easy way to punish someone, but it's not fair.

I know a woman who makes a lot of money, and her husband, who is only in his forties, declares himself "retired." When his family business sold, he was out of work and never got another job. She makes enough money to support them, but she gets perpetually irritated that he hasn't gotten a job. She tells him she doesn't care what kind of job he gets, but he finally admitted to her one day, "Look, I can never compete with you. I can never make close to what you make, so if I even try, it will just feel pathetic to me. I'm better off helping out at home where I can support what you do." Logically this makes perfect sense, and he does help out at home in ways that allow her to do her work, but she still finds herself getting irritated (logically or not) that he's not contributing financially, and he still feels inadequate (logically or not) because he's not the provider. There are men who rest on their laurels and have no inspiration or motivation to do anything, and there are men who are doing what they can financially. It's not always easy to find a job in this economy, especially if you are older. Figure out which describes your situation and be as understanding as you can without letting your spouse take advantage of you.

If you want the relationship to work, you have to work on the money piece. Even if you only do this internally (because you know deep down that the problem is really just you and your attitude), do the work. Teach yourself to get over your pettiness by sheer force of will and habit.

When getting serious in a relationship, consider having both joint and separate bank accounts. Talk this through. Perhaps you will share a checking account but each have your own savings accounts. In my professional experience, I think it's generally better for most couples to have *both*—separate accounts for their own spending and then a joint account to manage/pay household bills. A separate account gives each person financial independence and autonomy (so neither of you has to ask "permission" to buy stuff). But the joint account helps keep you together as a team, committed to shared financial goals and responsibilities.

—LYNNETTE KHALFANI-COX, THE MONEY COACH,
WWW.ASKTHEMONEYCOACH.COM

If the gap in pay is a large one, it's important to recognize that *it will be a problem*. Whenever there is a big difference between two partners—different religions, different cultures, a big age gap—it has the potential to be a problem because you aren't coming from the same place. This is especially true with money, and even more true when it is the woman who makes more money. Nobody blinks if the husband is a multimillionaire and he has a hot young wife who doesn't have a penny to her name, but switch that and society gets all riled up—and so do the people in the relationship. Let's say you make a lot of money and you are used to a certain lifestyle. If you fall in love with somebody who can't even pay for the normal things required to live the life you live (whatever is normal for you), it's probably going to become an issue, whether you think it will or not. I'm not saying it can't work. Sometimes it does work. I'm just saying that you have to know going in that it's going to be a problem and that you're going to have to figure it out, rather than ignore it until it explodes. Because it will explode. Oh yes it will.

Often, money issues aren't really about money. They are about the principle of the situation and what it reveals about character. Is it right that your boyfriend will let you pay for an expensive dinner because he doesn't make as much money as you, but then he will turn around and buy a really expensive watch for himself? Or is he generous with what he has, taking you out for pizza or cooking you dinner at home in a way he can afford but that is also a gesture of care and affection toward you? It definitely isn't about the price tag of the gesture. It's about the meaning behind the gesture. A generous person will take care of you in the ways that he can, and that can feel great, but someone who is grabby and wants you to take care of him will be a turnoff.

Money will always be a hot-button topic, and it will always bring out the worst in people. This is something that people in relationships may always have to fight. Let's say you make more money than your partner. You pick up the checks for expensive dinners, but then you learn that he has allocated $1,500 for himself to gamble twice a year. Is that irresponsible? Not necessarily. If he's not asking you for that $1,500, then that is an expense he has built into his budget. Why shouldn't he be able to do that? It's a fine line, and the person making less shouldn't be taking advantage and sponging off the person with more, but if they are financially responsible in their own context, then you don't really have anything to complain about. The provider is in control, but that doesn't give the provider license to be cruel or manipulative or unreasonable. You can watch all your own dimes, but you don't have to watch every dime the other person spends, as long as the other person isn't taking advantage of you. This is hard to do if you are fastidious about money, but it is necessary in unequal money partnerships. Personally, I don't like spending a lot of money on sunglasses or jeans. But I will spend money on other things, and I wouldn't want someone else telling me where I should and shouldn't spend my money.

It's also crucial to know where you stand. In a new relationship (not just dating, but when you think it could really turn into something), it's worth having a relaxed, no-pressure conversation at some point (maybe not on the very first date, but soon): "What's your philosophy about money? How do you feel about money in a relationship? How was money handled in your family growing up? How would we both feel comfortable if we went on vacation together, or went shopping, or moved in together someday?"

It's very important to be both unemotional and honest with yourself during this conversation. Will you feel bad if he never pays for anything? If you would, you need to say this. It is very common and normal for a woman to have trouble respecting a man who doesn't define himself by being a provider. You have to be a big person with the ability to rise above those (probably fading) stereotypes to make that work. Even if you think you can handle it, I can guarantee that other people will say things that will make you doubt yourself and your partner. Why shouldn't the man stay home with the kids if you make more money, for example? It's a legitimate question, but you have to answer it with total and complete honesty. The truth will set you free to work on your issues or recognize that you won't be able to overcome them. You can't be who you're not and no matter how you think you "should" think, often money noise programmed into you from childhood or your background will prevail.

You also have to remember to talk about money calmly. You don't want to say something you will regret, because the next time you are both standing in a store together, he will remember everything you said. Make it theoretical rather than pointing fingers. "So what if this were to happen?" rather than "When that happened . . ."

Finally, there is an incredibly important rule you have to follow if you make more money than someone you want to be in a relationship with: *Never emasculate the man.* Making money a big issue is one of the quickest ways to do that. Men feel biologically programmed to be the provider, and when they aren't the provider, or don't earn as much as you, it is an automatic ego blow, even without you saying one word. Even if you don't like the situation, you do like your husband or boyfriend, so what are you going to do? You are going to help him feel like a man. You are going to take the high road. This can save your relationship. Here are some ideas:

- **Let him go public.** Split expenses in a way that is reflective of how much each person earns, but let him have the more public expenses, while you take the private ones. This allows the guy to save face and feel like a man, at least in front of other people. For instance, maybe you pay for rent but he pays when you go furniture shopping. Maybe on vacations, you pay for the flight and the hotel online ahead of time, but he pays for all the incidentals, like meals and activities, so he's the one handing the server his credit card. This can feel unfair if you have an ego about money, and that's something you should know about yourself. I have a girlfriend who wants the credit for being the breadwinner, and she often takes it at the expense of her boyfriend's ego. She's making a choice, but the relationship isn't going well.

You don't have to nitpick about groceries and dry cleaning and every little thing, but I get it. If you are paying a lot more and it's all behind the scenes and he is getting all the credit when he's paying a fraction of what you are paying, it's easy to start feeling resentful. It also might seem sexist. Why should he have to be handled so carefully? Because that's just the way it is. You have to handle him carefully when it comes to money, and he has to handle you carefully when it comes to PMS. Fair is fair. It might sound old-fashioned, but if that's how your guy is, then that is how he is. If you don't let a man feel like a man, he will wither before your very eyes (or he'll find someone who makes him feel better about himself than you do).

- **Don't rope him into your extravagance.** Sometimes I like to take extravagant vacations, but I can't expect somebody I'm with to split that with me. I'm the one who wanted to take the vacation, and if I want him to go with me, then I can pay. Let him pay for the things that he wants to do for you. If he can't afford it, he would never take you on a vacation like you might choose for yourself, but he might do other things. Even if he buys you a muffin and coffee or a lipstick you like, that means something to him and it should mean something to you. It's the principle, remember?

- **Factor in the price of effort.** Life isn't just about money. Look at everything your guy does for you that makes up for the finance piece, which is just one small piece of your relationship (even if it sometimes feels like the biggest piece). When a man mows the lawn or carries the heavy packages up the stairs or shovels the snow or washes your car, that's supporting you, too. When a man volunteers or works to make the world a better place even if he doesn't get paid for it, factor in that contribution. When a man is motivated with passion for what he does, even if it's not particularly profitable, that's worth a lot. When a man treats you with respect and chivalry, that's worth major man points. I love it when a guy doesn't let me open the car door, or lets me order first, or puts a protective arm around me in a chaotic situation, or carries my bag. It makes me feel safe and valuable. This is him taking care of you, and it makes up for a lot of the financial part that may be missing.

. . . .

MAN-FORMATION

Unfortunately, when a man feels emasculated by not making as much money, sometimes he can turn into a bigger jerk and won't try to make up for his lack of financial contribution at all. He's angry and that can make someone controlling. He might be competitive in petty ways, he will always want to be right, and he will cut you down as punishment for your success in a warped effort to prove that he is better than you in other ways. If this describes your situation, you need to talk through the issue and get on the same page, and if that doesn't work, you might reconsider the relationship.

. . . .

- **Show him your appreciation.** If you make more money but you truly value your partner's efforts, *tell him*. Positively reinforce this kind of thing and say how much it means to you. It will mean everything to him to know you appreciate and value his contributions, even if they aren't financial. Remember when they came out with those news stories about how much a house-wife should earn for the work she does? Just imagine that situation is flipped and how hard that is for a man to swallow. (We're not the only ones who have to make an effort to swallow.)

- **Find the soft/hard balance.** You have the right to make more money *and* want your man to act like a man, but if you want that, then you have to help him feel like a man. Make a space for that. Stop talking over him. Stop belittling him. If you don't think you do that, then really pay attention because you might do it more than you think. Also stop bringing up money all the time. Try being soft sometimes. I can be known as a hard person, but believe me, even though I'm hard on the outside, I'm soft on the inside. Everybody has a soft side, even men. Maybe you can't be soft all the time, but find where you can be soft. Maybe it's in the bedroom. Maybe it's during your alone time. Maybe it's with family. Find it and you will feel more balanced, and give your man a chance to stand up and flex his muscles (even metaphorically).

· ·

JUST THE TIP

If you are the provider, paying for everything, and your partner really is contributing to society in some way, respect that. However, if he's just running around waiting for the world to give him money and has no problem letting you take on that whole burden, then you have a right to withdraw your respect. You shouldn't be working like a dog while he's out playing golf. If somebody has no issue with being supported by a woman and letting other people pay all the time, or if he has no idea how to work and is entitled, wanting things to be handed to him all the time, run like a thief in the night.

· ·

- **Indulge in generosity.** It's easy to slip into the stereotype that the man should be generous with the woman, but you can be generous and bighearted, too. This is easy for some women, a lot harder for others, but what can it hurt? If you do it with real generosity rather than expecting something for it, it will make you both feel good. I was recently with my guy when we met his friends for a large and very expensive dinner. When the bill came, he picked it up. I glanced at it and saw it was $600. He's a guy, so he felt the need to pick it up since the dinner was his idea and because guys feel so much pressure around money issues and who pays what. I knew it would be stretching things for him to pay that bill, so I subtly handed him my credit card under the table and whispered, "Let's split it." He could be the big man and pick up the tab, and I could feel good about helping him out in a tight spot. This wouldn't always work, and you have to do it in the right way. You have to take a man's temperature at certain points regarding how he is feeling about money. If I would have made a big show about picking up the tab, or if he was already feeling sensitive about me paying for everything, he might have been offended, but because I did it without letting anyone else know and because he is a confident man, he really appreciated that gesture.

There are other ways to be generous, not with your money but with your expectations. Maybe he really wants to pay for dinner all the time. It is generous to take the pressure off for it to be an expensive event every night. Maybe you say, "Hey, let me cook for you tonight," or "I'll buy the groceries since I'm getting home first today," or "Tonight let's just get Taco Bell and chill out." If you don't make it about the money, but instead make it about your time together, you take the pressure and stress off the guy. Don't make him stretch the limits of his financial capabilities just to prove he really likes you.

A generous person will take you out for $2 pizza and make you feel like he's a big shot. People who are cheap get anxiety when the bill comes. I was once with somebody who was terribly cheap, who never minded me paying for everything, but if he had to pay, then as soon as the bill came, it was always uncomfortable. He would scan it to make sure nothing was added and get this look in his eyes like he was physically in pain. A cheap guy I had been dating for about 3 months took me to Chelsea Piers on Valentine's Day and when I said I wanted to get a muffin, he let me pay for it. Later, we went to Greenwich Village and I picked out some $60 perfume. He let me pay for that, too. On Valentine's Day. A little thought or gesture would have gone such a long way. It wasn't about the money, it was about the attitude. I should have run. Later in my life, a guy I was dating, who was very generous but didn't have a lot of money, bought me a pair of sunglasses I admired one sunny day when I had forgotten mine. That made my life. It was such a small thing, but every time I wore those sunglasses, I felt proud.

JUST THE TIP

A generous partner is a valuable partner, and a cheap partner is a burden. Chronic cheapness is very hard to cure. It's like a sickness and it's a huge turnoff. Some people are naturally cheap, and it makes everything to do with money uncomfortable. Being cheap isn't the same as being thrifty. People who are thrifty are smart with their money and don't waste it. I'm a frugal person, but I will buy people Christmas presents from Hermès. However, I will go crazy on my assistants if they waste money. Once I asked them to FedEx something from the Hamptons to the city, and they spent more on the shipping charge than the item was worth. I was furious. I get crazy about wasting money, but I don't think I'm cheap. I think I'm sensible. I'm definitely not wasteful.

• **Share life.** No matter who makes more money, you have to have something together that you share the expenses on, so you both feel like you are contributing. When you take a vacation or go out to eat, you should both at least contribute something—if you pay for dinner, he can pay for the cab. If you buy the plane tickets, he pays for dinner. Not only do you help balance the power struggle, but you are working together to create memories and experiences. That's worth a lot.

I think it's also important to share a bank account—but not your only bank account. In my opinion, a couple living together or married should have a joint account for joint expenses, but they should both also have their own accounts. You each have your nest eggs, and you each have an account for buying personal things like your beauty supplies and salon expenses and his golf fees and electronic gadgets (if I'm going to be totally stereotypical but descriptive of my own experience). You use the joint account for the things you do together, from paying the rent or the mortgage to taking vacations and dry cleaning. You could structure how much each person contributes to that joint account based on income, then pay things out of it evenly. But always have your own account, whether you make more or not.

- **Be proud of yourself.** As a woman in a man-centric world, you get to be powerful enough to be in a role that most women just fifty years ago couldn't have dreamed of. The fact that the first section in this chapter is about when the woman makes more money is a testament to that shift in our culture, and it's awesome. Go, you!

. . . .

JUST THE TIP

If you don't share an understanding about where you both stand with your financial situation, you risk losing respect for each other. If you degrade him for not making enough money, you can lose respect for him, and if he is constantly injured by your attempts to punish him for not making enough money, he can lose respect for you. This shows up most obviously in the bedroom. Mutual respect is directly connected to the sexual dynamic, so if things aren't working there, it could be a sign that there is a money or power issue.

. . . .

Strategies for When Someone Else Supports You

If you are in the more traditional role of the wife or girlfriend who is financially dependent on a partner, your issues will be the flip side of the issues I've been discussing. For women who depend on someone else, self-esteem can be a huge issue.

I was once in a serious relationship with a man who was much richer than I was. Once we were at a blackjack table gambling, and he suddenly looked at me and said in front of everyone, "You're playing like you don't even care. You're not paying attention, and it's not your money anyway." He didn't know I had just spent $1,500 I couldn't afford on a surprise sailing trip for his birthday, but his words said everything to me. He was using money to control me because he who makes the gold makes the rules.

Everything in the previous section applies to you and your partner, only flipped. At the heart of it all is communication. You have to work out a way for you to both feel comfortable, and if your partner is in the habit of undermining you and belittling you because you are not the earner, then you need to say something. Know your value and know what you bring to the relationship. Are you supportive? Do you give great advice? Are you a good mother? Do you keep a nice house? Value is not always financial. This is a hard role to be in because you cannot force someone else to change, but you can definitely let it be known that your contributions, while not financially as significant, matter for your lives together, and you need to be respected for that. If you are sitting around watching TV and eating candy all day, sure, maybe you need to find something more productive to do. However, if you have stayed home to raise your children, or you have a job you are passionate about but it just doesn't pay very much, then that should never be disregarded. Show your partner the first part of this chapter as a starting point for discussion.

Part of the problem could also be you. If you don't respect yourself because you don't make enough money, then you can do something about that. Refer back to chapter 6, "Get a Life."

. . . .

GIRL TALK

Always have your own money. *Always.* I cannot emphasize enough the importance of having a stash of money that is just yours, that nobody else has any say over. Add to it whenever you can because the more you have, the more powerful you will feel. Especially if you are not the breadwinner, you need to know that you have that money, just in case you need it. You never know what life will throw at you—divorce, financial collapse, death. Bottom line: Don't buy those shoes or buy them on sale and stash what you save. Pride yourself on creating a nest egg for yourself. Be a hoarder. Be a chipmunk. It can come and go in an instant.

. . . .

When the Balance Shifts

Just as with control, the power related to money can shift. Maybe your husband made more, but then your kids got older and you got a great job and now you make more, and he suddenly feels threatened. Maybe your husband made all the money but then made some bad decisions or the economy negatively affected his line of work, but you're at home with the kids and can't work and are suddenly in dire financial straits. This can make you resentful and angry at him for failing as a provider when you can't help out. Maybe you were the breadwinner but then he suddenly got a promotion and now he makes more than you and you're the one who feels threatened. Or what if you made all the money for many years, but then the tables turn when you lose your job and your partner starts making the big bucks? This is confusing and it makes things like divorces crazy. If a woman is with a man for twenty years supporting him while he earns his professional credentials or works his way up the ladder, does she deserve half of everything when they get divorced? And what if they were only together for a little while? What if the genders are reversed? Is that the same? It's a sticky gray area for sure, and you should always be ready for it by knowing how you both feel about financial issues and having a plan (and a prenup!).

The most important thing to remember is that the flow of money, like the flow of energy, is always changing, and if you pin all your relationship hopes and dreams on money, you will be disappointed eventually. He who makes the gold makes the rules, but the rules change, and the gold changes, and today's rich man can easily be tomorrow's poor man.

A relationship is about you and another person, not about the bank account balance. That connection has to be strong. But never underestimate the power of the bank account balance to erode your connection. It can happen to anyone. You have to ride it out if you want to stay together, and you have to talk about it. Sometimes, a frank discussion without emotion can strip money of its power over you, at least temporarily. Keep talking. What triggers you? What can you deal with? What do you need? What does your partner need? It's your best weapon and your best defense, because what remains unspoken has the most power of all.

I have been in the position of standing in front of my partner while he held his hand out to me, wanting me to fill it with money. This disgusted me, but I think it may have also disgusted him. I sensed that it made him bitter and angry, and maybe it wouldn't have been quite the same if the genders had been reversed, but the power dynamic remains. This is what has to come to the surface. "Where are we with money? And how can we handle it so it doesn't tear us apart?" I don't have all the answers, but at least now I know that I have to keep asking the questions.

· ·

DR. AMADOR SAYS . . . .

If you or your partner make a lot of money (or if both of you do), this raises a special problem: Am I desired because of my money, or for who I really am? There is no question that wealth makes a person more attractive. We don't need research to tell us that. Nevertheless, the research has been done, especially with men (it's much less clear, at least according to the studies, whether money makes a woman more attractive). For both sexes, in my experience, money creates insecurity about being loved and sows seeds of distrust. It's the third person in the room. Being able to talk about money is key to resolving these feelings, and if your partner won't talk about it, that is a problem and may be a warning sign.

—Xavier Amador, Ph.D., president,
LEAP Institute, www.leapinstitute.org

. . . .

CHAPTER 9

• • • • • • • • • • • • • •

Getting It On

*If you kiss on the first date and it's not right, then there will be
no second date. Sometimes it's better to hold out and not kiss for
a long time. I am a strong believer in kissing being very intimate,
and the minute you kiss, the floodgates open for everything else.*
—JENNIFER LOPEZ

You can think up a million rules about how you should and shouldn't
have sex, and then you could break them all. They say you should never
have sex on the first date, and that's often true, but I've been known
to have the occasional one-night stand. Sometimes it's a disaster. Once,
however, I had been miserable and hadn't had sex in a long time. I met
this guy, and he was a total player, aka "a dog." I knew it wouldn't go anywhere anyway, so we had sex knowing we would never go out again. Afterward, it was so good that we looked at each other and we both wondered,
Wait, do we really like each other? Wasn't this hookup supposed to be a joke?
We actually ended up together for a long time. Neither of us wanted
anything out of the relationship, and that took all the pressure off. If we
hadn't had sex on the first date, we probably never would have connected
at all. We broke all the rules, and somehow, it worked out anyway.

Sex is a confusing, exciting, always-interesting topic, and in many
ways it defines relationships. There are a million ways to have sex. Hot
and heavy, slow and sweet, quickies, all-nighters, morning wake-up calls,

nooners, middle-of-the-night half-awake sex, acrobatic sex, lazy sex, role-playing sex—and then there are a million more positions, from the most traditional missionary styles to those often-hilarious attempts to imitate the weirdest pages in the *Kama Sutra*. Oral sex, back-door sex, breakup sex, makeup sex . . . hold on, did it just get hot in here, or is it me?

Sex is a foundation in a relationship. It is a symbol of your connection. It's not the only foundation, but for most people, it's pretty important. I asked a lot of friends about this, and most of them agree that when sex is working, everything else works a little better. Good sex doesn't solve all your problems, but it is an indication of a good connection and communication in a relationship. When it's not working, everything else feels a little bit off, even if you both pretend (sometimes for years) that everything is fine. You might have to live without it, or without as much of it as you would like. Sometimes there are barriers, like postpartum periods and menopause or erectile issues. Sometimes there are trade-offs and you decide that sex isn't as much of a priority as other things, like companionship or financial or emotional support. But for most of us, sex matters and is a revealing barometer for a relationship.

In the same way that you have to face your money noise and deal with it before it destroys your relationship, you also have to deal with sexual issues. Sex can be hard for some couples to talk about because some people get embarrassed talking about sex. If you have trouble talking about it, or relaxing when you do it, or obsessing about it, or wanting a lot more of it or a lot less of it than your partner, these are issues to get out in the open, no matter how embarrassing one or both of you think it is. *Let's talk about sex, baby!*

. . . .

JUST THE TIP

Good sex usually means good communication, but sometimes you can use it as an excuse not to deal with a problem. You tell yourself that everything is okay in your relationship because you just had good sex. However, the rush of the hormone oxytocin you get after a good orgasm is like a drug that makes you believe everything is wonderful.

It can be a temporary escape but it doesn't solve any issues. Enjoy sex and use it to communicate, but don't use it as an excuse.

• •

Come out of the Closet

The number one thing I would like to tell women about sex is that it's okay to like it. Even love it. It's also okay to talk about it. Thanks to the TV show *Sex and the City*, a lot of us are more liberated in being able to talk about it as well as like it. If you are in a relationship and you like sex, there is no reason to hide it. Embrace it.

This used to be hard to do, but it's changing. A girlfriend of mine told me that when her mother caught her in a compromising position with a boy in high school, she was taken aside and asked in all sincerity by her parents: "Why would you *do* something like that?" She remembers wanting to say, "Um . . . because it's *fun*?" This was in the 1980s, and she remembers feeling too ashamed to actually admit she enjoyed it. Her parents just assumed the boy was pressuring her, and she didn't correct them. She just shrugged and said something about how *he* wanted to do it. This was true but certainly not the whole truth.

I recently read that at least 30 percent of pornography viewers are women (although women are much less likely to pay for porn). I won't go into the politics of pornography here, but suffice it to say that *we are interested*. We want to get turned on and we want to get off.

Being a sexual person doesn't mean you want sex all the time. I'm a Scorpio, and they say it's the most sexual sign, but to me it's more about quality than quantity. I want sex to be amazing, but I don't need it every day. Sometimes I just want physical contact, even if it's just being cuddly or putting a hand on an arm while listening intently. That's okay, too. All kinds of physical contact are okay if both of you like it.

But sex also comes with a lot of complications, like:

- When should you do it? How soon is too soon? What if it's bad?
- What if you do it before you know you should?
- What if you have no sexual chemistry?

- What if you lose your sexual chemistry?
- How do you get your groove back?
- What if you can't have an orgasm?
- What if he can't get it up?
- What do you do about sex after divorce?
- What do you do about sex after childbirth?
- What do you do about sex when you have children?
- What about masturbation?

Let's talk about all of it, because everybody has an opinion and we all want to know what the rest of us are thinking about sex.

. . . .

MAN-FORMATION

There is a stereotype that men want sex all the time and women don't. This has often been my experience, but I also know a lot of people who seemingly have the opposite problem. The woman needs and craves the physical contact and emotional benefits of regular sex, but the guy, for whatever reason, just doesn't go there very often. Although some people say that this can be a sign that he is having an affair, I think more often it is a matter of low self-esteem or stress or even a physical problem. In my opinion, *all guys want sex all the time*. It's just that some of them might not be able to follow through, for a variety of physical and/or emotional reasons.

If this happens to you, maybe you can talk about it and make a deal to have sex more, but if sex doesn't work for a guy, it is a very sensitive topic. Tread lightly. Just like a guy's ego can be destroyed when he doesn't make as much money as a woman even if she never says anything, a guy's ego can be destroyed when he can't get it up even if she never says anything. If this is a regular problem, seriously, make an appointment for him to see a doctor. Or maybe the problem isn't that he doesn't want to have sex, but that he doesn't want to have the kind of sex you want to have. Maybe you want him to go down on you more often, but he doesn't really like to do that. Would you rather have a guy who goes down on you all the time even if you're not attracted to him? If you have great sexual chemistry but you don't share all the same likes and dislikes when it comes to technique, this is something worth working on, or even doing without. Can you get that same kind of enjoyment in some other way? What about the handheld shower attachment? What about toys? What about fantasizing? You have options. He might wish you would give him blow jobs more often or have anal sex, but if the chemistry is there and you have a real connection, he's not going to end the relationship over it if you aren't with doing that stuff. It can go both ways. We all have a right to our preferences.

In the meantime, refer to the section on masturbation later in this chapter. It could change your life.

· ·

The First Time

The first time I ever had sex, I was sixteen years old and it was Valentine's Day. I was in love with my boyfriend, and we were at a friend's house, staying over after a party. It was romantic for a first time. I know it isn't always. I got lucky. I got lucky with a guy I was recently dating. The first time we had sex, we had it several times, and again the next morning, and I felt like it made us closer. We got to know each other. We connected, and the connection was strong. But I've had other first times that didn't go so well—first times that were awkward or uncomfortable. Sometimes you do it all wrong, or the other person messes it up, or the chemistry is off, or the rhythm is off, or you regret it the next day. So how do you get it right?

When you first meet someone and connect and you have that chemistry, it's not going to take long before you both start silently wondering when sex is going to be on the table. (Not literally on the table. Or maybe literally on the table . . .) This can be a time of game-playing. A woman can have a number of dates or days in her mind that she is supposed to wait to be respectable. A man can be focused on the conquest and getting sex as soon as possible, even if he knows, logically, that the relationship isn't ready for it yet. The natural evolution of when sex should happen is often somewhere in the middle, but the internal question about it is likely to happen after just a few dates . . . or halfway through the first date.

This is all part of the buildup. Never underestimate the power of the buildup! There is a reason why when there is a TV show with sexual tension between two people, they try to draw it out as long as possible. Sexual tension keeps people watching. If they let those characters have sex too soon, the bubble bursts and people aren't as interested in the show anymore. This happens in real life, too. There is an exciting and productive tension in the relationship time before you have sex, and once you do it, you can never get that time back. Don't rush through this stage. It's fun and it's also a fact-finding mission, because you are clearheaded in a way you won't be after you get physically intimate.

Part of this tension is an element of cat and mouse. That tension and banter and give-and-take are all part of the dance. We draw them in. We entice them. We imply that sex with us will be great, but then we hold them off because we know we shouldn't do it too soon and we don't want to be "that girl," or we genuinely aren't ready but want to keep the other person interested until we are. We advance and retreat, advance and retreat. We play the traditional roles—the man trying to get the woman to say yes, the woman saying no until she doesn't say no anymore—or we flip the roles, with the woman in pursuit and the man playing hard to get. Either way, it's a game.

MAN-FORMATION

Men like a good game. They don't want it to be too easy. They don't want *you* to be too easy, unless they are already pretty sure you are one of those girls they will have fun with and then move on from. If that's what you want, too, then you don't need to read this. Just go do what you want. But if you want something more, then you should know that men are intrigued and driven crazy (in a good way) by the tease of the possibility of sex and the delayed gratification of not getting it right away. As long as they think there is a good chance they will get it *eventually*, they are happy to play the game with you.

What is the point of this and why don't we all just bang it out the first time we meet an attractive stranger? Because sex is pleasurable, but it's not just about pleasure. It's too important to treat like an ice-cream cone or a box of movie candy. Overindulge too soon and there will be consequences. If you value a relationship or see long-term potential, neither one of you wants to screw it up. And premature sex *can screw it up*. Here's why:

- **Your reputation.** Right or wrong, if it gets around you had sex on the first date, it can influence your reputation. Right or wrong, a guy will see you differently after you have sex. No matter what else is going on, they *will* see you differently. Know this. If you go for it, own it.

- **Low stakes.** If a guy thinks you are too easy and not a challenge, he will get bored sooner. You have to give him something to strive for and anticipate. And don't you want something to anticipate, too? Waiting can be fun—tense and exciting and something you can build up in your mind and look forward to, like gazing at a cake in a bakery window and knowing you can't have it until your birthday.

- **That awkward moment.** Sex changes things. It changes your dynamic and it can feel awkward afterward. You don't want to change things before you even know what they are, or you won't ever really know what they are apart from the mind-altering influence of sex. If you aren't ready, you also may not fully realize the implications of what you've done and that can take some time to figure out.

- **The clingy/needy factor.** Premature sex can make people clingier and needier than they would be if they waited longer. Sex sets up expectations for both partners and can make people feel unreasonably jealous or petty about things that wouldn't otherwise matter.

- **Imbalance.** If your emotional connection hasn't matured before you have sex, then the relationship gets out of balance because it is physically way ahead of where it is emotionally. This will involve playing catch-up. Your emotional relationship has to catch up to your physical relationship, and that can be confusing for everyone.

- **Delayed gratification.** Delayed gratification builds excitement, so when you do finally have sex, it will not just mean more but be more exciting.
- **Ignorance.** The quality of premature sex is not indicative of the quality of long-term-relationship sex. Before you really know somebody, it's hard to know how to make love to them (or bang them). That goes both ways. If you botch it, that can stick. If he is clumsy or awkward, you will remember that. There are exceptions. Sometimes the chemistry is there right from the start and it's always awesome. Sometimes the chemistry isn't there and it's never going to be awesome. However, if you give it some time, you'll both be more confident about what you're doing because you will really know each other.
- **You haven't hooked him yet.** If he hasn't fallen in love with your personality yet, if he is not emotionally hooked on you yet, then the sex better be mind-blowing. Otherwise, you have no leverage. You can come off as promiscuous or destroy what might have been a promising relationship. When you don't know someone very well, you have to keep your game tight, and that's not easy with your clothes off or in the morning with a hangover. If you look sloppy or have bad breath at the beginning, it's just gross. When someone really loves you, it's charming. I read an article recently that said men reported not caring about giving an orgasm to a hookup, but they did care about giving an orgasm to a girlfriend. Maybe wait for the orgasm. The exception: Rarely, a very strong initial connection can override the other factors. It can happen.

All that being said, every rule has an exception, and maybe that's you. I know a few examples of couples who had sex on the first date and ended up married anyway. Either the connection was just very natural, or they managed to work through the extra hurdles that premature sex created. It can work, but it makes things more difficult. If you aren't emotionally ready for sex, if your physical relationship has jumped ahead of your emotional relationship, then you will probably have to do some backpedaling if you want to save it.

So when should you have sex? There are no hard-and-fast rules. It depends on who you are and what kind of relationship you want. What are your goals for the relationship? It's not the 1950s, where you're supposed to wait for marriage. In the twenty-first century, that would be a little weird (although not unheard of). How will you know if you are sexually compatible, or even whether you should move in together, if you haven't bonded on that physical level? But the first date is almost always too soon, and in the majority of cases, so is the second. But the third real date, when you are connecting? Go for it. On the other hand, sometimes you just want to have sex, and it doesn't matter that much to you who you have sex with. Then again, maybe you are fifty-two years old and divorced and you just want to get laid, so who cares about a commitment or a relationship? Maybe you are in your thirties or forties and you've been through it with someone and now you just want to have fun without all the bother. It is what it is, and when you are all adults, you can do what you want.

If your vagina has cobwebs on it, you might need to just jump in and do it. If your vibrator battery has burned out from overuse or you are rubbing yourself against the washing machine on the rinse cycle, you might be long overdue. This is low-stakes sex, and it doesn't have to be a big deal. If the chemistry isn't there, trust and confidence and a little booze can help. Get it out of your system, and then move on with your life. Eventually you will find somebody worth the sexual tension of waiting longer.

For a good prospect, I can't possibly tell you how many dates are right to wait. It really depends on how your relationship is progressing and who you are. You won't always do it right. I've had a couple of one-night stands, and some of them have been fun, and some of them I regretted. I've had sex too soon and had to do some damage control by backing off and not being needy like I wanted to be, and other times, it turned out not to matter (which means it actually wasn't too soon). The only way to know for sure is to know yourself and never do anything that gives you a bad feeling or makes you uncomfortable, including when you consider the aftermath.

If you really want to be sure you don't screw up a promising relationship, consider these tried-and-true signs that your new relationship is or is not ready to withstand the new set of pressures that come with a sexual relationship:

YOU'RE NOT READY	YOU MIGHT BE READY
It's the first date. This is true almost without exception. I did fall in love one time on a first date, but that's very unusual. First date sex usually turns into a one-night stand, which is fine if you know that's what it is. It's either instant gratification and it's fine, or it's just awkward and you never quite recover.	You've had multiple dates and your sexual chemistry keeps getting stronger. You both like and respect each other, and you feel confident that the other person will call you the next day.
Your main reason for wanting to sleep with him is that he's hot.	Your main reason for wanting to sleep with him is to deepen a connection you both already feel. (He can also be totally hot.)
You are obsessed with having it, but you never think about how you will feel afterward. You just want instant gratification.	You are in sync. You feel trusted and respected, and you are pretty sure the other person will be gentle and generous in bed.
The other person is pressuring you to do it.	You are not in any way pressured to do it.
You aren't sure you totally trust the other person.	You totally trust the other person, not because you want to but because that person has already proven himself trustworthy.
One of you has no interest in a committed relationship, and one of you definitely wants a committed relationship. You're not on the same page.	You both have the same feelings about commitment—either you could both see your relationship going in that direction, or neither of you is interested in commitment and you are both fine with that.

YOU'RE NOT READY	YOU MIGHT BE READY
You aren't sure the other person likes you, but you think sleeping together might help win him or keep him.	You know the other person likes you, and the feeling is mutual. You don't need sex to prove it.
There are some red flags, and you hope having sex will fix or override them. You think if he knows how good you are, you will suck him in or change him or he won't leave you.	You both think very highly of each other and feel lucky to be together. You can't believe you have such a great person in your life.
You only want to have sex when you drink too much. In the cold and sober light of day, he's not attractive to you. Alcohol is a panty dropper. Beware because you won't feel the same tomorrow.	You want to have sex with him *every time you see him*. Even in the morning.
You're just lonely. Or you want to have a boyfriend. You don't necessarily care who it is.	You have your own life and you are happy, but when he's around, he makes you happier and you feel even better about yourself.
You feel like the other person just wants it. It doesn't really have anything to do with you.	You can talk about the future together without tension, even if you are both undecided about what that means.
You don't really feel like it.	You both just want to do it. And you do. And it's fine.

The bottom line is that it's probably up to you. No guy is "different from the others." Every single guy has the goal of getting laid, and every girl says her guy is different, that he's not like that. I'm here to tell you that if he's not like that, he is gay.

That being said, guys don't actually want you to sleep with them on the first date if they really like you. Remember that they want to pursue. Don't make it too easy. They will take it if they can get it, but it will

change their opinion of you. Even if it works out, they will always remember that you let them have it on the first date, and they might always
wonder if you were like that with everyone. Maybe you were, and you're
okay with that, but if you aren't, it's something to think about. Go ahead
and do it, but know that you are rolling the dice. You might not make that
connection. You have to be willing to lose the guy.

Sometimes it's worth it, though. Just don't sleep with somebody's
friend. The world is very small and that's not a good look.

If you really think about it, you will probably know when you are
ready—maybe you won't be 100 percent sure, but 80 percent sure is pretty
good odds. Don't let yourself get talked into something you don't really
want to do, but don't hold out for longer than you really want to just because external pressures tell you that you should. Know why you are doing
it, and know you can handle it. Most important, know this: You do not owe
sex to anyone. Not even if he spent a lot of money on you. (*Especially* if
he spent a lot of money on you.) A gift, a nice dinner, even a trip does not
obligate you to have sex. You do not *ever* have to have sex with someone if
you don't want to. Sex should *always* be mutual. Never forget that.

Oops! You "Accidentally" Had Premature Sex

So maybe it's too late for my fancy chart and you've already done the
deed, and done it too soon. Maybe you drank too much and your inhibi-
tions and judgment were off. Maybe you needed it and you couldn't resist
it. Maybe you had a one-night stand. Maybe it was fun at the time but in
the morning, you knew you'd fucked up. You weren't ready, or he wasn't
ready, or whatever. So the question is, what do you do about it?

You have to get the ball back.

The first line of defense is to be light about it. Laugh. Leave, and don't
offer your number. If you really want him to call, say thanks, you had a
great time, give him an awesome kiss, and say you have to go. Be confident, never needy. Let him feel good and get out before he can regret anything. Keep it light, bright, and casual, then forget it, like you are never
going to see him again. Don't text. Don't call. This is way more easily said
than done, but you've got to do it if you want to get the ball back. This is

the best way to get him to pursue you, even though you gave up the goods a little too soon. If it doesn't work, it wouldn't have worked any better if you had been needy and called him every fifteen minutes, and at least you get to move on with your dignity intact.

. . . .

JUST THE TIP

You've seen it in romantic comedies and maybe you've actually said it or heard it: the premature "I love you," an often innocent or off-the-cuff comment followed by chirping crickets and a look of alarm in the person to whom it was directed. Oops. What do you do now? How do you get your foot out of your mouth, or smooth it over if someone said it to you too soon?

1. If you are the person who said "I love you" too soon, make a joke, like, "Of course I mean I love you, I love myself, I love my dog, I love everyone!" or even, "I said 'ya,' right? I love ya. Because that's totally different."

2. If someone said it to you too soon and you can tell they are panicking about your response, smooth over the situation. Smile warmly and change the subject. If the "I love you" warrants a more serious approach, you could say you are guarded and it's hard for you to open up, but when you do it is major, so you hope he will be patient with you. If you know you don't feel it and you're not sure you ever will, don't lead the person on. Don't say it if you don't mean it. You could be totally honest: "I appreciate that you feel like that, but it's too soon for me to say it in return honestly."

. . . .

When You Finally Do It

You finally did it. It was awesome, and the earth moved, and you both woke up all cuddly and moony and romantic and you can't get enough of each other. Or not. Maybe it wasn't as good as you thought it would be. Maybe you are confused or disappointed, or pleasantly surprised. No matter how you feel after you've done the deed, make no mistake: Your relationship has now changed. You don't just know each other. You *know* each other. You are now officially more vulnerable, and you have more to lose. But you also have more to gain.

If your relationship progresses from here, my one piece of advice is to take it easy. This is not the time to make demands, including the demand to know what it all means. Figure out what it means to you before you require your partner to say what it means for him or her. Do not start obsessing, or clinging, or hovering over your phone waiting for a text. This is hard to do, but it is essential to let things progress in a healthy way from here. This is the time to let the relationship breathe. You have made a major step forward in intimacy, so you need to be sure you also maintain your separate identities and don't collapse into each other and become a codependent mess.

Maybe this will be easy for you, but for some women, it's a huge challenge. We are programmed to cling, to some extent. The release of estrogen and oxytocin that happens with physical contact and especially with orgasm actually changes your brain, and you will want to hang on to that other person with a death grip. You will want to call and text constantly, to spend every second together. When you are apart, you might feel like you will die if you don't see the other person. These chemicals make a new relationship feel like love. You might tell yourself you are deeply in love, and maybe you are. However, enduring love is what grows over the long term. This is chemistry, but it's a natural impulse that can actually have the opposite effect from what is intended in our current culture.

. . . .

DR. AMADOR SAYS . . .

I respectfully disagree that women are "programmed to cling." The reason I disagree with this is that I see it as a form of negative self-talk. If this is what you are telling yourself, even as a joke or to disarm or to be sarcastic, such comments can change something good and natural about you into something bad and abnormal in your own mind, and this is harmful. Women do have an evolutionary and social imperative to value relationships more highly than men, but that is not "clinging" and is not a bad thing.

—Xavier Amador, Ph.D., president,
LEAP Institute, www.leapinstitute.org

This is why you have to be so careful. Your logical mind can override your impulse to cling and smother, but you have to know and recognize the impulse and then choose to moderate it. Know this and know yourself, and take a deep breath. You can do this. Let intimacy grow naturally from here. It can't grow if you smother it. Most importantly: Be yourself. Don't take everyone's advice right now. It's about you and your partner, and what's right for both of you in terms of together time and emotional vulnerability totally depends on your dynamic. Just be open and real and give the other person just enough space to get perspective.

JUST THE TIP

You don't always have to be in the mood to have sex and it isn't compromising yourself to have sex with someone you love even if you don't necessarily feel like it that minute. Maybe it becomes part of your relationship's natural give-and-take. Your partner might not like shopping, or might rather eat at McDonald's than the health food café you love, but he might do it sometimes because you like it and because you will return the favor in the bedroom. You can provide oral sex (or whatever the desired act might be, assuming you are okay with it), you can cook dinner in a negligee, you can play naughty French maid or whatever it is that turns your partner on, not because you are necessarily dying to put on a French maid costume but just because you know your partner would love it. You might also know the relationship needs it, if you haven't had sex for a while. Then it's time to go to the mall or watch that romantic comedy. He'll be in a much better mood for compromising. Everybody gets what they want, and nobody is overly inconvenienced. It's win-win.

. . . .

Sexual Chemistry

If you were to ask some of my exes if I was a sexual person, a few of them might say the bed felt like a sheet of ice. That would be fair enough, and the reason is because with some of my former partners, I liked them as people but I wasn't sexually attracted to them. In other words, we didn't have sexual chemistry.

Sexual chemistry is a mysterious thing. Either you have it or you don't. Sexual chemistry is impossible to fake. Just think about movies and the characters who do and do not have chemistry. Ryan Gosling and Rachel McAdams had it in *The Notebook*, but Ryan Reynolds and Sandra Bullock did not have it in *The Proposal*. Brad Pitt and Angelina Jolie had it in *Mr. and Mrs. Smith*, but Johnny Depp and Angelina Jolie did not have it in *The Tourist*. You've probably had it before. It's that feeling that makes you a little bit weak in the knees, that hijacks your brain, that gives you butterflies when you think of the other person. When you have it, physical affection, even holding hands, can make you swoon. When you don't have it, physical affection can feel unpleasant. I know that for me personally, I can't fake it. If I have sex with somebody and there is no sexual chemistry, it makes me feel dirty and upset and I get anxiety. It's just a bad feeling.

You can't determine sexual chemistry with logic, but your gut knows when you've got it and when you don't. If you aren't paying attention, or if you are focusing on other things, like a man's reputation or job or money or cool car, you could trick yourself into getting too involved with somebody who doesn't really have long-term relationship potential. However, if a relationship does not have sexual chemistry, then trust me when I say that you will have a problem, if not today, then somewhere down the line. It might not be an insurmountable problem. You can live without sexual chemistry (see the next "Just the Tip" box). However, if you are pretending you have it because the guy looks good on paper, you are fooling yourself, and the relationship probably won't last, unless you are not a sexual person.

• •

JUST THE TIP

What if you're not sure whether or not you have sexual chemistry? Maybe the sex is "good enough." Maybe you don't think sex is that important to you, but you're not sure because you've never had really great sex. Maybe you associate great sex with flings and your stable, vanilla sex life makes you comfortable, even without the fireworks. Maybe your partner can't always get you off, but you're fine with pleasing yourself to fill in the gaps. You don't have to get everything from your partner. Or maybe you are crazy for your partner but you're still not quite sure if he feels the same. There are ways to gauge your chemistry. Do you sense small hesitations in yourself or your partner? Do either of you have a reluctance to fully engage? Is your partner selfish, meeting his own needs and leaving you to have your own orgasm, or is that other person trying really hard to please you but it's not happening? The next time you are with that person, tune in to the sexual chemistry. Listen to your body, and carefully observe your partner's body. Bodies don't lie, even if minds can trick you. Do you have a physiological response to that person? Does that person lean in to you when you talk and touch you at every opportunity? Is there a magnetic pull between you or a distance? Is there electricity, or is there dead air? Do you feel like your gestures, emotions, and energy are fully reciprocated or one-sided? Being honest about these questions can help you determine if your relationship has what you need.

• •

Relationships end the way they begin. In the beginning, if your gut isn't totally turned upside down by the thought of that good-night kiss, if you don't go a little bit weak in the knees when you remember what he did to you last night, then you probably never will. Maybe you can live with that and maybe you can't, but don't lie to yourself and say the earth moved when the whole night was actually kind of boring and what you really liked was telling your mom you went out with a doctor.

Maybe you're thinking, *But . . . it was a* Ferrari! or *But . . . he's in medical school!* or *But . . . my biological clock is ticking and he's nice* enough! or *I probably can't do better than this*, or *But my mother/sister/friends really like him!* None of that matters. I don't care how many experts you consult. I don't care what books you read or what vibrators you get. You cannot fix a lack of sexual chemistry.

Maybe companionship and/or financial security and/or prestige are enough for you, if sex isn't that important to you. However, know yourself and don't fool yourself into thinking sex doesn't matter when it actually does. If you spend all your energy convincing yourself that you don't care about sex, you might end up having sex with the golf pro before you know what hit you.

Although you can't define sexual chemistry, it does usually involve some concurrent qualities, like good communication, trust, and mutual respect. You can have sex with someone you don't respect or don't trust, and you can have superficial sex, like with a supermodel, and you can have mind-blowing revenge sex or even hate sex, but over the long term, none of that will be really *good sex* that fulfills you and makes you feel valued. Sexual chemistry isn't necessarily about having sex by the book. It doesn't have to involve people who are necessarily hot or young or agile or experienced or whatever. The chemistry between you and another person, no matter who you are, how you look, how old you are, or anything else, is entirely unique. You have to feel it. And if you had it once, even if it faded, then you can have it again.

Are your personal insecurities holding you back? The most important thing when it comes to great sex is to be good to each other and good to yourself. Maybe you aren't comfortable in lingerie. So forget about that. Some guys don't even like lingerie, but they love a cute pair of boy shorts and a tank top. Find what you are comfortable in and what looks good on you, then own your body. Confidence is the most attractive feature you can have. You can be the most gorgeous girl in the world, but if you aren't confident, you won't be sexy. The girl who really owns it is the girl who comes across as hot. You don't have to be thin to be sexy. You don't have to have big boobs or a big butt or a tiny waist to be sexy. You don't have to be twenty-five or have great hair or skin to be sexy. Everybody looks terrible sometimes. Everybody has bad breath sometimes. Everybody feels gross sometimes, so feeling that way does not disqualify you from the right to have good sex. I just heard that one of the beautiful, famous musicians we all know and love spends $25,000 every day on her glam squad. Don't compare yourself to that. It's an unrealistic image, and probably most of her pictures are airbrushed anyway. Just be you. That's enough. If you have stretch marks or a scar from a C-section or you've had a mastectomy or something else that makes you feel self-conscious, the trust of a committed partner can really help to fuel your desire and help you to let yourself go a little. We spend so much time hyper-focusing on the external physicality of sex symbols and comparing ourselves to those airbrushed images and people whose job it is to look good all the time that we forget what sexy really is. None of that has anything to do with real people and real sex. Sexy means confident. Confidence is everything. Know what makes you feel confident as well as what your partner likes. There are many ways to be sexy and many ways to feel connected to another human being. If you know you are sexy, it doesn't matter what physical attributes you have. You will *be* sexy.

Reclaiming Sexual Chemistry

What if you had it and then you lost it? Pizza is delicious, but if you eat it every single day for twenty years, you're going to get sick of it. A lot of couples who have been together for a long time, especially those who have been married for a decade or two, naturally experience lulls in sexual activity. Many couples get out of sync. They focus on the kids or money or career and forget to focus on each other. Other things can interfere, too—health issues, emotional issues, resentment from issues you aren't dealing with, body image issues, baby weight, hormones, all that shit. Sometimes you are drifting apart and going in different directions. This can cause a sexual relationship to slow down or even stop—the reason why everybody jokes that sex stops after marriage. We all get too busy, too tired, too distracted, too whatever. But if you had it before, you can have it again. If you both want to rekindle the relationship, there are ways. They might not be the same things that got you going when you first met. People change and grow, and you know someone in a different way after years than you did at first. If it's been a long time, it might feel weird or awkward or embarrassing to try something new. This is the time to take a risk. Step out of your comfort zone. Do something a little crazy.

The best way to break out of a rut is to leap out with unexpected behavior. Try something new. Try moves you've never tried before. Be experimental. Not everything will work. Some guys don't want you to touch their hair, but they might go wild if you kiss their ears. Maybe you buy a slinky new nightgown or cute sexy pajamas. Maybe you even bring up watching porn together. Men like a freak in the bedroom, so this is not where you need to be classy and appropriate. You don't want to get raunchy and disgusting. You don't have to hang from the chandelier with whips. Just try adding little bits of spice into your sex life, like you would into a recipe, and watch it heat up. You don't have to be a screamer, but some sexy moaning is always appreciated. If you have limitations or hesitations, communicate them, which will only make your intimacy more meaningful. Be that girlfriend or wife your partner thinks about when you're not around because of how great it was last night. If you push against your insecurities and your dull habits and let your sexual self go a little, even when you don't feel like it at the moment, you will get a lot more out of sex—not just physical enjoyment, but long-term relationship bonding.

. . . .

DR. AMADOR SAYS . . .

I feel compelled to add a word of caution here: Sexual chemistry is an awesome thing. However, beware. Like alcohol and drugs, it can lead to an emotional eclipse—blocking out your gut reactions, logical mind, and good judgment.

Sexual chemistry is not a solid foundation for lasting intimate relationships. It can be one of the cornerstones, but it is never enough on its own. Please don't misunderstand and rename me Dr. Killjoy. By all means, enjoy the chemistry when you have it, and if it's lost and you can reclaim it, revel in that. But like drinking, beware of using it as a means to escape your feelings and worries about what's going on in your relationship. Enjoy, but use with caution.

—Xavier Amador, Ph.D., president, LEAP Institute, www.leapinstitute.org

. . . .

Or maybe that's not really your style but you could see arranging a date night with no cell phones and certain subjects off-limits for conversation (kids, work). Maybe you book a trip together, or you find a new hobby to share. Maybe you join a cycling club together, or take a tai chi class, or learn to surf, or maybe you learn how to work on cars with him or he learns how to do yoga with you—or both, to make it fair. Be present with each other, during sex and at other times, too. You can rejuvenate a connection just by being focused on each other. Look your partner in the eye, touch, respond. Show your enjoyment.

When you get back in sync, the sexual chemistry usually kicks back in. Knowing you once had sexual chemistry is the foundation.

Another way is to just focus on each other more. Be flirtatious. Touch the other person more. Do something unexpected—if you are romantic, put sweet little notes in his pocket or briefcase. If you are daring, text a sexy picture. Or just ask. Your partner might be just as frustrated as you are and might be dying to mention something but not sure you will be receptive. If you let him or her know you feel the lagging passion, too, then you can get creative together.

. . . .

JUST THE TIP

There is nothing like childbirth to kill your sex drive and bring everything to a screeching halt. For six months, everything is pretty messed up down there and your hormones are telling you to stay far away from the penis until you heal. Your husband or boyfriend, however, didn't have to push out a baby. He's feeling fine and tapping his foot, waiting for the green light. It's hardly fair and women can feel this pressure. Even when the doctor says it's okay, that doesn't mean you're ready. Sex feels weird after you have a baby. Your body has been through a lot, whether you had your baby naturally or had a C-section. All the hardwiring inside is out of whack, and it can feel wrong, psychologically as well as physiologically. Basically, you're rusty. You also might have issues with feeling attractive. You might not have lost the baby weight and still don't feel like yourself, or like the way you look. There are a bunch of different reasons why this can be an issue, but just know that it takes a while and should be treated with sensitivity. Eventually, however, it's like riding a bike. You never really forget how to do it. Don't do it if you really don't feel ready, but the sooner you get back into it, the sooner you will start enjoying it again.

Living Without Sexual Chemistry

If you are already in a relationship without much or any sexual chemistry, you might be struggling with this issue. Or maybe not. If you have many other reasons to stay, that can be okay. It just depends on how important sex is to you. For many people, it really isn't that big of a deal. I have a friend who gives her husband a blow job every few days and sends him on his way, and that's enough for both of them. They really don't get into anything more complicated or messy very often, and they're both fine with it. I have another friend who says she and her partner really don't do that much but neither of them minds. I have other friends who do it constantly, even after a decade. Everybody is different.

However, if the lack of sexual chemistry in your marriage nags at you, you may have to realize and accept the fact that you've chosen a life of companionship, safety, and security instead of a life of passion and sexual thrills. I know a girl who married a man battling cancer, and because of the medications he was on, sex simply wasn't on the table. She knew this

and it was a struggle at first, but she got so much love, financial and emotional support, encouragement, and companionship from him that she
decided it was worthwhile. They had their issues, but he was her greatest
fan, was her biggest supporter, and believed in her dream. She lost him
eventually and got into another relationship that was very sexual in nature, but she always looks back fondly and is grateful for how much her
deceased husband changed her life.

I know another woman with an amazing sex life. She and her husband
both have very high sex drives and have sex at least once a day (which
sounds awesome to me—I think sex is one of the most important things
in a relationship, and a good sex life is something to be proud of. Embrace it and don't take it for granted, if you have it). This couple truly
connects physically, but he has no interest in spending more than about
two minutes on a conversation. He's basically a caveman who is good in
bed. It's a trade-off. She spends a lot of time with her girlfriends and gets
her conversational and emotional needs met with them. Then she goes
home for her nightly awesome orgasm. It works for them. A lot of women
I know would hate that kind of relationship. They would rather have the
conversation and the emotional bond, and maybe sex every week or two.

My point is that nobody gets everything out of a single relationship.
What do you really need from a partner, and what do you need from your
friends and family? The more people you have in your life, the more likely
all your needs will be met. If sex is what really matters to you in a partner,
find someone who can give you that. If sex is less important than someone who makes you feel really good about yourself or who can talk for
hours about anything with you, then maybe that's just fine for you. Some
relationships are even "open," where the couple has a strong bond but has
agreed that one or both of them can seek sex outside the relationship. A
lot of people would have a problem with this, but it definitely works for
some.

Whatever you do, don't compare yourself to others. Instead, sit down
with yourself and think about what's most important to you. Don't fool
yourself into thinking something is more important than it is. Picture
yourself living your life without your partner in order to find somebody
who can give you what you think you aren't getting now—but picture

what you might not get from somebody else that you have now and cherish. A rose has petals and thorns, and a relationship has its beautiful parts and its thorny parts. Every relationship. You can't have one without the other, so which thorns are you willing to accept, and which ones are deal breakers for you? Sexual chemistry might not be as important to you as you think—or it might be more important to you than you have been convincing yourself it is. Know yourself, and you can figure out what you need. Then you'll know what you need to do to get it.

. . . .

JUST THE TIP

Don't bring other people into your sex life. Too many cooks spoil the sex, and your sex life should not be a dinner party joke. "Yeah, we used to have sex, but now we're married, ha ha," or "We have sex every night, don't you?" Don't do that to each other—or your dinner guests. Either people will think one of you is having an affair and will secretly congratulate themselves about how they have more sex than you are obviously having, or they will think your "every night" claims are BS or that you are bragging, and you will always have to live up to that standard. Ten years from now, do you still want your friends to be asking, "So, are you still having sex every day?" It's nobody's business, and if you keep it private, it becomes a relationship builder instead of a relationship wrecker.

. . . .

Married Sex

You know what they say about marriage—it's the sex killer. Unfortunately, this is sometimes true. Marriage can take the wonder and excitement and danger out of sex. You are safe and content now, so sex can become predictable, and predictable isn't that exciting, and may eventually give way to other things, like too much TV or spending too much time on Facebook or just working too much and being too tired. On the other hand, with married sex, you can take even more sexual risks because you know you have a foundation of trust.

I know a couple who vowed, when they got married, to have sex every single night. They thought it was romantic and that it would keep them in touch. They did it every single day for the first two years of their marriage. Then one day, one of them said, "You know, we don't really have to do it tonight," and suddenly it just stopped. One night off turned into weeks off, and months. She stopped wearing lingerie, he stopped being romantic, and while they remained friendly and companionable, sexual interaction gradually seemed awkward. Then one night, they decided to meet at a hotel bar, get bombed, role-play a little, and boom—they were back on track. They didn't do it every single day, like a duty, but they are on a several-times-a-week schedule, and now it feels more spontaneous, and they feel more connected and intimate with each other than they ever have.

• •

CELEBS SPEAK OUT

*The romance doesn't have to fade. It's all about keeping it
fresh. I still want her to look at me and be like, "Yo, this is
the man I want to be with." So you gotta keep yourself up,
keep up your p's and your q's, and keep your lady happy.*
—Ice Cube

• •

You don't have to live the stereotype. I get it—life is busy and exhausting, especially if you have young kids. If you were sexually thrilling to each other once, you don't have to keep up that pace as you get older and busier and that seems less crucial, but you should keep that sexual connection if you can. As you get older and more experienced, sex can get more exciting, and even more frequent, just because you live together and have easier access and an automatic willing partner. (Or mostly willing.)

A lot of married couples I know still have sex a lot. Some maybe a couple of times a month, but plenty of them have sex once a week and a few I know still have sex daily. It's not unheard of. Sexual rhythms ebb and flow like a wave. If you go with that, being okay with the periods when you do it less often but always being open to the movement toward doing it more often, then you will stay in touch.

You can also give yourself options. Some people don't want to go on the whole journey the whole time. Sometimes you just want a quick release, or you want to give your partner one without getting undressed. Sometimes you just want some contact without an orgasm. Sometimes a make-out session can make your day. When you take off the orgasm pressure, everybody can loosen up a little. You can fool around for twenty minutes and then move on feeling good about each other. Sex isn't always about scoring a goal. All roads lead to Rome.

• •

CELEBS SPEAK OUT

After being together twenty-one years, I think the key is you have to start out hot for each other in the first place. Then make time to create a space so you can be intimate. Have fun, be creative, get kinky—whatever works for you. Go for it and have fun! Also, respect respect respect! Nothing is hotter than respecting and honoring each other for who you are and they are.
—LISA RINNA

• •

Sex After Divorce

Divorce is heartbreaking and brutal, and even when the breakup is "civil" or "friendly," it's still the source of a lot of misery, regret, self-flagellation, and guilt on all sides, even if your ex doesn't show it. Maybe you were only married for a short time, or maybe for years, but either way it can feel weird and uncomfortable to get out there and try to meet people again after it's over. Maybe you've even forgotten how. Maybe you are gun-shy. You don't want to get hurt again. Maybe you are cynical now, sure there is no such thing as true love. Maybe you are determined never to marry again, but you're lonely and you would just like some companionship, somebody to go out to dinner with or see a movie with or hey, maybe even have sex with every now and again.

But you can meet people again, and you can rediscover those atrophied love muscles (are you doing your Kegels?). You can find that part of you again that is fun and flirty and carefree and loves your life. If you've been in a bad marriage, this might be easier than you think. You are finally free. This is a time to get back in touch with yourself and with the outside world.

The most important thing to remember about dating again after divorce is not to dump your shit on someone else. Don't be that person who whines, "We never had sex," or who confesses, "This is the first time I've done this in years!" Unless you're going to make a joke. Saying, "I haven't had sex since they invented fire," can lighten the mood. Just don't do it in a needy way. Enjoy who you are and what brought you to this place. You are starting over, so don't drag your old baggage with you when you are trying to connect with someone new. You are a different person than you were before your marriage and definitely different than you were before your divorce. Now it's time to discover who that is.

If you really haven't had sex in a while, it can feel very awkward. If you're fumbling with condoms or not sure what to do with your hands or you are self-conscious about your body because you're not young anymore, this can put a crimp in things until you're used to having sex again. You might not have an orgasm very easily or be sure how to help your partner have one. All I can say is that you have to just jump right in and practice. If you are having trouble, get a toy for yourself and use it to get your body back into the mode of feeling sexual. This can really help move things along in the vagina department. Also be patient, because if you are with a man who is older, he may be having a similar problem. Divorced sex has to be a no-judgment zone!

If you have kids, this can be a plus. Many people find mothers very attractive. They are mature and nurturing but earthy and sexy in a grown-up, evolved way. Mothers aren't bimbos. Not every man wants to date a woman with kids, but if you are a single mom, you don't want those men anyway.

There are some definite perks to dating someone who is divorced. You aren't the woman who obsesses about getting the ring so you can say you've been married. If you already have kids, you're not hunting for someone to have kids with. You are a little older, more established in your life, and more interesting because you've had more life experience. Having your own life really helps make you more attractive.

When you have a child, this can also set the pace for a new relationship. Because children always come first, you won't be able to jump in and obsess about a relationship. You are busy being a mom, so things will naturally move more slowly, which is good for you after a divorce. You need time to assess what really went wrong so you don't make the same mistake again. Having a child can enforce that extra time for self-reflection.

. . . .

JUST THE TIP

After divorce, where do you even meet people? A lot of people try online dating and have had some interesting dates that way. I've heard some people are on there just for sex, but others are actually looking for relationships. You can also meet people through friends (if they are friends who really know you) or through your kids. There are a lot of single and divorced parents at the park, picking kids up from school, or at any kid activity. If you want to meet somebody, be open but not desperate. Make eye contact. Smile and be natural. Don't try to force every interaction into a potential relationship. Go easy and it will happen when it's time.

. . . .

But having sex when you are a single mom (whether you've been married before or not) can be a touchy subject. A newly divorced friend of mine was at a party once, talking to another friend who had been divorced for five years. The more "experienced" divorcée said to her, "I would *never* bring a man home to meet my children or even let my kids know I was seeing someone unless I knew we were getting married." Ouch. Extreme, but I totally get it. Especially if your kids have already been through divorce, the last thing you want to do is put them through more disappointment or let them get attached to somebody else who isn't going to stick around. Kids come first, period.

Although it depends on the age of your children, you do need to consider at what point you'll introduce your kids to a possible new romantic partner. If you are friendly with your ex, you might be able to discuss this, but don't rush into the introductions. If you have been with someone for six months, it's probably safe to introduce that person to your kids, but you can always say that someone is just your friend. I have a lot of friends, both men and women, and my daughter has met many of them. She doesn't necessarily pick up on the different kinds of relationships and I don't make it obvious.

If your kids are over age seven, they may pick up on the difference, so ease in. If your kids need the reassurance, you can always tell them that you are not replacing their dad. You are just finding new grown-up friends. Even if you get remarried eventually, every child with two involved parents needs to know that you are not replacing one parent with a new one. There can be many adults in a child's life, and as far as I'm concerned, the more positive role models who love a child, the better. On television, I once saw an interview with Tiger Woods's ex-wife. The interviewer asked her if it bothered her that her ex-husband had a new woman in his life around her kids. She said that the more people who love her kids, the better. I thought that was very evolved.

· ·

EXPERT ADVICE

Kids can be tricky when dating post-divorce. They can become possessive with the fear of losing you, or feel caught in the middle as they attempt to manage their loyalty. Be considerate when introducing your children to your dates. They don't need to meet everyone that you date. Unless a relationship is very serious, I don't advise involving your children. Reassurances about their role in your life can go a long way. Tell them that you will always answer any questions that arise and do it. Remember your love interest is just that . . . yours! Don't shove the relationship down their throat.

—Janet Taylor, psychiatrist, New
York City, www.drjanet.tv

. . . .

Masturbation

Let's talk about this. The word "masturbation" makes some people cringe, but masturbation is sex, and it's pretty handy when you can't get it from someone else. It's quick, you're in and then you're out (literally?), and you feel so relaxed afterward. It helps to lower your stress level, it's great for your skin tone, and it puts you in a good mood. It can relieve menstrual cramps and headaches, and it burns calories, too! Masturbation can also be an empowering experience. It's independent. It's taking care of yourself. It's saying, with your own two hands, "I don't need a man. I can do this on my own!" If you aren't doing it, maybe it's time to give it a try.

A survey of men and women in the United States showed that men masturbate more often than women but that women still do it. The peak age for both men and women is between twenty-five and twenty-nine, during which time 68.6 percent of men and 51.7 percent of women reported masturbating in the last month, and 83.6 percent of men and 71.5 percent of women reported masturbating during the past year. But the numbers don't exactly plummet after that. In their thirties, 62.9 percent of women report masturbating within the last year, and 64.9 percent of women in their forties say the same thing. Even women over seventy do it—32.8 percent admitted to masturbating within the last year. An even more recent study reported that 92 percent of women overall regularly masturbate, which is higher than previous studies reported. Either women are doing it more now than ever, or they are more willing to admit it.

So what's stopping you? Maybe you just haven't really considered it. I know a woman who was divorced but on friendly terms with her ex-husband. They had a few sessions of "ex sex" until he met someone and told her, apologetically, that he didn't feel right about doing that anymore. She complained that she was in her sexual prime and he said something like, "So, you masturbate, right?" She told me she was totally shocked when he said that to her—but less shocked by the idea than by the realization that she never, ever did that. Why hadn't she thought of that herself? Why had she been relying on other people to bumble around down there trying to give her an orgasm and only being successful about 25 percent of the time? She went home that day and promptly gave it a try, and yowza! She realized she could have an orgasm a lot faster than she'd ever had one before, with a 100 percent success rate. How efficient.

Personally, I never masturbated until I was thirty-one years old. It just didn't occur to me. A guy I was dating once said to me, "You need to get a toy." I tried it, and it really does work. (I've also used the jets on the Jacuzzi in a hotel, just FYI.) Masturbation can be great for the many women who can't seem to orgasm easily during sex or who only orgasm with oral sex, because let's face it—you can't always get somebody to do that for you. According to another recent study, 75 percent of women never reach orgasm from intercourse alone, without extra help from a toy, a tongue, or a hand. Ten to 15 percent never have an orgasm at all.

I can't speak for everyone, but I think that masturbation is the ultimate way to know yourself. You can learn, at your own pace, exactly where you like to be touched, what turns you on, what you don't like, and how you have an orgasm. Everybody is different and there is no wrong way to do it, but if you don't masturbate, you might never know the right way for you. You might never have a really good orgasm. If you can't give one to yourself, how can you expect somebody else to do it?

Masturbation is also a great tension reliever. If you're stuck or on a deadline or you can't get to sleep or you're just cranky, lock the bedroom door and have at it. It's great for breaking through creative blocks, getting stuff done, and helping you sleep. It can even make you look healthier and give your skin a nice flush. You can't exactly do it at work, but you can always do it when you get home, if you don't have somebody around to oblige you.

Finally, masturbation fills in the gaps when you need more sex than you are getting or just want to get your body back in the mood for more sex. It is a gift, something you can do selfishly without involving anyone else. Explore your body. Touch everywhere, not just in the obvious places. Literally love yourself. Find your sensitive spots, your ticklish spots, your OMG spots, and see where you can go with them. It's like a sexual fitness workout, and way more fun than a regular workout. It tunes you up and increases your sensitivity and sexual awareness, so you can be a more responsive (and orgasmic) partner. And if you tell your partner about it? It sounds naughty, in a good way, and it might just make "regular" sex better, too.

CHAPTER 10

· · · · · · · · · · · · · · ·

Don't Let Cracks Become Craters

*The meeting of two personalities is like the
contact of two chemical substances: if there
is any reaction, both are transformed.*
—C. G. JUNG

It's ironic that we obsess about and try so hard to get and keep the perfect relationship, and yet we are the very ones who sabotage those relationships. This is something I've had trouble with my entire life. I pour a ton of energy into relationships. I focus on relationships more than I focus on my business, which I know sounds crazy, and I still don't get it right. I still overthink everything. It's a big challenge for me. I've gotten a little better recently, but I still screw up all the time.

My biggest problem has always been my failure to step back and let things breathe. Even though I know, logically, that men need this, that sometimes it's the only way, I still can't seem to remember or stop myself from messing with an already inflamed situation. You can't mess with the engine until you let it cool off, and you can't fix a relationship in the heat of an argument. I know I'm controlling. I know I'm afraid to feel love. I find it scary to be vulnerable. Sometimes fear makes me say things I regret or try to control things it's not my business to control. Sometimes I don't want to let the other person have a life because I'm afraid of what might happen, but then in fear, I sabotage what's good. Sometimes I find it very difficult to know how to balance my own life with wanting someone else in my life. I can be very confusing. This is why I suck at relationships. But then again . . . don't a lot of us suck at relationships, at least some of the time?

• •

DR. AMADOR SAYS . . .

I have to step in early here and say that Bethenny is too hard on herself. When she labels herself a saboteur, she is taking too much of the blame. I have had the privilege of being allowed into her inner life, and I disagree that she sabotages her relationships. Bethenny has great courage, insight, motivation, and many strengths. Relationships are often difficult, and when they don't work, it's because the two pieces just don't fit together. Yes, sometimes we misbehave and do things we regret, but I have seen relationships recover from infidelity and worse.

Taking all or most of the blame for a failed relationship stops you from self-reflection. Blame, including self-blame, leads to blindness. Reading this chapter, you will benefit from many hard-won insights Bethenny has uncovered. If she was truly and wholly to blame for the relationships that didn't work out, she would never have uncovered the lessons you will benefit from as you read on.

Why do so many of us persist in negative self-talk? Simply because these old habits of self-blame and even self-hatred die a slow death, even when you are working on yourself. Bethenny has come a long way and I know she will succeed in going the distance. She is right to be optimistic.

—Xavier Amador, Ph.D., president,
LEAP Institute, www.leapinstitute.org

• •

Relationships are hard to maintain. New or old, married or single, they all suffer normal wear and tear because life is hard. They get cracks, and if you don't patch the cracks, they become craters, and then the whole thing falls apart. If you've ever burned a pot of rice, you know that even though only the bottom layer is actually burned, the whole pot tastes burned, and you can't get that taste out of your mouth, your food . . . or your relationship. Better not to let it burn in the first place. As soon as you notice all the water getting absorbed, add more before it burns.

Whether you let yourself go because you think he doesn't care how you look, or you constantly criticize, or you can't stand his annoying habits one more second, or you think you can be rude and thoughtless and self-centered because you already "have him," or you never openly discuss what's wrong under the surface, or you are embarrassed by his friends or embarrassed by him when you are around your friends, or you keep having the exact same fight over and over again for years, you can probably do a better job at relationship maintenance. You can own your stuff and even fix it. This chapter is about preventing cracks when you can and recognizing them when they are still small and fixable—like when the rice just starts to get brown, and you catch it in time, and throw away the crusty parts, and the rest is still good. Rice doesn't have to be perfectly cooked to nourish you.

Relationships are like eating a healthful diet. They have to work in your life or you won't stick with them. Your relationship should be challenging and delicious and result in personal growth and positive changes in your habits. It should not be suffocating and constricting and full of deprivation, and you should not have to white-knuckle it all the time. You can't force healthy eating and you can't force a relationship. You can set up rules, but sometimes you will break them, and you can't throw it all away because you did something wrong. You need to give it space, let it breathe, work with it, and not fight it. Like that song in the movie *Frozen* says, you have to let it go. Let it become what it is, let it organically grow into your life. A relationship is like a wave, and you can't fight a wave. You have to go with it or get out of the water. This chapter is about how to go with it. (And I know this is easier said than done!)

It Can Happen to You

Maybe you know people whose relationships look perfect. They are not. Maybe you think your relationship has its problems but you won't ever have any serious issues. You are wrong. The biggest mistake you can make is to assume your relationship can't crack. No relationship is indestructible, and even the best ones can go bad if you neglect them. It creeps in, almost unnoticeable. There are different styles of dysfunction and people can be very repressed. Many of us don't express ourselves when we could or should, and before you know it, you are harboring resentment, and then suddenly you've experienced years of deterioration, and then it explodes. Relationships take maintenance, just like a house or a car or a body. If you don't take care of things as you go, the repair bill or the medical bill is going to be huge. You get out what you put in. You don't put crappy fuel in an Aston Martin if you want to enjoy having an Aston Martin.

If the slightest sign of relationship trouble or any bad behavior on your partner's part sends you running or makes you shut down and refuse to face the issue, then it won't take long to develop a crack. Don't do what I did and turn the other way or mess with the crack until it gets bigger and bigger. It's like picking a pimple—it won't get better if you mess with it. Don't complain to your friends and roll your eyes and gag at your husband behind his back but never tell him that you are having an issue. This just creates more tension inside of you. You tell yourself a story, and when you say it out loud to other people, the story just keeps getting bigger and bigger. It's your own internal dialogue getting blown out of proportion, and eventually you're going to spin out. I have two friends who have both been married for many years. They are both miserable in their marriages and cannot stand their husbands. Once they were making lobster for a dinner party and one of the lobsters was dead before they cooked it. I heard them arguing about which of their husbands they were going to serve the rotten lobster to. I also heard one of them say she always poured heavy cream in her husband's coffee, hoping it would give him a heart attack. Do you want to end up like that? I don't.

So let's fix it.

Just Say No to Crack

Relationships develop cracks for a million different reasons. If you aren't paying attention, you could miss them. See if you recognize your own relationship cracks here, and then find out what you can do to repair the damage now, before your relationship looks like the surface of the moon.

Crack #1: Relationship Atrophy

This happens when you get too comfortable and entrenched in a pattern, or you're just bickering all the time and are in a funk. The relationship becomes blah. Nothing exciting happens, you begin to take each other and the relationship for granted, you stop noticing and appreciating each other, and you get bored or a little depressed. You are in a rut because the relationship has stalled. You aren't evolving and changing. One danger of this is that your mind starts wandering (or your partner's does). One or both of you might start thinking about how a new relationship could be exciting, stimulating, and new. This is the fallacy of the "bigger, better deal." It's tempting to think that something better is just over the horizon, but the mistake is not seeking that excitement in your current relationship. You think you would be better off without the relationship, when you're really just not thinking clearly.

Repair Strategy: You are stalled and you have to get the motor running again. What you are doing now isn't working, so you need to change something. One way to do this is to do exactly the opposite of your impulse. If you want to nag your partner for leaving you alone to play golf again, do the opposite. Say, "I think you should go play golf. You deserve a break." Be sincere and kind about it, not mean and sarcastic. When you want to yell, speak softly. When you want to criticize, say something nice. When you want to lie around in your yoga pants, put on something a little sexy. If you don't feel like having sex, turn over in bed to face your partner and be receptive. Reach out. When you really just want to strangle the other person, let out the rope and let him hang himself, and he can't blame you for holding him back.

Remember that *Seinfeld* episode where George Costanza started doing exactly the opposite of every tendency he had, and his whole life got better? This can actually work. You know the character of your relationship and you know your habits, so go the other way and see what happens. You might notice that when you let your partner go free, freedom isn't quite so appealing. Sometimes people do things out of opposition. If you are sweet about your partner's desires, he might change his mind and want to spend more time with you, especially if you've suddenly stopped nagging. When you want to hold on to an argument, just let it go. Force yourself.

Crack #2: Letting Yourself Go

I've been known to hang around the house in baggy sweatpants with no bra and mascara smudges under my eyes. This is fine some of the time (probably not as often as I do it, although with my career, I have to get decked out all the time, so this is my balance). You should be able to feel comfortable and relaxed in your own living space, but if it's a chronic problem, then it's disrespectful to the relationship in the same way it would be disrespectful to a job to show up unshowered and in your pajamas. Letting yourself go is like saying, "I don't need to make any effort to look good for you." You don't have to wear kitten heels all day every day, but when you do, be sure your guy gets an eyeful. When I'm going out to an event and I get all dressed up, I make sure the guy I'm dating gets a chance to see me looking so good, to balance out all the times when I don't.

This goes both ways—it's definitely not just a woman's problem. I have a friend who says that sometimes she looks at her husband when he hasn't showered in a couple of days and his hair is all messed up and he is unshaven and dirty from doing yard work, and she thinks, *He looks like a homeless person. I am a successful and attractive woman and I'm married to a homeless person.* Even if you walk around wearing baggy T-shirts covered in baby spit-up (which you can't always help, but it shouldn't be your go-to look) or you've gotten in the habit of skipping exercise and eating badly and now you're always too tired for sex, and even if he's got perpetual stubble (not in a good way) and sits around watching sports all weekend over the top of his beer belly, you can both pull it together. I have a friend who prides herself on never dressing up, but it can become uncomfortable for others when her hair is all over the place and she's not wearing a bra. Sometimes you have to pull it together.

Repair Strategy: Sometimes it doesn't take very much effort. You don't need to put on a fancy dress and stilettos. I went out one weekend wearing overalls and a half top with a faux tattoo. The guy I was dating thought it was sexy and it really turned him on. It was a little thing, but I put some thought into it and it worked. You can get back in the habit of taking more pride in your appearance by establishing some rules for yourself. Be comfortable at home, but when you go out or spend time together, make an effort. Put on a dress. (A clean dress, not the wrinkled one on the floor.) Get your hair blown out. Get a pedicure. Wear heels or sandals or red lipstick or do whatever is natural for you, that makes you feel good and sexy. Even if the thing you change isn't something your partner will specifically notice (like your toenails), it will make you feel better about yourself, and that translates to sexy and confident. Sometimes, letting yourself go is a sign of low self-esteem, and you just need to take care of yourself a little. Have some me time so you can start to feel more positive. That confidence will not only help you to get out of your rut of bad health habits or lazy hygiene but can also make you appear sexier even without changing anything else. Do it for yourself, not just for your partner.

If it's your partner you're trying to make over, don't criticize. That just makes you look like a bitch. Instead, try positive reinforcement. "I love it when you smell like soap and aftershave." "You look so handsome in that new shirt." "Let's get dressed up and go out tonight—you always clean up so nice." "You look hot tonight!" Or drop some hints. "After the game is over, do you want to go to the gym with me?" "I love how soft your face is after you shave," or "Let's take a bath . . ." Reward any efforts with lots of attention and/or a blow job, which is a highly effective positive reinforcement tool.

Crack #3: Having the Same Fight Over and Over

Why do we have the same fight over and over, in the same way, using the same words? This is the definition of insanity. It's time to stop arguing and start talking. Obviously this is a rule you will break a million times, but the goal is to discuss, not argue. Arguing doesn't work. It is a zero-sum game. Somebody always loses. Instead, you need to define a new style for your communication, calmly and clearly.

The reason people have the same fight over and over is usually because the fight is not about what it's about. You need to get to the core. Maybe you argue about the dishes or the laundry, but the real problem is that you resent how much time he spends with his friends, or he resents how much money you spend, or you both resent how little sex you are having. Maybe one of you can't get over a past infidelity. If you aren't getting to the real problem, you have to find another way in. What is the real problem? You have to keep asking yourself that so you don't get distracted by stupid things that have nothing to do with the real problem.

This is really hard to do because you legitimately might not know what the real problem is, or if you do know, you just might not want to deal with it. You don't want to talk about it, or your partner doesn't want to talk about it. If you aren't prepared to have the real discussion, then sometimes arguing about something peripheral feels safer. The dishes really don't matter all that much, so the fight can blow over, but what if you actually admitted you were unhappy or had lied about being over the cheating, or had to say something embarrassing like, "I need more sex"? That's scarier. Sometimes you just want to talk because you are having all these feelings, but if you don't really understand the issue emotionally, uncontrolled talking can do real damage. If you want to save the relationship, sometimes you have to have the hard conversation, but only when you understand what the issue is, not just intellectually but also emotionally. The good news is that once you have it out for real, then you can stop having the arguments that masquerade as the real issue.

· ·

JUST THE TIP

Sometimes the real issue comes up all by itself. I have a friend who is extremely against smoking. To her, smoking is a deal breaker for any relationship. Then one day she found out that her husband of twenty years had been smoking throughout their entire marriage, on business trips, on poker night, or whenever she wasn't around. To her, this was a major betrayal and she felt almost like he'd cheated on her. She was devastated, not only that he lied to her all those years, but that all their friends knew he smoked and nobody told her. They had to sit down and work it out immediately or it could have ended their marriage. It took them a while to get over it, but they did. And he quit for real.

This wouldn't be a deal breaker for everyone. Everyone has the things that bother them. A cigarette when you're not around might not bother you. To her, it mattered. That's the point—you have to have your own boundaries, not boundaries set by anyone else. You have to know what matters to you and then be true to yourself.

• •

Repair Strategy: Here's what you have to remember: *The argument isn't as important as the relationship.* Does it matter who wins, or will winning only make the other person feel like a loser? When you are both calm and not fighting about something else, you can talk about anything, as long as you stay unemotional. You are likely both at fault in some way. It takes two to fight, and couples get very good at pushing each other's buttons because sometimes, fighting reduces excess tension. But there are always casualties.

Work on listening, not reacting. Work on stepping back and not attacking. Work on sticking with it instead of running away. You have to find your way in. Being soft is the best way. If you already have your ideas about what's wrong and you come in with guns blazing, the other person probably won't hear you. They might never hear you when you come in hot, no matter how cleverly you phrase it, because they are already on the defensive. Instead be soft and open and bring it up gently without emotion. If they are already defensive, completely avoid saying the word "you." This is hard and you won't always succeed, but make it a goal.

Once you get good at this, you can actually anticipate arguments and head them off. Recently, a guy I was dating was planning to watch a marathon that his friend was running in. I figured he would probably be up all night partying afterward, but instead of not knowing and texting him all day wondering where he was and if he was coming back and whether I would get to see him and feeling resentful and frustrated and thinking he was inconsiderate, I decided to ask: "I know your friend is running today—will I get to see you today, in the morning or for dinner?"

"Definitely for dinner," he said. And that was that. I felt the freedom to let him go out and do his thing without being harassed, and I felt calm knowing I would see him and what the plan was. For me, that is important, so I made it happen. If you need to know, make a plan and structure it. Ask for what you want.

There is nothing wrong with saying, "Hey, let's spend some time together tomorrow. I know you're going out, but will you come back at some point and hang out with me?" So many people don't want to impose, but then they impose even more by calling and texting to see what the other person is doing. What women don't always understand is that men don't see time the way we do. To them, time spent watching TV together is the same as time spent having lunch together on a bench in the park. If you happen to be there when they are hanging out with their friends, they consider that quality time, too. We want more out of our time together, but we won't get it by being passive-aggressive about it. We have to ask for it, structure it, make it happen. Once your guy gets a taste of what quality time is really all about, he just might learn and seek it out himself. Fighting about it just causes unnecessary damage and gets you nowhere. Push gently to the core of the issue instead of dancing around it and you can stop having the same fight over and over. The point is to be up front.

Another thing people do when they keep having the same fight is to focus completely on what the other person is doing wrong. They build a case, accumulating evidence for some imagined trial in which they can prove, point by point, how wrong the other person is. They repeat to themselves, "I can't believe he did that" or "I can't believe she said that," and that becomes the whole focus. This is a form of emotional abuse. You are beating the other person up, making them feel worse, even hopeless. It makes them hate themselves and then, in turn, hate you. One good way to stop doing this is to take the focus off the other person and put it on yourself. Nobody is perfect and we all make mistakes. Everybody is a constant disappointment, but what are you doing to make it worse? How are you being a disappointment? Because I can guarantee that sometimes, you are. You don't want to start keeping score, because if your partner starts keeping score, too, you won't like the results. Instead, ask yourself how you can be better. What case might someone build against you? This puts the energy into something you can actually fix, and when you stop your own negative behavior that you were ignoring because you were busy accusing somebody else of something, you become a better partner and less likely to fight. It helps you realize that you are not perfect either, so you become more forgiving.

Another thing people tend to do, no matter how big or small the issue, is to pick and pick and pick at a wound so the swelling can't go down. Whether it's taking out the garbage or getting a divorce, you have to give inflammatory issues time to settle down. Leave it alone so the wound can heal. Men in particular, but also a lot of women, tend to retreat in the face of a serious issue, and badgering only makes it worse. People like this do not want to talk things out, even though they know they should. These people need space to retreat and breathe so they don't feel trapped and react like a wild animal. Really, we are all animals. Some of us are like wild animals trapped in a cage. If you poke at an animal in a cage or in a corner, it will be more likely to cower and retreat or play dead. Other people are like wild animals that sting or attack when threatened. If your partner feels trapped in a cage and you're busy stinging and attacking, the situation will get worse and worse. If you step back, your partner can get out of the corner or stop stinging and you can regroup and be calm again. Sometimes it just takes time. This is excruciating for people like me who want to deal with every issue in the moment it comes up, but sometimes it's just not productive and makes things worse.

If you really look at all these patterns, you might discover that you need to reconnect because you've been in a bad phase, arguing and feeling like you've never gotten along in your whole lives. You might not need to say something as formal as "Hey, let's reconnect!" You can be more casual about it. "Let's go to the cabin this weekend." "Let's go to that party." Don't tell him what you are trying to do, especially if he can't stand you right now. Just soften up and stop doing what you've been doing. Let it breathe. Reach out without being threatening. You can heal it this way.

Crack #4: Fighting Dirty

Every couple gets into arguments. It's not about never fighting, but it is about fighting fair. There are many nasty ways to fight dirty, and they can cause cracks in the relationship that can be hard to repair and hard to forgive. When someone fights dirty, the other person builds up walls for protection, and eventually, intimacy becomes impossible. Some examples of fighting dirty:

- **Genderizing or De-genderizing.** Gender is tricky and when you bring it into a fight, it can be nasty. There are multiple ways this can work, with both opposite-sex and same-sex couples. Emasculating a man is definitely fighting dirty. If you say things like, "Why can't you be a real man?" or "Why don't you get a job?" or "I can't depend on you" or "Why do I have to make all the money?" or "What did you do all day?" or anything to even imply weakness, this kills a man's spirit. Once in a while, a guy might need to be told to be mature, but sometimes it's the last thing he wants to or is able to do, and you need to be there to listen. No name-calling!

  Men can do the same thing to women, by making them feel either weak for being a girl or inappropriate for being strong because they're "acting like a man." People are who they are and everyone is a mix of soft and hard, assertive and receptive, male and female. Nobody should ever be made to feel ashamed of their gender traits, whether they are stereotypical or not. Maybe there is always pressure on you to be in charge and you are never allowed to be vulnerable. Maybe you feel victimized by the attitude that you are weak, are incompetent, and can't do anything for yourself. If someone says things to you that make you feel less than you are, that diminish you or separate you from your natural identity, that's fighting dirty. Criticize a situation or a behavior all you want, but in a good relationship, both partners encourage each other to be who they are and who they need to be, even as that changes throughout the relationship.

- **Threatening.** If you threaten divorce or a breakup with every argument, that's fighting dirty. You can't keep playing the divorce or breakup card if you don't mean it, or you will turn into the boy who cried wolf. If you ever really do mean it, your partner won't believe it. Or your partner will believe it and be so traumatized by having to grapple with constant potential relationship destruction every time you have an argument that he may just decide to beat you to it and call the whole thing off.

- **Creating or feeling jealousy.** Jealousy is a destructive emotion in any dosage other than the most mild. No matter how tempted you are to flirt with other people when you are angry or say things like, "So many other people [or worse, a specific person's name] would treat me so much better than you do," and no matter how often you want to succumb to paranoid suspicions about your partner, you have to stop.

Repair strategy: Be kind, even when it's hard. Don't push buttons, even when you really want to. And don't involve anyone else in your relationship issues. This is not about which of all the men out there would be nicest to you, or who thinks you are sexiest, or who wants you, or comparing your partner to anybody else. All that is irrelevant because you are with the person you are with, not all those other people. You have chosen, and those others are out of the running so it's not fair to bring them up. Work with what you have and stay with your partner, physically and emotionally. Also, don't act irrationally jealous. You have to get over this problem. See a counselor if you need help with this. There is definitely a line—sometimes jealousy is reasonable, if your partner is acting inappropriately. You need to figure out whether it's justified or not, and if it's not, you need to get past it. Otherwise, jealousy is one of the fastest ways to create an irreparable crack.

· ·

GIRL TALK

It's very hard for many women to accept the idea that someone might not want to be with them all the time and might like going out and doing their own thing, but that does not mean the person doesn't love you. However, what women don't always realize is that guys, as much as they like to go out and hang out together, also feel peer pressure.

A long time ago, I was hanging out with a guy I was dating and a lot of his friends. They asked him if he wanted to go out with them.

He turned to me and said, "I don't really want to go out with those guys. I'm tired. Let's just go home after this." That felt really good—I felt like we were going to get some quality time together. Then one his friends told him which bar they were going to, and he turned to me and said, "I guess I'm going to go."

What? I calmly said, "That hurts my feelings. I feel like I've just been shafted. I thought you were coming home with me. Why is everybody else more important?"

He said, "I can't leave my guys to go to a bar without me!" He really felt the pressure to go, like he owed them his presence. They were a group of guys, and they wanted all the group members there. He felt pressure to be a "guy's guy."

I said, "And I'm not one of your guys?"

Suddenly, he totally got what he hadn't seen at all before. His whole face changed and he said, "Oh my God! You are my *best* guy!" And he came home with me.

I wish men would understand that they don't always have to say yes to something they don't feel like doing, especially when they would rather spend time with us. It's not weak to want to go home and have quality time with your girlfriend or wife. It's actually strong, because it takes the courage of your convictions.

Somewhere in the middle, there is a sweet spot—where guys and girls can both go out with their friends without their partners being threatened or feeling neglected, but where they can also spend enough quality time together to nurture their relationship.

. . . .

Crack #5: Thinking You Can Build the Perfect Partner or Change Someone at All

People don't change. Behavior can change, but only because somebody decides to change their own behavior. You can't change somebody else, and if you go into a relationship thinking it's a fixer-upper, you risk major disappointment. That's not to say a relationship won't change and people can't evolve. They do. I've seen it firsthand. When people are younger, their expectations can be set too high. Everybody is flawed. The bottom line is that if someone really loves you, they want you to be happy, but why would they want to make somebody happy who is constantly bitching and picking at them? You don't get to step in and decide to mold somebody into your idea of the perfect partner. It's not going to work, and it can eventually make you feel like your partner is your enemy if he doesn't change the way you want him to change. If you spend all your relationship energy trying to change someone instead of getting to know and appreciate who that person actually is, your relationship will never evolve and will probably eventually dissolve when your partner is tired of your nonacceptance. If you think you can make the perfect person, you will always be disappointed and you will be much less forgiving about every mistake that person ever makes.

The other problem with focusing on making someone else perfect (besides the futility of it) is that you will be much less likely to see your own faults or try to work on them. Every relationship is an opportunity for you to be a better person, to learn more about yourself, and to evolve in the way you handle relationships, even if the one you are in isn't meant to last. Always work on your own perfect and until you achieve it, don't expect it from anybody else.

Maybe someone will change when they meet you because of the way your relationship evolves, but you can't force it. Instead, just watch for it. Instead of asking for it or demanding it or even expecting it, just let it happen naturally. Often, it will. I've been in a relationship with someone who entered the relationship as a boy and then became a man. When someone realizes that their life will be better with some fundamental changes, that person may be more likely to change. Your partner has to change because he thinks that you have made life better, and this is what it will take to keep you around. But it won't be because you told that person to change, or forced it, or nagged it to death. It will grow out of the relationship organically. You really have to love somebody to change for them. You can't just love them on paper. If you can't imagine life without that person, that can be powerful enough for you to deal with qualities you might not accept in someone else, and also to actually change your own worst qualities.

For example, I have a friend who met a guy who was a player. He was hot and on the make all the time. He loved to go out at night and drink a lot and pick up women. Every weekend, he had a new one, and he never committed to any of them. When they met, this was him, and she was fine with that because she wasn't looking for anything either, and he was totally forthcoming about who he was and what he was doing. She was just out to have a good time. However, he liked her instantly (maybe because she didn't want anything from him). She realized she really liked him, too. She decided that his habits didn't make him a bad person. They were just bad habits. She accepted him, even though he knew his wild ways bothered her, and after a few months, he started to change. He didn't want to go out as much. He wasn't interested in other women. He was all about her.

Then he had a relapse (and a relapse can happen any time—in six months, or in 20 years). They got into a routine and he thought the grass might be greener in other pastures. He wanted to be single again and hang out with his friends. This was very hard on her but she saw it as a mistake, a blip in his personal growth, and not as a character flaw. Instead of getting all over him about it, she pulled back. She gave him enough rope to hang himself. She was calm and honest and told him that she would like a relationship, and it was up to him to decide if he wanted one, too. She knew that if he didn't make the decision himself, she wouldn't really have him. She was willing to walk away, and he came back to her.

If she had been trying to change him into the perfect person, he probably would have felt even more pressure to go out and be a player again, but she never did that. Now he's practically a model boyfriend. Even players get tired of the lifestyle and when they meet the right woman, they might decide to change all on their own. A good partner is proud of his relationships, appreciates together time and family time and romance, and appreciates those small connected moments. He never thought he would become that kind of person, but today, that's exactly who he is. You can't always know what someone will decide to become.

Repair Strategy: Sometimes, what you see is what you get, and you will have to make a decision: Can you accept the person or not? If you are a perfectionist, this is a hard question because you still probably think, deep down, that you can change your partner. People are who they are, and if you can't love who your partner is right now, with all the imperfections that come with being human (and there will be many), then you can't love who your partner really is. Loving who someone is doesn't mean you don't want them to keep improving and evolving. It doesn't mean accepting physical, verbal, or emotional abuse. But it does mean supporting and accepting a faulty but good person you love and respect, who loves and respects you.

A friend once told me, "Love is unconditional, but relationships are conditional." Of course they are. But if you want a relationship, if you love the person and want to make it work, then you have to stop expecting perfection and stop trying to change and mold your partner into who you want him to be, and just let that person become who he really is. Personalities are dynamic, not static, and there is always the potential for evolution (and devolution). However, if you can't accept who that person is right now, then the only fair thing to do for both of you is to move on. If you're married, obviously, you can't just walk out because you decide you don't like who your spouse is or has become. It's not that easy. This actually happens a lot because marriage is long and people grow in different directions. If this does happen, you need to work a lot harder to figure this out. You need to look at each other and rediscover who you both are now. Can you get back to where you were or find common ground the way you are now? As long as you are both willing, you can work out nearly anything. If one of you isn't willing to compromise or work together to build the relationship, that's a different (and sad) story.

Meanwhile, work on *yourself* and your own problems with acceptance and tolerance. Do you tend to get jealous? Are you often irritable? Are you intolerant? Do you let people push you around? Identify the areas that you feel you need to grow in, and start there. You can't be someone else for your partner any more than your partner can be someone else for you, but you can change and evolve and grow because you want to and choose to. Ironically, total acceptance from a partner tends to bring out peoples' best sides, and that's when they tend to change for the better, all on their own. But life is a mirror. Look at yourself and you'll see who and what actually needs to change.

. . . .

JUST THE TIP

A mistake I've definitely made in the past is revealing my internal dialogue to somebody else. We say a lot of crazy shit to ourselves, but some of it should stay private. If you hate somebody in the moment, don't say that, because it might not be true later. Your partner thinks bad things about you, too, and if you heard the things he thought about you, you would probably never speak to him again, which is why he doesn't say them out loud—and you shouldn't either.

Also, definitely don't say anything negative you feel about his mother, his past, or his friends. Never trash his friends, ever. Once it's out there, you can't ever take it back. Even if your bad opinions are true, they cause damage and you don't need to express them. Another thing not to say out loud is that you aren't a happy person. Don't say that. Don't tell other people. It puts them in an impossible position because nobody else can fix your unhappiness but you. In fact, try never to say something negative to somebody if it will make them feel bad and they can't do anything about it. (Venting to girlfriends doesn't count—that's expected and necessary.) Deal with your stuff yourself or with your therapist. If you are unhappy or hate people, that's your work, not your partner's. Remember, you never have to say everything you are thinking, and in most cases, you shouldn't.

. . . .

Crack #6: Faking It

Do you show your true self to your partner? Are you authentic in your relationship? At least at first, you probably aren't. We all do this. We are on our best behavior in the beginning, but eventually everybody reveals their true nature. You can only be who you think someone else wants for so long before the mask starts to slip. If you've faked it for too long, it's not only exhausting, but it can feel like you were lying when the real you peeks through.

A woman I know fell in love with an artist whose work she found fascinating. She thought he was cool and edgy, and he showed her all the pieces he'd done and talked about his career like he was really in it. She got the impression that he was a working artist. It wasn't until they were married that it became clear he had no intention of being a working artist anymore. He had a small inheritance, so he didn't really do much of anything. She felt like she'd been duped. She loved him and stayed married to him, but he wasn't the person she thought he was at first, and she had to figure out how to deal with that disappointment.

This often goes both ways. I have two married friends who met when they were both young. She loved to go out and have fun and he loved to stay home and relax and be more private. However, when they met (and were in their twenties), he acted like he liked to go out more than he did, to impress her, and she acted like she was more mellow and more of a homebody than she really was, to impress him. Ten years later, they are married and he always wants to stay home and she always wants to go out. This continues to be a source of discord for them both. To handle it, she hangs out with her friends and compartmentalizes her really social side. She has decided to accept that most of the time, he wants to stay home, and he has decided to accept that she likes to go out more than he does. Yet their marriage works because fundamentally, culturally, and morally, they are very similar. They like the same hobbies, they have the same attitudes, and they are going in the same direction.

Of course, really getting to know someone, including their habits and traits, not to mention their best and worst qualities, takes time. Obviously you don't want to lay out all your cards on the first date. That takes all the mystery and fun out of getting to know someone (and it will make you look crazy). Letting the information out gradually isn't faking it. However, if you act like you are somebody you're not, eventually you'll be found out. You will be building a relationship on a shaky foundation.

Also, you have to make allowances for the reality that people change, and you might have to support that even if you don't love the change. Maybe someone was always a fun guy, but he was an alcoholic, and then he went to rehab. Maybe now he's not as boisterous and fun, but he's getting his life together. You have to support that. Maybe somebody loves to go out to eat and celebrate and be indulgent, but then she decides she really wants to get healthy and lose the extra weight that is hurting her health. She pulls back on the indulgence and maybe she doesn't seem as fun or carefree anymore, but she is trying to do what is good for her. You have to support that. Maybe somebody lost a family member. That can change someone's personality. He may not be as happy or fun as he used to be. He might be sad for a long time. You have to support that, too. A relationship is about being there for each other, even if it's less fun for awhile. In most cases, the person undergoing the change will be able to reclaim their fun or happy or boisterous side, but it may take time to figure out how to do that in a new way. If you love the person, then those superficial changes shouldn't damage the heart of the relationship. Help them get through it and you could become even closer.

Repair Strategy: Be yourself, right from the start. It's the only way. It sounds cliché, but this is how you forge an authentic connection with someone. You don't have to be your whole self right this minute. Let your authentic self out a little bit at a time if you've already been faking it and you need to fix it. Or just cop to it. Admit you've been giving a false impression, and explain why ("I really like you and I wanted to impress you, but you need to know that I'm not crazy about football." Or *Star Wars*. Or sushi. Or whatever it is.). Or maybe decide to get a little bit into football or finally watch *Star Wars*. Be open to new experiences. You don't have to make them part of your identity, but it's a way to reach across the aisle. (And then maybe he'll be willing to try yoga!)

Whether you like dogs or prefer cats, admit to yourself who you are, what you like, what you want, what you need. Sometimes people like to think of themselves the way they want their partners to see them, instead of seeing themselves directly. I hear examples of this all the time. People hide extreme views, a shady past, difficult family members, and personal failings. They fake ambition or exaggerate their accomplishments and they totally hide or minimize their transgressions and failures. That's not even covering all the little things we don't think to mention that happen to be at odds with the other person's preferences—things like whether you are a morning person or a night owl, whether you like sex every day or if once a week seems a little extreme to you, and like my friends, whether you are a social butterfly or a homebody. Some men are charming in public but not at home, or charming at home but not in public. There is nothing wrong with being any of these things, but if you and your partner are at odds on these basic traits, it can cause constant low-grade irritation.

I know of a very successful woman in the world of fashion who has not been successful in her relationships. The men she has dated say she is a chameleon. She makes the man she is with believe that she totally loves all the same things he loves, but it never works in the long term because eventually, they find out who she really is, and it is nothing like how she advertised herself. At some point, when there is trust, you have to reveal your own personal crazy to your partner. They need to know. Are you obsessive? Do you have an eating disorder? Do you have a crazy mother? Do you dote on your father? Do you have an unnatural connection to your dog? You have to show it at some point. You can't hide it forever.

Successful people in general also tend to be complicated and relentless. I am the girl who is up writing books at four a.m. while the guy I'm dating is probably out getting bombed at some sports bar. He says he is envious of my ability to multitask, but I am envious of his ability to sleep in all morning when he can. I can't do that. I have many complicated and conflicting emotions, I have high standards for myself and everyone around me, and I don't mince words. I'm not that easy to be around, let alone be in a relationship with, and I know others like me who are particularly challenging partners. If this sounds like you, the trick is never to misrepresent yourself. Don't pretend to be someone who's easygoing, simple, pleasant, laid-back, and always in a good mood if that is definitely not who you are. You can be that way sometimes—I do it, and it's always a relief, but I can't sustain it. If you need constant stimulation, if you thrive on stress, you need a partner who can handle that. Be your whole self right this minute, and then let the chips fall where they will.

If it turns out the two of you are just fundamentally different, but you still really like each other and you have good chemistry, you can make it work. For example, I like to stay home and the guy I'm dating likes to go out. Now I go out a little more than I would otherwise, and he stays home a little more than he would otherwise. We meet in the middle. But sometimes, I'm just not interested. I happen to be a private person, more so than I used to be. Now that I'm on TV or being interviewed so often, that has changed me. Now I'm more of a homebody. Because of the stresses of my job and life, I need to stay home and rest when I can. I need to decompress from that life and I need someone who can support and understand that. At the same time, I need to support and understand a partner's need to go out and socialize and get crazy even if I don't feel like coming along. You can't be a jealous person in situations like this, but if there is trust, then you can both make room for who you both are rather than constantly demanding that each of you becomes more like the other person. Unless you are both honest about who you really are, it won't even be good when it could be great. Let your authentic self out—it might be more endearing to the person who loves you than you thought it ever could be.

Crack #7: Making Decisions by Committee

Everybody has an opinion. In a relationship, your opinion matters, and your partner's opinion matters. As for everybody else, some of your friends and family members might have good advice, help you put things in perspective, or give you a much-needed reality check now and then, but if you let the opinions of people who aren't in your relationship interfere with your relationship, then you can get into trouble, because nobody really knows the true dynamic of your relationship but you and your partner. But this is very hard not to do. We all want someone to give us a simple solution to our complicated problems, but most of the time, letting everybody else solve your personal issues will get you in more trouble than if you really looked honestly at what was going on from your own perspective and the perspective of your partner, and acted based on that.

Believe me, I know about this. When I was on reality TV, I had the details of several of my relationships out there for the world to see. People who watched saw part of the truth, not the whole truth, but some of them thought they could judge the relationship based on what they saw. I got a lot of unsolicited advice, and if I had tried to follow it all, I would have been spinning in circles and in a much worse place than I am now. It's not that different with your friends. They get your very biased side of the story, and they want to support you, but they won't necessarily give you good or objective advice. Often, they will advise you based on what they want and their own reality, even if they think they are being helpful and objective. Some people are married and they want everyone else to be married. Some people are divorced and they want everyone else to be divorced. Some of them don't remember what it's like to be single, or haven't had kids, or they have a particular like or dislike of your partner for some personal reason of their own. Nobody can know the truth about anyone's relationship beyond those who are in it. Even if you are quite sure your sister should get a divorce or your best friend should take her relationship more seriously because she has "such a good guy," you don't know. And nobody knows the truth of your relationship either.

This is why you should never make decisions by committee. You can talk to your friends to get things off your chest, and sometimes friends do give good advice. You can certainly consider it, but ultimately the decision you make has to be yours and you have to feel in your gut that you are making the right move. But don't let someone else who only has incomplete and biased information tell you what you should or shouldn't do with your relationship. When you start letting other people in, it can be poison.

Repair Strategy: Just because you don't know what to do in your relationship, that doesn't mean anybody else knows better. If you really want advice, ask for it, but always, always take it with a grain of salt. It's so easy to get swayed by a passionate friend who is just so sure she has the answers for you. Never forget that the person giving you advice only sees your side, or at least a biased and incomplete side, so they are not in a position to really tell you what you should do. Only you can decide that. If you can remember that, then you should be okay. Meanwhile, if you really aren't sure, never default to someone else's advice, unless you feel inside that it is the right thing *for you*, considering everything you know about your partner and your relationship. If you still aren't sure, then just wait. Don't act. Things become more clear with time, and the advice you got might turn out to be spot-on . . . or dead wrong. Know yourself, and eventually, with time and consideration, you will know what you should do.

Crack #8: Fostering Contempt, Disdain, and Disgust

This is a tough one. If you get angry often enough, or if you are disappointed too often, especially if you don't express it, it can fester inside and turn into contempt, disdain, or disgust. It's that feeling you get when you can't stand to look at that person anymore, when everything he says grates on your nerves and you just want to roll your eyes or leave the room because you can't stand your partner anymore. This is a toxic situation, but strangely enough, some people hold on to those feelings and use them as a weapon of power. I like to say "the least interested party always wins," but a totally uninterested and even disgusted party doesn't win at all because life is miserable that way. You both have to want to be in it.

We all feel disgusted with our partners some of the time (especially during PMS—or football season). People are gross sometimes. They burp, they fart, they leave their shit on the floor, they neglect each other, they are selfish, they can be spoiled and unreasonable. I'm only talking about *everyone*. We all have our less-than-glorious moments. However, if you have a feeling of contempt about your partner all the time, even when he clearly doesn't deserve it, something's got to change because the relationship is rotting from the inside out. Nobody wants to feel dead inside. Either you need to look at why you feel that way and get it out of you (talking, counseling, fighting, forgiving, whatever), or you need to move on. This is no way to live. The stress of feeling disdain and contempt for the person you are supposed to love is huge and overwhelming, and it's unsustainable. You need to do something about it, for your own sanity.

Repair Strategy: When you feel stuck on a hamster wheel of contempt and you can't snap out of it, you need to change what you're doing. Find a way to stop the bleeding. Exercise. Take a trip. Clear the decks. Don't be rash. Instead, find your way back into the heart of your relationship. Maybe you sit down with that person and decide to forgive them fully and completely with the condition that X, Y, and Z must never happen again. Maybe you take a hard look at yourself and realize you are unhappy or unfulfilled, and you figure out what to do about it. Maybe you feel like you've given up too much, and you need to get some of your independence back. Whatever it is, you need to make a move and then let go of those bad feelings. Stop blaming your partner for things he can't help or never even did.

Or maybe you need to leave. Maybe the relationship just isn't working any longer. Maybe the love and passion are really gone. Sometimes (often), you can get it back if you had it once, but when you no longer have the will to fix your relationship and you have only negative feelings about it and no desire for repair, then you need to set yourself free. It can be the best feeling in the world, to escape that oppressive existence. I'm definitely not telling you to break up or get a divorce, but I am telling you that if you aren't happy, then *you* need to figure out whether you need to break up or get a divorce. Sometimes it feels like it's really over and you have to come in and out of it a little bit, if only in your mind. Take a night off. Give it time. You might be madly in love but you have to change the vibe. Break the negative flow. Turn it around.

If you feel like the world is coming to an end and you can only see the negative, and you feel like you don't even know the other person anymore, take three days off. Even what you feel is the worst marriage ever might look okay again after a break. If you feel like you are getting hurt, you need to end it, but if you aren't getting hurt, if you are just annoyed and irritated and disgusted for your own crazy reasons (and maybe some legit reasons, too), imagine your life without that person. What would it feel like? If you don't like that thought, if you can't imagine that reality, then you need to get back in and fix it. Sometimes all it takes is a gesture. Just say, "Hey, can I have a hug?" or "Wonna be friends?" or "I know, let's pretend we like each other" or "Let's hold hands." Sometimes a peace offering can completely reverse the bad energy.

The fact is that if you get rid of this person and look for another one, this perfect guy you imagine finding is just going to be a different kind of asshole. Maybe you need to accept the asshole you already live with. He's *your* asshole. Not if he is cruel, not if he is abusive, not if you don't love him, but if you do? We can all be assholes some of the time. Don't you want to be forgiven when you act like one?

Crack #9: Too Much Intervention

Sometimes you just have to let things be. Are you making a big deal about every little thing because it's not exactly the way you want it or the way you would do it? Is he doing something trivial but annoying, like chewing too loudly or reading the paper over breakfast instead of talking to you? Is he cooking something or cleaning something the wrong way because it's not the way you would do it? You can ruin a perfectly good day, or date, or vacation by trying to intervene too much in what your partner is doing, saying, thinking. It's easy to get into the mode of seeing and feeling only the bad and not remembering the good. Sometimes we get short-term memory loss, but the good is in there, too. Sometimes you just need to let the bad go and find the good.

Repair Strategy: It's time to stop obsessing. Step back and look at the big picture—he's there, he's with you, he's trying to help, he means well. Or at least you hope he does. Call a friend so she or he can talk you down. Get some perspective. Is there really a big huge horrible problem, or are you just irritated about something stupid? Sometimes things really aren't that big of a deal but you need to get some perspective before you can really see it. It can be more worthwhile to let it go than to talk about it. Sometimes, you can't just let something go, of course. If something is really bothering you, then it needs a discussion, but think before you speak. Maybe let it go for a short period of time. Think of it like a juice cleanse. You'll go back to it in three days, but for now, you are cleansing. Give yourself time to calm down, for the wound to heal, for the anger to abate. Then choose your words carefully.

Don't say things you will regret later. This will hurt you and is a sign of self-loathing. Tone is everything. I have a friend whose husband tells her not to listen to his tone and to just listen to his words, but that's impossible. A tone of disdain or disrespect will negate anything you say, and veiled threats or unfair attacks or bringing too many problems up at once will totally cloud the issue. A tone of gentle respect and consideration works almost every time.

For example, you might be tempted to say, "You're selfish. You never think about me. It's all about you. I need more. This isn't good enough

for me. I can do better. So many men would treat me better than you do."
But try saying how you feel without using the word "you": "It really hurt
my feelings when I was left alone last night. " Remember not to bring up
all the other shit that bugs you. Just stick to the one thing. Just the one
thing. Stay on the path, be calm, and don't attack. This is very difficult
when you feel like your partner is finally really listening to you, but as
soon as you start piling on your other complaints, he will suddenly be unable to hear you, so don't go there.

If you just can't stop picking at every little thing your partner does and
says, then maybe you need to look at why you care so much about things
that don't really matter or aren't even about you. It actually might be you
who is the problem. Maybe it's a sign of your commitment issues. ("I can't
possibly be with him! Because those eyebrows!") Or maybe there is a bigger problem underneath but it's easier to complain about how he makes
the bed the wrong way and you simply can't live like that. Maybe you're
just feeling particularly needy, and this is a way to get attention. Maybe
you're just in a bad place or feeling vulnerable. You need to get to the
bottom of that and realize that you're the one stirring up the trouble. Or
maybe you're genuinely not getting what you need out of the relationship
and you are just trying to find whatever you can get, even if you're focusing on the wrong things. Talk it out with a friend (or a counselor) to see
if you can get to the bottom of it. Your obsessing might be a sign of something more serious, or it might just be a sign that you need to let it be.

Crack #10: Forgetting Where You Started

I always say that things end the way they began. If your relationship
began strong, if there was chemistry and love and a bond between you,
and in the meantime nobody has betrayed anybody or done anything
really terrible, you can get that back. It's easy to forget where you started
when someone is getting on your nerves or isn't acting the way you think
he should act, but if you started strong, all those feelings are still down
there somewhere. Remember where you came from, why you love that
person, and remember that if you have love and respect and a good connection, it really doesn't get any better than that. True love is hard to find,
so excavate it from beneath the layers of bad habits, dull routines, and
taking each other for granted. Wouldn't it be a shame to throw it all away?

Repair Strategy: Go back to your foundation. Think about what got you together in the first place. Sit down together and ask each other: Are we a team? Are we a partnership? Can we let some of the bad habits go? Can we compromise? Where can we meet in the middle? Who can give a little here and who can give a little there to get us back to that place where we started? Think about tearing down an old rotting house and rebuilding it from the foundation. Any relationship can do that at any time, if both parties are willing.

Know Thyself, Know Thy Partner, and Know Thy Relationship

My final advice for preventing the cracks that can eventually destroy a relationship is to know thyself, and know each other, and know thy relationship. If you decide to be partnered, then you need all three of these in your consciousness to really flourish. You need to be able to know who you are and be who you are, but you also need to know who your partner is and let your partner be who he is, too. And then you need to know and understand the nature of your relationship, and let that relationship be what it is. Don't beat yourself up. Don't beat up your partner. Don't beat up the relationship. Let them alone when they need to breathe, and be there to care for them when they need attention. And by "they," I mean all three of you: you, your partner, and your relationship, which is a living, breathing thing.

That means trying not to do any of the things in this chapter and being aware of your tone when you speak to each other. It means not making veiled threats and taking the other person's feelings into account. Some people think they can treat their partners worse than they treat total strangers, but it should be just the opposite. (Not that you should be nasty to total strangers, but you know what I mean.)

The best place to start is to decide what you really need right now in your life, and then figure out if your relationship is providing it. If it isn't, can you both evolve so you are both getting what you need, keeping in mind you can't get everything from one person? For example, I've recently assessed what I think I need in a relationship. This is my list:

- I want someone who is a partner in life.
- I want someone to grow with.
- I want someone who can make me laugh.
- I want someone I can respect.
- I want someone to learn from, who teaches me things I didn't know before.
- I want someone who loves my daughter and wants to be part of a family.
- I want someone who can be a good co-parent.
- I want someone who is a good son to his parents.
- I want someone to spend time with and have fun with.
- I want sex, love, passion, and connection.
- I want someone to hug.
- I want someone to make love to.
- I want fidelity—I don't want to be cheated on.
- I want someone who understands me.
- I want someone who isn't threatened by me.
- I want someone I feel passion with.
- I want someone who wants to be in it for the long haul.
- I want someone I can trust, who trusts me completely.
- I want someone who doesn't want me for financial reasons, but just for who I am.
- I want someone to take care of, who also wants to take care of me.
- I want to be happy as much as possible, and I want to make someone else happy.
- I want a relationship I can be proud of.
- I want to feel safe and loved.
- I want to feel like the luckiest girl in the world.
- I want someone to notice what's important to me and help me do those things, or do them with me. That could mean doing yoga with me or walking on the beach or just being romantic once in a while.
- I want someone who knows how to practice moderation and balance.

- I want someone who considers my feelings as important as his own.
- I want a partner who appreciates who and what I am.
- I want someone who isn't perfect but whose dreams I can believe in, and I want someone to believe in me and everything I still want to accomplish.
- I want someone who will lean in when I lean out, who will bring me closer when I get scared or try to run away.
- I want a partner who thinks of us as an "us."
- I want someone who can compromise and help me compromise.
- I reserve the right to think of more things I need.

• •

DR. AMADOR SAYS . . .

A final word from me: I really love this list Bethenny has compiled. If I had to choose one item that I believe encompasses all the others, one that speaks to the heart of the matter, it is this one: "I want to feel safe and loved."

When we feel safe and loved, we take chances, we grow, we deal with our fears, we argue in ways that bring us closer, we don't lose ourselves, we feel appreciated, passion becomes possible, and we become partners. That's what it's all about.

—Xavier Amador, Ph.D., president, LEAP
Institute, www.leapinstitute.org

• •

This is mine, but I hope you will make your own list. I know my list would have been quite different in my twenties, but now that I'm in my forties, there are things that are much more important to me than status or money or good looks. I know myself better now, and after all the wrong partners I've chosen over the years, I have a much better idea of what will be right for me. That's all I want for you. Try your hand at your own list, and then see how your partner measures up. If you have a good person who is good to you, who trusts you and loves you and whom you trust and love, then that is the main thing. Everything else isn't really that important. If you have what you really need, then patch the cracks and your foundation will keep getting stronger. We all want a strong relationship that will see us through, and nobody wants to grow old alone. As you get older, these are the things you think about. Maybe you still look forward to marriage, or you have a faulty but good marriage and you look forward to a long future together. Maybe you're divorced and you hope to find love again—maybe marriage, maybe not, but love, support, and companionship.

Whatever it is you want, it's okay to want it. Humans are social animals and we need each other. We need family. We need friends. We need love. And we can find it.

I know we can. Just remember that in the end, the most important relationship you can have is the one with yourself. And that even though you might think you suck at relationships, just know that I suck at relationships so you don't have to.

Remember Who You Are

Never forget what took me a lifetime to learn:
You have only one heart. Be true to it.
—ANGELINA JOLIE'S CHARACTER IN
THE MOVIE *BEYOND BORDERS*

Now that this book is coming to an end, I realize there is one more thing I really want to leave you with. This is something important to me that I want you to take away from this book, if you take away nothing else. Here it is:

No matter how much you want to be in a relationship, no matter how much you long for companionship and someone to share your life with, no relationship should ever come at the price of you.

It starts with you, it ends with you, and a good relationship can make your life better, but a relationship doesn't make you who you are, and a relationship can't take away who you are. A relationship that isn't right for you, that diminishes you, or that forces you to be somebody other than your genuine and authentic self in every way will only make your life worse. Good relationships let both of you be who you are, fully and completely.

No matter whom you love and who loves you, no matter how in love and committed you are, no matter how long you have been married, you will always be an autonomous individual, and you should always know who you are and be able to make it on your own if you have to (even if you never actually have to). The best relationships are not made of two people becoming one, or one person subsuming or submitting to another, but of two people hand in hand, supporting each other's individuality and going through life together, headed in the same direction. In order to do that, you need to be a whole person yourself. You need to maintain your identity. You need to know who you are and remember it, no matter how much you want to be with somebody else. A relationship should be bigger than the sum of its parts.

When you get caught up in a relationship, it's easy to forget who you are. It's easy to think of yourself as vulnerable, flighty, crazy, or smitten, rather than remembering that you might sometimes be all those things but that you are also strong, independent, and autonomous, and that even though you want someone in your life, you don't *need* someone in your life. The most important advice I can give you is to never love someone more than you love yourself.

So I want to end this book with a final list, just for you. You can do all kinds of things for other people, and you probably do that every day, but you can do just as many things for yourself. A lot of women find it easier to do things for others than to do things for themselves, but this is an important list. A crucial list. This is a list about how to be yourself and be good to yourself. You deserve it. The very best way to be someone that somebody else will love is to be someone that *you* love. You can look good for you. You can be sexy for you. You can dress nicely for you. The fact that somebody else might also enjoy those things too is secondary.

1. Never settle for less than you deserve. If you are not being treated well, be willing to walk unless conditions change. "Having" somebody is never, ever worth the price of being treated disrespectfully or abusively.

2. Have confidence in your own beauty and power. How do you think celebs like J.Lo get with hot guys twenty years younger than they are? Because they walk into a room knowing they are beautiful and feeling confident. Nobody doubts them because they don't doubt themselves.

3. When you feel insecure, seek security from within, not from someone else. Others can certainly make you feel better temporarily, but

if you don't find the power to recover on your own, you'll always relapse. You have it in there and you can find it by accessing your authentic self. Who are you? When you feel grounded in self-knowledge, you will feel secure. You just need to reach down and get it.

4. Accept yourself exactly as you are right now. So you have some weight to lose? You could use a nicer wardrobe? Your job sucks? So what? That has nothing to do with who you really are as a person— your values, your actions, your talents, your capacity for love. Confidence is the most attractive quality a woman can possess. It makes you beautiful and sexy. Why wait to be the most interesting woman in the room? You can always work toward and achieve goals, but if you don't like and appreciate yourself for the exceptional human being you are right now, those goals will keep getting further and further away. Not to get too maudlin about it, but imagine yourself as a young child, when you were four or five years old. Think of how beautiful and unique and precious you were. Think of how much love, support, and affection you needed and deserved. You still need and deserve all those things, no less than you did then. As an adult, you can give that to yourself. Cherish and love yourself. You are precious and unique.

5. Don't compete with younger girls. You were there once. Those hot young girls don't know who they are yet because they haven't experienced enough life. You are where you are right now. Embrace your age and the wisdom and confidence you've gained because of it. It makes you even more complex and beautiful than someone who is beautiful simply because of youth.

6. Notice when someone brings out your best, and notice when someone brings out your worst. That goes for romantic partners as well as friends and even family members. The ones who bring out your best are the ones who really see who you are. Those are the ones to keep in your life. The rest are expendable.

7. Never be afraid to leave a relationship that isn't giving you what you need and deserve or forces you to be someone you are not. A relationship should make space for you to be yourself and live your dreams. If you need to get out, get out. The truth will set you free,

and sometimes facing it is the most courageous and important gift you can give yourself. Ask for help if you need it, but make the move.

8. Be with people who are proud to be with you, who brag about you, who want to show you off. Never waste time on people who are ashamed of you. Shame on anyone who dares to be ashamed of you. Even when you make mistakes or do bad things, even when you are ashamed of your actions, never, ever be ashamed of who you are. Make amends, fix it, apologize, but do not live in shame.

9. Don't make emotional decisions because of money. I understand that sometimes you have to stay with someone because you can't afford to go out on your own. I totally get it, but every day, you find a way to get a little bit further out on your own. Inch by inch, you can get there. Don't let anyone own you or control you because of money. Have your own money, no matter what, and build it up. Also know that you will never, ever be happy if you marry for money. Maybe you will hit the jackpot and fall in love with someone who also happens to have money. If so, you are the luckiest girl in the world. However, you will never learn to love somebody because they have money. What you will learn is to hate yourself. You will always feel controlled. It does not work. Have your own money!

10. Respect small changes in yourself and others. Small changes can be a sign of eventual big changes. As long as you and the ones in your life are moving in the right direction, there is always potential for improvement.

11. Don't live a mediocre life. You can have mediocre moments. We all do. But your life can be exceptional, just like you are. Do what you need to do in this life so you can look back over your life in old age with pride rather than regret. There's no time like the present. Don't waste another moment. Relationship or no relationship, let your life shine.

Visit my website at www.bethenny.com for news about the new I Suck at Relationships Forum, where we can all have real conversations about the relationship issues that plague us—because we all suck at relationships sometimes, but together, we can all get better.

Acknowledgments

I cannot believe that this is my eighth book. I remember writing *Naturally Thin* and it feeling like the most daunting task yet the most liberating because it simply poured out of me.

I must acknowledge you, the readers. You're the reason I feel so safe and comfortable to express and expose myself with the intention of hoping that I might help you to get through something difficult or that you might relate to something crazy that goes through my mind or occurs in my life.

Thank you to Touchstone, the publishing imprint that has been with me since my very first word on paper. Thank you to Matthew Benjamin and David Falk, my very communicative, supportive, and passionate friends at Touchstone. Thank you to Zachary Schisgal and Jeremy Katz (the first people in publishing to give me a shot). I never forget who helped me out when I was irrelevant in this biz.

Thank you to Eve Adamson. We have definitely had a great impact on each other's lives, and I love being on this journey with you. You are an incredible and trusting support.

Thank you to my Skinnygirls: Alex, Julia, Leslie, and Meghan. I am not easy. The job isn't easy, and for the past two years the environment hasn't been easy. I appreciate your passion, drive, and dedication. Leslie, I truly appreciate what you have been through and I will never forget it.

Thank you to Bryn, my love, my peanut. You are the purity in my life, and the element that gives it all meaning and makes so many other things so insignificant. I love you with all my heart and soul. You are the greatest gift in my life.

Thank you Cookie. You have been at my feet for every word I've ever written. I've spent more time with you than any other living creature. I love you more than words can say.

Thank you to my "BIG." You inspired the idea for this book and you have inspired me and taught me so much about relationships. Beginner's luck? 143.

Thank you to my girlfriends Sarah and Teri. You're my therapists. Xo.

Thank you to all of you—for watching, for reading, for writing, for connecting, and most of all for being so fearless and honest.

You have made me a writer.

We really are in this thing together. I am forever grateful.

Index

abandonment, 31, 36–37, 211
abuse, 184, 192, 280, 296
  in breakups, 201, 204
  control and, 134–35, 137
  fear of, 189
adolescence, 34
advice, cautions about, 285–86
affairs, *see* cheating
age:
  commitment and, 175, 177–78
  fear related to, 191
  marriage and, 26, 180
  masturbation and, 261
  maturity and, 146, 259, 297
  sex and, 256
age gap, 178, 219
  comfort zone for, 72–73
  in dating younger men, 15, 296
alcohol use:
  arguing when influenced by, 18
  effect on relationship of, 57–58,
    132
  and emotions, 32, 64
  as escape, 252
  excessive, 174, 201
  when to avoid, 193, 209
Amador, Xavier:
  on blame and negativity, 164, 265
  on clinging, 245–46
  on complexity of men, 13
  on confidence, 77
  on couples' therapy, 200–201
  on emotional thinking, 32–33
  on emotional triggers, 36–37
  on exiting an argument, 60–61
  on financial control, 212–13
  on fundamental relationship goal,
    293
  on gender gap in understanding,
    10–11
  on gender stereotypes, 150–51
  on getting married, 181
  on gut instinct, 166–67
  on healthy fighting, 17–18, 20,
    60–61
  on letting go of control, 121–22,
    129–30
  on losing your identity, 147, 150–51
  on PMS, 63
  on proximity, 155
  on relationship game, 91
  on restraint in electronic
    communication, 54–55
  on sexual chemistry, 251–52
  on talking, 57
  on trusting your emotions, 70–71
  on vulnerability, 125–26
  on wealth, 230–31
American Academy of Matrimonial
  Lawyers, 207

"Amnesia," 28
analyzing, obsessive, 24, 32, 34, 38
anger, control and, 130–32
apologizing, 64, 96, 189, 298
appearance:
    for dating, 75
    taking pride in, 136–37, 158, 171,
        266, 269–70
arguing:
    anatomy of typical fight in, 185
    disengaging from, 60–64, 159
    fighting dirty in, 17, 274–77
    gender gap in, 16, 24
    with a know-it-all, 138
    men's avoidance of, 16–18, 24–25
    money as topic of, 214
    pinpointing the issue in, 130
    repeating the same fight in, 270–74
    strategies for diffusing, 272–74
    techniques for healthy, 17–18, 20,
        60–62
    timing in, 18–20, 54, 64
    women's mistakes in, 61–62
arrogance, confidence vs., 77
attainability, challenge and, 82
attention, need for, 127–28
attraction:
    gender gap in, 28
    independence and, 100
    of money, 230–31
    mutual, 65–66
    unequal, 101
authenticity:
    and identity, 295–98
    pretense and, 281–85
availability, adjusting your, 85, 86–87,
        102, 105–7, 109, 111–12, 144,
        159, 197

bachelors:
    chronic, 103, 111
    connotations of, 25
Baldwin, Alec, 26

bank accounts, separate and shared,
        219, 227, 228
Being Single in a Couples' World
        (Amador), 147
BET (breathe, exit, think) technique,
        60–61
Beyond Borders, 295
biological clock, 67, 69, 84
blame:
    accepting, 35, 287–88, 290
    avoiding focus on, 273–74
    for failed relationships, 265
    misplacing of, 62
booty calls, 145, 173
boyfriend/girlfriend, use of term, 175,
        176
bragging, 43, 83, 171, 255
breakups:
    amicable, 195
    deal breakers in, 71, 186, 188,
        201–2, 215, 271
    "Don't-Do" list for, 208–9
    emotional response to, 163–64
    finality in, 196, 197–98
    gender gap in, 26–27
    gradual, 197
    how to get over, 98
    making decisions about, 184–93
    of marriage, *see* divorce
    premature, 31–32, 187–88
    recovery from, 208–10
    relationship evaluation before,
        186–89, 197
    reversing, 198–99
    with serial monogamists, 114
    strategies for, 195–99
    by text, 142
    threats of, 275–76
    timing for, 177, 195
    "To-Do" list for, 209
Bro Code, 22
Bryn (author's daughter), 4, 43, 123
Bullock, Sandra, 247

Burner Method, 98–104, 199
  how to play, 100–103

careers:
  fulfillment through, 162–63
  importance to men of, 12
  resuming, 188–89
  role of, 35, 36
cat and mouse game, 89, 94, 104–7, 113, 120
  sexual, 237
celebrities:
  relationship commentary by, 26, 76, 113, 128, 178–80, 256, 257
  sexual chemistry of, 247, 250
  see also specific individuals
change:
  being supportive of, 282–83
  as potential improvement, 298
  unrealistic expectations of, 277–81
cheapness, thriftiness vs., 226
cheating:
  and divorce, 201–3
  gender differences in, 42–43
  habitual, 201
  jealousy and, 139
  reasons for, 96, 201–3
  suspicions about, 140–41, 235
  texting and, 144
  trust betrayed by, 138
childbirth, sex after, 235, 252–53
childhood:
  author's, 211
  character influenced by, 117, 212–13, 221, 297
  emotional triggers from, 36–37
  gender stereotypes based in, 150
children:
  control of, 121
  in divorce, 137, 141–42, 190, 200–201, 205, 207, 258–61
  in effect on relationships, 68, 70, 84, 94, 179–80, 201, 235, 256

  parenting of, 136–37, 228
  and stay-at-home dads, 139, 221
chivalry, 172
chores, 130–31, 182
clinging, 111–12, 158, 243–46
clothing, sexy, 75
codependency, 156, 190
cold turkey, 196, 197–98
colleagues:
  caution about relationships with, 102
  as guy friends, 104
comfort zone:
  in assessing new relationships, 72–73
  going outside, 86
commitment:
  determining whether to end, 184
  early levels of, 175
  fear of, 36, 84–85, 89, 111, 191
  forcing, 149, 158, 174
  gender gap in, 28, 67, 160
  making a, 103, 177–80
  from a player, 110–13
  risks of, 75
  security of, 52
  sexual, 49, 103, 104, 177, 251
  signs to determine attainability of, 170–74
  timing for, 174–78
  ungettable, 113–14
communication:
  curbing emotions in, 16–17
  electronic, 1–2, 37, 39, 41, 44, 54–55, 142–45
  fear of, 36
  in financial issues, 220–21, 228, 230
  focusing on the topic in, 53–54, 270–71
  gender gap in, 9–10, 13–14, 19, 20–21, 30, 34, 37–41, 48–49, 50, 53, 148–49, 160

communication (*cont.*)
  importance of timing in, 18–20,
    53–56
  in marriage, 182
  in sexual chemistry, 249
  in sustaining relationships, 266
  taking a break from, 40–41
  see also arguing; talking
communication cleanse, 40–41
compromise, 201, 284, 291
confidence:
  as attractive, 76–77, 112, 158, 170,
    249–50, 270, 296–97
  life changes as threats to, 163–64
  in relationship game, 96
  undermining of, 138
confrontation, avoiding, 50
contempt, chronic and ongoing,
  287–88
control:
  abusive, 134–35
  anger and, 130–32
  author's issue of, 117–18, 264
  of boundaries of new relationships,
    77–84
  as cry for help, 134
  as disrespect, 128
  dysfunctional types of, 135–45
  equality of, 119–21, 135
  financial, 124, 131–32, 211–14,
    220, 228
  in fixing relationships, 110
  going with the flow vs., 124
  househusbands and, 139
  how to gain, 135, 243–44
  how to lose, 135
  influence vs., 119
  jealousy and, 139–42
  letting go of, 121–28
  money as, 69
  in need to be right, 138
  by partner, 133–35, 146–47
  regaining of, 133–35

  in relationship game, 93
  in relationships, 117–45
  replacement strategies for,
    122–28
  of self, 128–33, 145, 150
  by spying, 138
  total management in, 136–37
  when to relinquish, 109, 119–20
control freaks:
  partner as, 133–35
  red flags for recognizing, 135–45
  yourself as, 121–33
counseling:
  author's experience in, 3
  when to seek, 54, 135, 137, 138,
    158, 199–200, 202, 205, 276,
    281, 287, 290
couples' therapy, 199, 200–202
courtship, *see* relationship game
courtship rituals, 90
credit management, 207
credit scores, 215–16
criticism, obsessive, 289–90
crying:
  by men, 24–25
  as therapeutic, 27
culture gap, 72, 177, 178–80, 219

Damon, Matt, 113
dating, dates:
  casual flings in, 101
  cooking analogy for, 98–104
  after divorce, 203, 257–61
  dressing for first, 75
  online, 259
  planning of, 78, 85, 171, 173, 177
deal breakers:
  in assessing relationships, 71, 186,
    188
  betrayal in, 271
  financial, 215
  in marriage, 201–2
de Beauvoir, Simone, 65

defensiveness, avoiding, 18, 55
de-genderizing, 275
de la Renta, Oscar, 146
demands:
  consequences of, 51, 53–54
  poor strategy for, 133
  strategy for presenting, 46–52,
    55–56
Depp, Johnny, 247
depression, 163–64, 192
DeVos, Rich, 211
discretion, necessity of, 42–46
divorce, 85, 165, 286, 288, 294
  author's, 3–4, 44, 123, 164
  children and, 137, 141–42, 190,
    200–201, 205, 207, 258–61
  considerations on, 199–208
  counseling for, 199, 200–201
  exes in, 137, 141–42
  financial and legal issues in, 207–8,
    229
  how to meet people after, 259
  making threats of, 51
  prenups and, 182–83
  recovery from, 208–10
  response to, 146, 163–64, 206
  sex after, 235, 257–61
  stigma of, 190
  strategies for getting over, 98,
    208–10
  threats of, 275–76
  your responsibility in, 206
drama:
  men's aversion to, 108
  women's tendency toward, 16, 37,
    38, 47, 57, 168
drinking, see alcohol use
drug abuse, 174, 184, 201

e-mails:
  practicing restraint in, 54–55,
    143
  when to use, 102

emasculation:
  avoiding financial, 139, 217–18,
    221–29, 275
  as fighting dirty, 275
emotions:
  in assessing relationships, 70–71,
    85
  in communication, 11, 47, 50, 52,
    53, 159, 272
  as culturally unacceptable for men,
    13, 24
  gender gap in, 127
  in men, 63, 99, 121
  men's avoidance of, 17, 20–21,
    23–24
  overreacting to, 30–32
  in sex, 238, 239, 251–52
  triggers for, 36–37
  women's focus on, 20–21, 23–24,
    52, 99
empty nesters, 163
Equifax, 215
estrogen, 245
ethnicity gap, 72, 177, 219
exaggeration, 62
exclusivity:
  gender gap in, 99
  sexual, 176
  as sign of commitment, 172, 175
  timing for, 173
exercise:
  obsessing about, 83
  for stress relief, 209
exes:
  avoiding talking about, 83, 141
  maintaining contact with, 101
  remaining friends with, 141–42, 260
  sex with, 262
  as Super Dads, 137
expectations:
  cultural, 217
  generosity in, 224–25
  unrealistic, 168, 188

Experian, 216
extravagance, 222

Facebook:
    posting status on, 148, 171, 173
    what to avoid on, 44
Facetime, 143, 145
falling in love, gender gap in, 26, 28
families:
    in assessing new relationships,
        73–74, 177
    avoiding criticism of, 281
    differing cultural backgrounds in,
        72, 177, 219
    and financial issues, 216
    illegal or unethical behavior of,
        173–74
    liking and being liked by partner's,
        108, 172
    men's relationships with, 22
    objection of, 178–80
    role of, 35, 128, 254, 285, 294, 297
    in separation, 194
    see also children; parents
father figures, 2
fatherhood:
    and abandonment issues, 36–37
    divorce and, 137
    marriage and, 26
    stay-at-home dads, 139
fear:
    author's, 191–92
    breakups motivated by, 191–93
    of commitment, 36, 84–85, 89,
        111, 191
    decisions made out of, 2, 208, 264
    gut instinct and, 189–92
    of losing partner, 150
    maintaining bad relationships out
        of, 190–91
female bonding, 23–24
FICO, 215–16
fighting, see arguing

fighting dirty, 17, 274–77
finances:
    author's issues with, 211–12
    control issues in, 124, 131–32,
        211–14, 220, 228
    divorce and, 206–8
    and happiness, 3
    management of, 211–31
    in marriage, 26, 131, 162, 182–83,
        298
    in paying for dates, 78, 220
    in relationship goals, 69, 298
    and sexual obligation, 243
    women's independence in, 139,
        180, 207, 214, 217–28, 298
financial inequality, 2, 43, 125, 139,
        162, 183, 211–31
    entitlement in, 224
    shifting balance in, 230–31
    strategies for protecting male ego
        in, 221–29
    when you are dependent,
        228–30
    when you make more, 217–28
financial infidelity, 202
5 Seconds of Summer, 28
flirting, 94, 102, 115, 148
    cat and mouse game as, 104–7
    jealousy and, 140, 276
    sexual, 252
    strategy for, 105–6
    by text, 144
food, obsessing about, 83
forgiveness, chronic contempt vs.,
        287–88
fun, 23
    in engaging a potential partner, 76,
        82, 112
    in multiple relationships, 101–3
    of new relationships, 152
    as relationship goal, 69, 172
future, attempting to control,
        124–25

gambling, 211
gay men, 22, 38, 104, 242
gender gap:
  in arguing, 16, 24
  in commitment, 28, 67
  in communication, 9–10, 13–14,
      19, 20–21, 30, 34, 37–41, 48–49,
      50, 53, 148–49, 160
  in emotions, 127
  in exclusivity, 99
  financial, 2, 43, 125, 139, 162, 183,
      211–31
  in guilt, 99
  in heartbreak, 26–29
  in marriage, 25, 84
  in problem solving, 13–14, 61
  roots of, 150–51
  in sex, 34, 109, 252–53
  in understanding, 9–29
genderizing, 275
generosity, 224–26
girlfriends (his), loss of identity in
    becoming, 146–48
girlfriends (yours):
  cutting off, 149, 154
  discretion in dealing with, 44
  supportive role of, 14, 35, 38, 87,
      126, 128, 135, 162, 164, 208,
      254, 281, 289, 294
girl talk:
  on arguing, 185
  on communication, 38
  on communication cleanse,
      40–41
  on control of self, 132–33
  on emotional gender gap, 127
  on financial independence,
      228–30
  on finding the right person, 155
  on guy friends, 276–77
  on multiple sexual relationships,
      99–100
  on neediness, 157–58

  on obsessing, 44
  on relationship conversations,
      159
  on solving relationship problems,
      110
  on women's relationship mistakes,
      82–84
Gosling, Ryan, 247
gossip, 22, 31, 46
guilt, gender gap in, 99
gut instinct:
  acknowledging red flags in, 165–67,
      172–74, 184, 188, 195
  in decisions on marriage, 180–84
  in ending a relationship, 195–210
  in evaluating progress of
      relationships, 174–80, 184–93
  recognizing positive signs in,
      170–72, 187–89, 194–95
  on sexual chemistry, 247–48
  trusting of, 1, 70–71, 165–210
  warning scenarios for, 168–70
guy friends (his), 31, 86–87, 109,
      134, 148, 163, 173, 175, 176,
      279
  allowing time for, 276–77
  avoiding criticism of, 281
  liking and being liked by, 108
guy friends (yours), 102, 104

hard to get, 107
heartbreak, 164
  in breakups, 198, 209
  gender gap in, 26–29
helplessness, 83
Hepburn, Audrey, 76
Hepburn, Katharine, 180
hormones:
  women influenced by, 30–32, 34,
      58, 99, 233, 245, 252–53
  see also PMS, and "crazy" behavior
househusbands, control issues for,
      139

Ice Cube, 128, 256
identity:
    being true to your own, 16, 78–79,
        90, 94, 112–13, 206, 254–55,
        272, 294, 295–98
    checklist for honoring your own,
        296–98
    after divorce, 258
    and finding your passion, 162–63
    finding your soft side in, 225
    losing your, 146–52, 275
    and personal growth, 277–78
    reclaiming your, 151–64, 209
    revealing your own, 85, 90,
        281–85
    self-acceptance in, 280, 297
    in sexual relationship, 245, 250,
        254–55
    signs of loss of, 149–51
    see also self-knowledge
illness, sex and, 253–54
imperfections, assessing of, 74
I'm Right, You're Wrong, Now What?
    (Amador), 17–18
indecision, 83
independence, 81, 82, 287, 296
    attraction of, 100, 111–12, 151,
        158, 160–61
    financial, 139, 180, 207, 214,
        217–30
    game, 96
    maintaining your, 146–64
    masturbation as, 261
    through finding your passion,
        162–63
infatuation, 148
infidelity, see cheating
insecurity, 62, 83, 87, 150, 296–97
    control and, 120, 125, 132, 138
    excitement of, 189
    financial, 211
    of men, 96, 185
    and sex, 249–50

instinct, see gut instinct
interdependence, 151
internal dialogues, 56–57
    keeping privacy in, 281
    toxic, 267
introspection, 265
    in divorce consideration, 199–200,
        204–5
    in regaining your identity, 153–54,
        164
Irish blessing, 122
I Suck at Relationships Forum,
    298

jealousy, 149, 285
    control and, 139–42
    in fighting dirty, 276
    as strategy, 148
Jobs, Steve, 165
Jolie, Angelina, 247, 295
Julia (author's assistant), 45–46

Kama Sutra, 233
Kev (Maria Menounos's boyfriend),
    178–80
Khalfani-Cox, Lynnette:
    on bank accounts, 219
    on credit scores, 215–16
    on dating after divorce, 203
    on prenups, 207–8
    on women as breadwinners, 207,
        217
kindness:
    in avoiding hurt, 103
    in breakups, 197–98
    when to show, 29, 268–69, 276
kissing, 232
"kitchen-sinking," 18, 55, 61–62

Lachey, Nick, 165
Leslie (author's assistant), 40–41
lightening up, 10, 14–16, 20, 38, 109,
    289–90

living together, 85, 144, 182, 226
    planting the seeds for, 86
    premature attempts at, 124–25, 159
    sex and, 240
loneliness, 69, 102
Lopez, Jennifer, 232, 296
love, loving:
    as fundamental relationship goal,
        293–94
    inequality in, 2
    premature declaration of, 244
    sexual chemistry vs., 245
    see also falling in love, gender gap in

McAdams, Rachel, 247
male bonding, 23–24
man-formation:
    on being nurtured, 21
    on being the pursuer, 107
    on change, 74–75
    on financial inequality, 223
    on friends and family, 108
    on having game, 92
    on priorities, 23
    on relationship time, 148–49
    on sexual challenge, 237
    on sexual dysfunction, 235–36
manipulation, control as, 120–21,
        170
marriage:
    acceptance in, 280
    author's ambivalence over, 4, 180
    avoiding oversharing in, 45
    cat and mouse game in, 106
    commitment in, 104
    compromise in, 201
    financial harmony in, 216, 226–27
    of former partners, 114
    gender differences on, 25, 84
    getting a player's commitment for,
        110–13
    independent game in, 96
    jealousy in, 140–41

    legalities of, 183–84
    maintaining your identity in,
        154–55, 160–62
    making a decision about, 180–83
    men's reasons for, 25–26
    open, 104, 254
    overcoming obstacles to, 178–80
    platonic guy friends in, 104
    pretense and, 281–82
    reinvigorating of, 114–16
    as relationship goal, 4, 69, 165,
        171, 177
    separation in, 193
    sex and, 240, 255–57
    societal viewpoints on, 25–26, 84
    strategies for presenting demands
        in, 51–52
masturbation, 235, 236, 240, 258,
        261–63
meditation, 122
men:
    basic concerns of, 11–12
    basic things to remember about,
        14–16
    financially dependent, 218,
        221–29
    friendships of, see guy friends (his)
    gender gap in understanding of,
        9–29
    inappropriate choices of, 101–2,
        113–14
    information on, see man-formation
    as insecure, 96
    likes and dislikes of, 79–84
    as platonic friends, 102, 104
    as players, 90–93, 97
    protecting the ego of, 79–81, 110,
        120, 218, 221–29, 235
    as providers, 124–25, 217–18, 221,
        229
    as pursuers, 45–46, 66–67, 82, 107,
        158, 244
    as romantic, 15

men (*cont.*)
　and sex, 242–43
　showing respect for, 35
　as simple, 10–13, 15, 20, 30, 32,
　　49, 64
　strategies for talking to, 46–52
　thinking processes of, 20–21, 26,
　　38, 44, 54, 61
　unmarried, 25, 103, 111
*Men Are from Mars, Women Are from
　Venus* (Gray), 14
menopause, 64, 72, 233
Menounos, Maria, 178–80
menstruation, 63, 64
micromanaging, 205
midlife crisis, 116
mind reading, 47, 49, 127
Miyamoto, Shigeru, 89
money, *see* finances
money noise, 213–15, 233
Monroe, Marilyn, 117
moodiness, 126–27, 158–59, 164
morals, differences in, 169–70
mothers:
　attraction of, 258–59
　single, 259–60
mourning, 164
Mr. and Mrs. Smith, 247
Mr. Might-Be-Right, 100–101
multitasking, 30, 118, 284
mystery, maintaining an air of, 42–45,
　93, 100, 110, 161, 282

nagging, as toxic, 15, 23, 83, 88,
　95, 112, 130, 199, 268–69,
　278
name calling, 17, 18, 55, 275
National Endowment for Financial
　Education (NEFE), 202
neediness, 30, 76, 80–81, 100, 112,
　125, 132, 149, 290
　Burner Method as cure for,
　　100–104

chronic, 155–56
　after divorce, 258
　in marriage, 160–62
　overcoming, 156–61, 199
　in sex, 238, 240, 243–44
negativity, 84, 108, 164, 265
　of chronic contempt, 287–88
　diffusing, 288
　focusing on, 289–90
　as toxic, 267
New York Times, 217
nitpicking, 274, 278, 290
Notebook, The, 247
nurturing, men's need for, 21, 26,
　134

observation, 122–23
　in divorce consideration, 203–4
obsessing:
　on the negatives, 289–90
　over partner, 98, 99, 100, 103,
　　147–48, 149–52, 159
　women's tendency toward, 10, 14,
　　19, 24, 30, 35, 44, 61, 83, 116,
　　174, 245, 259, 264
one-night stands, 232, 240
online dating, 259
orgasms, 233, 235, 239, 254, 257,
　258, 262, 263
oversharing, 42–46
　dangers of, 45
oxytocin, 233, 245

parents:
　elderly, 183
　meeting each other's, 85, 86, 103,
　　111, 171, 175, 177, 197
passion, 171
perfection, unrealistic expectations of,
　277–81
perfectionists, 118, 131
perimenopause, 116
pets, 180

phone calls:
  waiting for, 149
  when to avoid, 2, 112, 150, 159,
     193, 198, 208, 209, 243–44, 245,
     252, 273
  when to expect, 171, 175
  when to use, 78, 106, 143–44
Pitt, Brad, 247
platonic relationships, 104
players:
  chronic, 103
  defined, 90
  ethical, 93
  getting a commitment from,
     110–13, 279
  qualities of, 92–93, 97
  sex with, 232
playing the field, 97–104
PMS, and "crazy" behavior, 30–32,
     34–36, 52, 58, 62–64, 110, 120,
     132, 159, 188, 222, 287
political gap, 72
Porcupine Game, 104
pornography, 234
positives, focus on, 122–23, 205, 270
postpartum, 233
prayer, 122
pregnancy, 34, 43, 119
prenuptial agreement (antenuptial
     agreement; prenup; premarital
     agreement), 182–83, 207–8,
     230
pretense, authenticity and, 281–85
Pretty Woman, 165
pride, in partner, 23
priorities:
  differing, 169–70
  recognizing your own, 94, 206
  in relationship standards, 71–72
problem solving, gender gap in
     approach to, 13–14, 61
professional girlfriend, as term, 81
projection, 131–32

Proposal, The, 247
proposals, 181

racial gap, 72, 177, 219
Real Housewives of New York City,
     214
reality TV, author's experience on,
     123, 177, 214, 285
reciprocation, 50–51, 115
relationship atrophy, 268–69
relationship game, 89–116
  calling a time-out in, 95–97
  in marriage, 114
  as ongoing, 116
  players in, 90, 92–93, 110–13
  playing the field in, 97–104
  risks of, 92, 109
  testing the waters in, 89–92, 94,
     103
  when to play, 93–95
  when to stop, 90, 93, 97, 103, 104
relationships:
  acceptance vs. change in, 277–81
  advice for women in, 37–59
  age factor in, 15
  author's tips for, see tips
  balancing strengths in, 59
  being true to oneself in, 78–79,
     151–64
  breaking up in, see breakups
  control in, 117–45
  cultural gaps in, 177
  desperation as basis of, 170
  expert input on, see Amador, Xavier;
     Khalfani-Cox, Lynnette; Taylor,
     Janet; Ziegler, Vikki
  financial issues in, 211–31
  finding the truth of, 191–92
  forced, 1, 150, 157
  gauging progress of, 114, 174–80,
     185
  goals of, 91
  how to end, 195–99

relationships (*cont.*)
  losing yourself in, 146–64
  making decisions in, 285–86
  mastering the catch and release in, 65–88
  milestones in, *see* relationship timeline
  mistreatment in, 166–67, 173
  moving to the next level in, 96
  multiple concurrent, 98–104, 199
  mutual agreement in, 125
  open, 104, 254
  others' opinions in, 1, 178–80, 285–86
  past, 43, 101
  reassessment of, 176–77, 197
  reestablishing, 198–99
  repeating bad patterns in, 169
  resolving problems in, 185–93
  separation in, 193–95
  sex as barometer for, 233
  sexual, *see* sexual relationship
  signs to determine future direction of, 170–74
  strain of ongoing contempt in, 287–88
  strategies for repairing cracks in, 267–91
  temporary inequality in, 188–89
  timeline for, 114, 175–78
  trusting gut instinct in, 165–210
  understanding of men in, 9–29
  ungettable partners for, 113–14
  when to end, 28–29, 49, 51, 74, 79, 135, 137, 138, 139, 140, 143, 158, 174, 176–77, 184–93, 201, 223, 224, 280, 287–88, 296, 297–98
  when to work on maintaining, 187–89, 191, 194–95

relationships, author's:
  discretion about, 43–44
  failings in, 1–5, 10, 28, 30–32, 44, 66–67, 82, 141, 147, 165, 173, 180, 184, 191–92, 232, 240, 264–65, 293–94
  financial issues in, 211–12, 214–15, 225–26, 228, 230
  list of needs in, 292–93
  optimism in, 2, 4–5, 28, 298
  successful strategies in, 9–10, 49, 57–58, 90, 114, 117–18, 123, 134, 171, 177, 185, 198, 232, 236, 259, 277, 284–85
relationships, long-term, 69, 113, 144, 146, 154, 164
  breakup of, 208
  fostering and sustaining, 264–94
  going back to the foundation of, 290–91
  negative signs for, 172–74
  positive signs for, 171–72
  reassessing, 287–88
  sex in, 238, 239, 247, 250–53
  see also commitment; marriage
relationships, new:
  assessing your goals in, 68–75, 91, 291–94
  changing your strategy for, 86–88
  choosing a partner for, 65–68, 99–100
  early warning signs for, 167–70, 184
  engaging a potential partner in, 76–77
  establishing boundaries and rules of, 77–84, 94–95, 142–44
  evaluating of, 166
  evolving progress of, 84–86, 90, 91, 96, 187
  excitement of, 152
  as foundation for long-term relationships, 290–91
  gaining information about, 45

introducing your children in,
259–60
locking down the connection in,
107–8
mistakes to avoid in, 82–84
playing the game in, *see* relationship
game
riding the wave of, 108–9
strategies for advancing, 85–86
when to work on maintaining,
187–88
relationship timeline, 114
three-month milestones in,
175–76
six-month milestones in, 176–77
eight-month milestones in,
177–78
religion gap, 72, 219
remarriage, 260
reputation:
guarding your, 99–100
premature sex and, 238, 239
resentment, 53, 152, 218, 229
resiliency, 27
respect, 289–90
in financial inequality, 228
partnership as, 128, 138, 296
in relationship goals, 70
for self, 151, 176
in sexual chemistry, 249, 257
Reynolds, Ryan, 247
ring, as commitment, 2, 50, 174, 197,
259
Rinna, Lisa, 257
risks:
of cat and mouse game, 106
of commitment, 75
excitement of, 187
of playing the relationship game,
92, 108–9
of reversing breakups, 198–99
in separation, 193
in sex, 243, 251, 256

role-playing, 95
ruts, relationship:
changing strategy in, 86–88,
268–69
in marriage, 114–15
sexual, 250–53
spicing up, 104–5
using surprise for, 95, 106

same-sex couples, 7, 275
secrecy:
financial, 202
of men, 22, 93
value of, 42–46
security, 84, 101, 182
inner, 296–97
Seinfeld, 268
self-care, 132–33, 164, 269–70
self-control, 128–33, 145
self-knowledge:
in assessing your relationship goals,
68–75, 291–94
control and, 128–33
in divorce consideration, 206
importance of, 295–98
and sex, 254–55
for women, 30–64
separation, disconnection strategies
for, 193–95
serial monogamists, 113–14
seven habits of healthy fighting,
17–18, 20, 60–61
sex:
attraction in, *see* sexual chemistry
awkwardness with, 238, 239, 258
challenge in, 236–37
commitment and, 49, 103, 104, 177
complications of, 234–35
concurrent multiple partners in,
99–100
after divorce, 235, 257–61
exclusivity in, 176
and financial issues, 227

sex (*cont.*)
  first experience of, 236
  frequency of, 253–54, 256–57, 283
  gender differences in, 34, 100
  lack of interest in, 83–84
  low stakes, 238
  makeup, 16
  in marriage, 114–15
  options and variety in, 230–31,
    235–36, 246–47, 251, 257,
    261–63
  as relationship changer, 245–46
  in relationships, *see* sexual
    relationships
  risks of, 243, 251, 256
  sexting vs., 145
  as a single mom, 259–60
  talking after, 52
  traditional roles in, 237
  when to avoid, 101
Sex, Lies, and Videotape, 28
Sex and the City, 194, 234
sex symbols, 250
sexting, 145
sex toys, 236, 258, 262
sexual attraction, 28
sexual chemistry, 234–35, 247–50
  living without, 253–55
  strategies for reclaiming of, 250–53
sexual desire, individual differences
    in, 233, 235, 249, 253–54
sexual dysfunction, 258, 262
  in men, 233, 235–36
sexual relationships, 232–63
  goals of, 69–70
  maintaining privacy in, 155
  in marriage, 255–57
  open, 104, 254
  premature engagement in, 78, 82,
    112, 238–39, 241–44
  pressures of, 240–42, 257
  when to initiate, 234, 236–43
sexual tension, 237, 238, 239

silences, 37–39, 83
silent contract, 59
Simpson, Jessica, 165
sincerity, 81, 96
Skype, 143
slow fade, 197
smoking, 271–72
space:
  maintaining your own, 94, 154
  in separation, 193–94
spinsters, bachelors vs., 25, 181
stay-at-home dads, 139
stereotypes:
  gender-based, 150–51, 275
  of providers, 221
  of romance, 118
  of sex, 235, 256
  of women, 34
stress:
  alleviating of, 15, 192, 285
  men's, 30–31
subservience, 83
Super Dads, in divorce, 137
superiority, 84

talking:
  about breaking up, 185–86
  choosing the right time for, 53–56,
    58, 126, 159, 160
  excessive, 37–41, 82, 124–25, 160
  focusing on the real issues in,
    56–59, 61–62, 186, 290
  about love, 244
  in marriage, 115
  about money, 220–21, 231
  phrases for building a man's ego
    through, 80–81
  about sex, 233
  showing appreciation through,
    222–23
  straightforward and direct methods
    for, 46–52, 54, 85, 87–88, 112,
    125, 185–86, 199, 273–74

strategies for, 52, 58–59, 272–73,
    289–90
texting vs., 144
tone in, 58, 289–90, 291
topics to avoid in, 83, 281
see also arguing
talk show, author's, 40
Taylor, Janet:
    on children in divorce, 260–61
    on communication gender gap, 50
    on ending a relationship, 192–93
    on financial infidelity, 202
text-ervention, 144
texting cleanse, 145
texts, texting:
    control through, 142–45
    practicing restraint in, 54–55
    rules for, 143–44
    waiting for, 149
    when to avoid, 1–2, 37, 39, 61, 103,
        112, 150, 159, 193, 198, 243,
        245, 272
    when to use, 41, 78, 94, 106,
        144
3-2-1 Rules, 177
threatening, as fighting dirty, 275–76
thriftiness, cheapness vs., 226
time-outs, 60–64, 95–97, 102, 109,
        116, 159, 288
    in breakups, 197
    in communication, 40–41
tips:
    on apologizing, 189
    on being a girlfriend, 81
    on cheapness vs. thriftiness, 226
    on deal breakers, 271
    on discovering yourself through
        relationships, 161–62
    on exes as fathers, 137
    on fighting for a relationship,
        194–95
    on financial inequality, 224,
        227

on fulfilling your needs, 35
on gauging sexual chemistry,
    248
on handing men's emotions,
    24–25
on having guy friends, 104
on househusbands, 139
on independence, 153
on internal dialogues, 281
on maintaining contact with exes,
    141–42
on meeting people after divorce,
    259
on meeting the parents, 177
on mutual sexual compromise,
    246–47
on premature declaration of, 244
on privacy in sexual relationships,
    255
on sex and finances, 227
on sex as an excuse, 233–34
on sexting, 145
on sexual exclusivity, 176
on timing for talking, 52
on when to leave a relationship,
    174
Tourist, The, 247
toxic fighting, 17
TransUnion, 216
travel, time apart due to, 184
trust, 28, 285, 294
    cheating and, 138, 139
    control and, 123, 125
    in gut instinct, 1, 70–71, 165–210
    in revealing your flaws, 284
    in sexual chemistry, 249, 256
    spying and, 138
truth:
    fear vs., 191–92
    finding, 194, 209, 297–98
Twitter, what to avoid on, 44, 158

Unmarried Equality, 181

values, differing, 169–70
violence, potential for, 140
vulnerability:
   balancing independence and,
     81–82, 96, 296
   control and, 119–20, 125, 264
   revealing of, 17, 80, 87, 96, 97,
     125–26, 132, 145, 172
   sex and, 245

Wall Street, 45
wealth, 214–15
   attraction of, 230–31
weddings, stress generated by, 30–32
weekend getaways, 86
Wilde, Oscar, 9
Woman of No Importance, A (Wilde), 9
women:
   as breadwinners, 139, 207, 214,
     217–27, 229

as complex, 10, 11, 15, 21, 30, 32,
   33, 35, 74, 284
in credit management, 207
hormonal aspect of, 30–32, 34–36
and need for attention, 127–28
on a pedestal, 16–17
relationship needs of, 33–37
self-knowledge for, 30–64
sexual complexity of, 34
sexual liberation of, 234–36
strategic advice for, *see* girl talk
thinking processes of, 26–27, 30,
   34, 38, 61, 159–60
traditional role of, 162
unmarried, 25, 181
Woods, Tiger, 141
   ex-wife of, 260

Zen Game, 107–8
Ziegler, Vikki, 182–83

About the Author

Bethenny Frankel is the four-time bestselling author of *Skinnydipping, A Place of Yes, The Skinnygirl Dish,* and *Naturally Thin.* She is the creator of the Skinnygirl brand—which extends to cocktails, fitness, and health—and focuses on practical solutions for women. She has been named one of the Top 100 Most Powerful Celebrities by *Forbes* magazine, and has been featured in both *Health* and *Glamour* magazines. She is a graduate of the Natural Gourmet Institute for Health and Culinary Arts. Bethenny lives in New York with her daughter, Bryn, and dog, Cookie.

Dr. Xavier Amador is the author of many popular books, including *I Am Right, You're Wrong, Now What?*; *I Am Not Sick, I Don't Need Help!*; and *Being Single in a Couples' World: How to Be Happily Single and Open to Love.* Dr. Amador draws on thirty years of experience, including personal experience, as well as the latest academic and clinical research. A nationally respected expert and university professor, Dr. Amador has been featured on PBS *NOVA,* ABC *Primetime Live,* and NBC Bravo. Dr. Amador is frequently called upon by news outlets such as CNN, ABC News, NBC News, Fox News, CBS *60 Minutes, Good Morning America,* NBC *Today* show, the *New York Times,* the *Washington Post, USA Today,* the *Wall Street Journal, Cosmopolitan, Glamour,* and many others. Currently a visiting professor at the State University of New York, for two decades he was a professor of psychiatry and psychology at Columbia University in New York City. To learn more, or to contact him, visit: www.dramador.com.

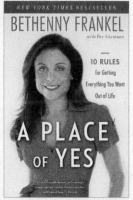
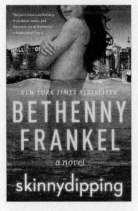